In Search of the Spirit of Capitalism
An essay on Max Weber's Protestant ethic thesis

In Search of the Spirit of Capitalism

An essay on Max Weber's Protestant ethic thesis

Gordon Marshall

Columbia University Press   New York   1982

Published in 1982 in the United States of America
by Columbia University Press

Library of Congress Cataloging in Publication Data
Marshall, Gordon.
  In search of the spirit of capitalism.
  "Appendix: Chronology of Weber's principal
writings in translation": p.
  Bibliography: p.
  1. Weber, Max, 1864–1920. Die protestantische
Ethik und der Geist des Kapitalismus.
2. Religion and sociology.   3. Christian ethics.
4. Protestantism and capitalism.   I. Title.
BR115.E3W434   261.8'5   81–18053

ISBN 0–231–05498–X   AACR2
     0–231–05499–8

Printed in Great Britain

Contents

Acknowledgements

This essay was written in response to a request that I compose a short text introducing undergraduates to the controversy that has surrounded Max Weber's famous thesis about the relationship between ascetic Protestantism and 'the spirit of modern capitalism'. Although I have written it very much as a sociologist, the argument is specifically addressed to a wider audience of historians and social scientists generally. My intention throughout has been to draw attention to the principal features of Weber's argument and then guide the reader as gently as possible through the complicated and often contradictory literatures that have grown up around these. I hope students will find in my commentary a useful companion to Weber's original presentation.

Howard Newby has generously contributed advice and encouragement far in excess of his editorial obligations. Linda George typed the manuscript quickly and efficiently. My thanks to them both.

The extract from Heinrich Rickert, Science and History: A Critique of Positivist Epistemology *(1962) on pages 47–8 is reproduced by kind permission of D. Van Nostrand Co. The extract from Eileen Power,* The Wool Trade in English Medieval History *(1941) on pages 114–15 is reproduced by kind permission of Oxford University Press.*

1   Introduction

Who now reads *The Protestant Ethic and the Spirit of Capitalism*? Almost everyone it seems. Despite repeated attempts to declare discussion of Max Weber's 'Protestant ethic thesis' closed,[1]* it continues to generate the steady stream of secondary and associated material that has made the ensuing controversy one of the longest running and most vociferous in the social sciences. New and retrospective articles appear each year in a broad spectrum of academic journals and publications. Most students of sociological theory, the sociologies of religion, industry, and development, of theology, and of the economic and social history of industrialization in the West are required, at some juncture, to assess the relative strengths and weaknesses of Weber's case. Immersing themselves in the literature, they will discover one tradition of commentary in which Weber's argument is dismissed as being wholly erroneous and another, equally established, in which it is so readily subscribed to, that it has attained the status of a domain assumption. Between those who have consigned the thesis to the scrapheap of false doctrine and those for whom it has passed into the realm of received wisdom has been generated a voluminous literature.[2] Perhaps, then, it might have been more appropriate to have begun yet another contribution to the debate by asking: 'Can there possibly be anything left to say about Weber's Protestant ethic thesis that has not already been said?'

It is my belief that, contrary to popular opinion, this question may be answered in the affirmative. Extant commentaries on Weber's thesis, it seems to me, offer the student little more than a series of choices between the devil and the deep blue sea, since attempts to proclaim the issue resolved, both by those in favour of and those against Weber's proposition, have rested on what are (in different ways) either patently inadmissible data or gross misrepresentations of his argument. His thesis remains as controversial as ever but, while

*Superior figures refer to the Notes on pages 181–207.

lively debate itself is to be welcomed, an apparently interminable confusion about even the most elementary aspects of Weber's argument makes the student's task of assessment unnecessarily harrowing. I hope to dispel at least some of this confusion by the discussion that follows.

Probably my most deep-seated objection to the extensive commentary that is already available on the subject concerns its avowedly partisan nature. Given the pre-secular character of Western society in the early twentieth century, it is perhaps understandable that among Weber's initial critics some felt that, as good Protestants or Catholics, they were obliged to defend their religion against Weber's 'slanderous' attempt to lay the evils of modernity squarely at its feet (in the case of Protestantism) or to dismiss it as inconsequential in the long history of 'economic progress' in Europe (in the case of Roman Catholicism). It is nevertheless discomforting to find modern commentators adopting similar aggrieved stances and, for example, conducting a moral crusade on behalf of Calvin in order to preserve the integrity of Calvinist theology against the 'unfair' as well as 'inaccurate' inter-pretation of that theology allegedly offered by Weber.[3]

More problematic than religious partisanship, however, has been the tendency among commentators to adopt entrenched positions behind disciplinary boundaries. Almost without exception, for example, historians entering into the debate about Weber's thesis have claimed that his argument can easily be refuted by referring to empirical data that are readily available and unambiguously damning: Weber's interpretation of Calvinism is false; the selection of religious texts that is cited is wholly unrepresentative; businessmen were behaving in a 'capitalistic' manner long before the Reformation; the proposed relationship between Protestantism and capitalistic development breaks down, for whatever reasons, in the cases of Scotland, Hungary, and Holland; and so forth. The self-righteous empiricism of certain historians[4] has, however, been met with an equally dogmatic refusal among sociologists to be drawn on empirical grounds. The latter have met objections based on documented instances where capitalism and Calvinism flourished independently of each other by referring to the grander methodological designs of Weber's essays. Thus they have accused historians of ignoring Weber's other sub-stantive investigations in the sociology of religion and maintained that his argument about the Protestant ethic makes sense only when the related analyses of Confucianism, Hinduism, and Judaism are taken fully into account; or, similarly, they have referred to the heuristic intent of the essays on religion as an attempt to illustrate the principles associated with the methodology of ideal-types, interpretative (*verstehende*) sociology, or meaningfully and causally adequate explanation.[5] One side claims to be in possession of the data while the other purports to hold the theory. Certainly there has been little or no meaningful dialogue between them.[6]

Criticisms cannot be rejected, of course, simply on the grounds that they are possibly partisan. Weber's own essays may have been no less so, although I believe this not to be the case. It cannot be denied, however, that the intensely polemical nature of the exchanges does make it difficult to assess their relative merits. What, for example, are we to make of Charles and Katherine George's extensive criticisms of Weber's interpretation of 'the Protestant mind of the English Reformation' in view of the fact that these authors declare at the outset (but only in a footnote) that as a matter of principle they choose to see religion as conditioned rather than conditioning in any historical situation? Such an approach is, of course, to rule out Weber's argument *a priori* on (unsubstantiated) theoretical grounds.[7] For sociologists to defend his thesis entirely in terms of Weber's supposed methodological objectives is, on the other hand, merely to sidestep the issues raised by obvious weaknesses in much of his empirical evidence.[8] The historical *critique* of his argument cannot be dismissed simply on the grounds that parts of it are 'rooted in misunderstandings'.[9] 'Misunderstood', as Michael Hill astutely observed, has been the most commonly used word in the entire debate, but it has often been the case that many who have used the term in reference to the works of others have gone on to make equally fundamental misunderstandings themselves. 'Please polemicise as sharply as possible against those of my views from which you differ', Weber once encouraged the economist Friedrich von Gottl-Ottlilienfeld.[10] He did not know it at the time but he had just spoken the epitaph for the whole controversy about his Protestant ethic thesis. It was with good reason that a cynic once described the exchanges about Weber's thesis as 'the academic "Thirty Years War" '.[11]

Against such a background this slim volume has only modest designs. My intention is to steer (as far as is possible) a non-partisan course through the controversy in order to assess the relative strengths and weaknesses of Weber's argument, and the force of certain of the subsequent criticisms, in a manner that may be useful to the second- or third-year undergraduate. It is as well to make it plain at the outset, however, that this essay does not offer a comprehensive review of the controversy thus far. An explicitly critical perspective is adopted throughout and the argument being presented does not depend upon pursuing nuances in the relevant literature.[12] No attempt is made to do equal justice to all of the parties concerned. I offer, instead, an interpretation and assessment of Weber's thesis which is specifically aimed at challenging accepted wisdom both among historians on the one hand and sociologists on the other. My general conclusion is that, while the latter have rightly corrected some of the more glaring errors committed by the former as a result of their ignorance of Weber's work outside his essays on the Protestant ethic, they have employed references to Weber's wider sociology as a means of avoiding relevant empirical issues altogether. This mutual 'talking past one another' has produced a curious situation whereby, in the opinion of this author at least, the recurrent criticisms of Weber's argument have been demonstrably the least telling whereas, ironically, the weakest parts of his thesis have only rarely been approached. For example, an irrelevant argument concerning usury has dogged discussion about the thesis from the outset, while the very serious problems faced by anyone seeking to document the changing 'spirit of capitalism' have attracted little or no attention.[13]

The approach adopted throughout this exposition therefore will be analytical rather than chronological. Chapter 2 is concerned with the origins of the concept that I consider provides the key to the proceedings – Weber's 'spirit of modern capitalism'. These are indeed complex, but it will be suggested that arguments here can be reduced to two broad perspectives – the 'genealogical' and the 'teleological' – and that the former, rather than the latter, provides the more suitable starting point for an understanding of Weber's text. In Chapter 3, I deal with the nature and implications of the concept of 'the spirit of capitalism' itself. The discussion is premised on the assumption – later substantiated – that many of those commenting on the Protestant ethic thesis have neglected to take Weber strictly at his word and investigate the relationship between the ethic of ascetic Protestantism and the mentality of the capitalist classes in early modern Europe. As a result they have failed to address themselves directly to the issue which, it is argued here, is fundamental to Weber's argument.

Chapter 4 takes up the related concept of 'the Protestant ethic'. My argument will be that Weber's discussion of Calvinism and its derivatives is the strongest part of his case – despite its consistently having been the object of severe criticism from all quarters. I hope to show that much of this criticism has been as ill informed as it has ill natured. Chapter 5 returns to some of the themes that will be raised in the discussion of the capitalist mentality and offers an assessment of the evidence for and against Weber's interpretation of the history of economic conduct in the West. The conclusion is reached that, while Weber has been ill served by many of his critics in this respect, his own case is empirically so thin that the only reasonable verdict for the moment would be one of 'not proven'.

Chapter 6 attempts to guide the student through some of the difficulties created by the introduction into the debate of Weber's other writings, of vast amounts of inconsequential historical materials, and of the inevitable comparison with the Marxist account of the rise of capitalism. Many of these betray efforts to resolve the central issue by default or on entirely spurious grounds. What in fact emerges from Chapter 6, more than any other single conclusion, are the severe and hitherto understated difficulties involved in subjecting Weber's argument to reasonable empirical scrutiny. Nevertheless, if those concerned do intend acting upon recent pleas to declare discussion of his thesis closed, then we ought at least to be clear about what, if anything, has been resolved and on what basis. My concluding remarks offer a short and perhaps surprising answer to these questions.

This approach has the merit of focusing attention on issues and eliminating unnecessary repetition of recurrent aspects of the controversy. However, the major disadvantage is that it obscures the history of the debate itself, so it might be useful to say something of chronology before commencing with the exposition proper.

Weber published his essays on 'Die protestantische Ethik und der Geist des Kapitalismus' in successive volumes of the *Archiv für Sozialwissenschaft und Sozialpolitik* (the learned journal which he edited jointly with Edgar Jaffe and Werner Sombart) in 1905. A complementary essay on Protestant sects was published in the following year. The immediate controversy between Weber and his German critics (principally the economic historians H. K. Fischer, Felix Rachfahl, Lujo Brentano, and Sombart himself) persisted until Weber's death in 1920, and saw Weber add to his original essays a number of lengthy replies to his critics, a series of comparative studies on the economic ethics of the religions of China, India, and Ancient Judea, and a plethora of revisions and footnotes which were incorporated into the versions of 'The Protestant ethic' and 'The Protestant sects' that were collated by Weber as the opening studies in his *Gesammelte Aufsätze zur Religionssoziologie* ('Collected essays in the sociology of religion') and published shortly after his death. Volume 1 of *Religionssoziologie* contains the essays on the Protestant ethic, the Protestant sects, Confucianism and Taoism in China (with an 'Introduction' and some 'Intermediate reflections' that were originally published alongside these), and an entirely new 'Author's introduction' to the assembled whole. Additional works by Weber, notably, from our point of view, his book length 'Sociology of religion' and a series of lectures on economic history, were published posthumously as, respectively, one part of *Economy and Society* and *General Economic History*.[14] Regrettably, some of the most important contributions to the 'German phase' of the controversy remain untranslated and mostly ignored (including some by Weber himself) and, as a result, a number of key issues and misunderstandings that were considered by Weber and the first generation of critics have reappeared at intervals in subsequent criticism, to the general annoyance of commentators familiar with the German material.

Between the end of the First and Second World Wars, the debate about Weber's thesis spread first to France and then to Britain and the United States. In France his argument was received critically by the distinguished historians Maurice Halbwachs, Henri Hauser, Henri Sée, and Henri Pirenne. In the English-speaking world, after some years of sympathetic (Forsyth, Fullerton, Parsons) and critical (Tawney, Knight) though generally ambivalent discussion, the 'Hamlet-without-the-Prince' nature of the debate was finally resolved here when Weber's essays on the Protestant ethic were translated into English by Talcott Parsons in 1930. What might be termed the 'classic phase' of the debate, which saw extended *critiques* of Weber's thesis by H. M. Robertson, Amintore Fanfani, and Albert Hyma added to the French and Anglo-American literature already mentioned, was symbolically closed with the publication in 1944 of Ephraim Fischoff's famous essay reviewing 'The history of a controversy'.

During recent years a thousand flowers have blossomed. Discussion has become more complicated as psychologists, economists, and philosophers have entered into the debate alongside the historians, sociologists, and theologians. Economic, social, and church historians have carried discussion forward along lines laid down during the earlier phases, inquiring into the precise nature and possible economic consequences of the Reformation and the Protestant mind. Probably the most notable contributions here are those of Christopher Hill, Hugh Trevor-Roper, Kurt Samuelsson, and the aforementioned

Charles and Katherine George, while Michael Walzer and David Little have amended Weber's argument by stressing the political implications of Puritanism. Still in the historical vein, some of Weber's incidental remarks about the relationship between the Reformation and the development of the natural sciences have spawned a parallel though separate debate involving a large number of philosophers and historians of the sciences as well as sociologists, notably R. F. Jones among the former and Robert Merton from sociology.

One of the most significant attempts to investigate the implications of Weber's argument in the modern world has been the cross-disciplinary attempt to apply his thesis to the study of the processes of development and underdevelopment in the Third World. Specialists from almost all the disciplines mentioned above have pursued such studies although, it must be said, some have been considerably more sophisticated than others in their use of Weber's argument. Wholly unsophisticated have been the numerous attempts to test the Protestant ethic thesis by investigating empirically the influence of 'the religious factor' on everyday and economic conduct in contemporary industrial societies. American sociologists conducting research along these lines have, with honourable exceptions, been guilty of a total lack of awareness of historical process where Weber's thesis has been concerned.

All the while, of course, a steady stream of more or less sympathetic literature has come forth, initially from German religious historians and especially Weber's friend and colleague Ernst Troeltsch, but increasingly from the pens of sociologists, including those of Parsons, Benjamin Nelson, and Robert Moore. Periodic escalations in the controversy have been occasioned by events such as the translation of *The Protestant Ethic and the Spirit of Capitalism* into French and by the widespread celebration of the centenary of Weber's birth, both in 1964, fanning the flames in France and Germany respectively.

The longevity of the discussion and proliferation of the literature has had two predictable consequences. First, as Bruun has rightly complained, 'Weber's . . . thought has been commented on, developed, modified, and attacked, so often, and in so many different contexts, that Weber himself occasionally seems to vanish behind a mountain of references and commentaries'.[15] Increasingly, as the debate wears on, we realize that Weber's original thesis is becoming lost in subsequent commentary. By the 1960s it is largely being approached indirectly via Parsons' reconstruction of Weberian sociology, or is simply equated with the arguments put forward by subsequent commentators such as, for example, that of Tawney, who was, of course, explicitly critical of Weber on several important points.[16] Weber has too frequently been dismissed on the strength of second-hand accounts of his argument and his thesis is more often referred to than really known. Moreover, the persistence of the controversy has had the additional effect of increasing the literature that is considered to be 'relevant' to the point where it has become unmanageable. How Weber's argument is to be read has become, in large part, a function of which of Weber's extensive writings, and what among the secondary literature, we elect to treat as part of 'the Protestant ethic thesis'. The following text, perhaps immodestly, offers the student some fairly strong advice on this score.

Finally, and by way of concluding these introductory remarks, a brief comment on Weber's style of writing. It is conventional, when discussing Weber's sociology, to remark upon the difficulties created by his manner of discourse. It is received wisdom that Weber's writings are complex if not convoluted: bedevilled with footnotes yet containing important gaps where essays and arguments are left incomplete; often critical and polemical and therefore unclear as to the precise nature of his own position. However, irrespective of the undoubted force of these criticisms where Weber's writings on, for instance, methodology are concerned, they have no validity whatsoever when levelled against the texts on *Religionssoziologie*. Even the lengthy footnotes to *The Protestant Ethic and the Spirit of Capitalism* are lucidly written. This is not to deny, of course, that these essays are open to several possible interpretations, nor that, at least as originally formulated, they are in places ambiguous. It is simply to argue that Weber has been badly served by many of his critics who, as he himself often complained, have read his text superficially or not read it at all. As a precise statement of an exciting but difficult argument Weber's essays on the Protestant ethic are unsurpassed in the subsequent literature as a whole.[17] His central concept of 'the spirit of modern capitalism', for example, may be ill-conceived and lack any empirical foundation, but the argument itself is certainly straightforward enough, as I shall endeavour to demonstrate in the following chapters.

2   The spirit of modern capitalism – 1

The central concept

The argument of Weber's famous essays of 1905 on the Protestant ethic turns on his concept of 'the spirit of modern capitalism'. In an early and important passage he describes the conceptual basis and peculiarities of 'the phenomenon of which we are seeking an historical explanation' in these terms:

> In the title of this study is used the somewhat pretentious phrase, the *spirit* of capitalism. What is to be understood by it? . . .
>
> If any object can be found to which this term can be applied with any understandable meaning, it can only be an historical individual, i.e., a complex of elements associated in historical reality which we unite into a conceptual whole from the standpoint of their cultural significance.
>
> Such a historical concept, however, since it refers in its content to a phenomenon significant for its unique individuality, cannot be defined according to the formula *genus proximum, differentia specifica*, but it must be gradually put together out of the individual parts which are taken from historical reality to make it up. Thus the final and definitive concept cannot stand at the beginning of the investigation, but must come at the end. We must, in other words, work out in the course of the discussion, as its most important result, the best conceptual formulation of what we here understand by the spirit of modern capitalism, that is the best from the point of view which interests us here. . . .
>
> Thus, if we try to determine the object, the analysis and historical explanation of which we are attempting, it cannot be in the form of a conceptual definition, but at least in the beginning only a provisional description of what is here meant by the spirit of capitalism. Such a description is, however, indispensable in order clearly to understand the object of the investigation.[1]

By way of a 'provisional description' of 'the spirit of modern capitalism' Weber offers the reader a number of lengthy quotations from Benjamin Franklin's *Necessary Hints to Those That Would be Rich* (1736) and *Advice to a Young Tradesman* (1748). Franklin's advice, according to Weber, can be reduced to the following maxims for everyday conduct: be prudent, diligent, and ever about your lawful business; do not idle, for time is money; cultivate your credit-worthiness and put it to good use, for credit is money; be punctual and just in the repayment of loans and debts, for to become a person of known credit-worthiness is to be master of other people's purses; be vigilant in keeping accounts; be frugal in consumption and do not waste money on inessentials; and, finally, do not let money lie idle, for the smallest sum soundly invested can earn a profit, and the profits reinvested soon multiply in ever-increasing amounts.[2]

Clearly, then, 'the spirit of modern capitalism' is the explanandum of Weber's original argument. This fact is not readily apparent, however, in the standard English translation of the essays themselves, which is taken not from the originals of 1905, but from the expanded versions that were prepared by Weber as part of the opening volume of his *Gesammelte Aufsätze zur Religionssoziologie*. It is important to realize that the 'Author's introduction' which appears in the English edition as the opening chapter of Weber's argument is *not* a part of the original essays, and dates instead from 1920.[3] It is an introduction to the *Religionssoziologie* series as a whole – not to the argument of *The Protestant Ethic and the Spirit of Capitalism*. This is no mere matter of bibliographical pedantry. As we shall see, countless distinguished scholars have failed to get to grips with even the most elementary aspects of Weber's argument precisely because they have been unaware of the history of Weber's separate texts and, therefore, of the different explananda of the 'Introduction' and the essays themselves. In the former Weber reflects at length on the diverse origins and the various social and cultural consequences of modern capitalism as an economic form or system (*Kapitalismus als Wirtschaftsform/Wirtschaftssystem*). The essays on the Protestant ethic, on the other hand, are concerned with the nature and origins of the spirit of capitalism (*der Geist des Kapitalismus*). The distinction between 'spirit' and 'system' or 'form' is of some consequence, as we shall see, and raises considerable difficulties for those seeking to document Weber's arguments empirically.

In his initial essays, therefore, Weber's task is to investigate the origins of an orientation towards mundane and economic activities which he sees as exemplified in Franklin's advice. Why should the origins of this world-view need to be explained? Indeed, why is this attitude towards money and its use in any way interesting or peculiarly modern? More generally, and remembering the above distinction between an economic 'system' and its 'spirit', why should Weber seek an historical explanation for the *spirit* of modern capitalism? To commence an argument by conceptualizing an 'economic ethos', and then proceed to search for its causes is, after all, a somewhat unusual programme. An understanding of the curious structure of Weber's argument, and the answers to these questions, are to be found in the intellectual background to Weber's original essays. How he wrote *The Protestant Ethic and the Spirit of Capitalism* is in large part a function of why he wrote it. To understand Weber's thesis, first of all we have to appreciate its intellectual origins.

Origins

Weber's essays on 'The Protestant ethic and the spirit of capitalism' have a long and complicated genealogy. Any number of more or less plausible personal reasons can be offered to explain his interest in their subject matter. From his earliest years, Weber seems to have displayed an intellectual fascination with religion, learning Hebrew on his own initiative at the age of 16 in order to study the Old Testament in the original language, and reading religious commentaries and attending classes in theology during his first terms at university.[4] His concern with the presuppositions and consequences of 'capitalism' was equally longstanding and can be related to the industrial and political situation of nineteenth-century Germany.[5] Although Britain was effectively industrialized from about 1850 onwards, the transition to capitalist industrialism in Germany took place only in the latter part of the nineteenth century, and under circumstances rather different from those which were associated with the British experience. Large-scale capitalist development was made possible in Germany through a forced process of political centralization secured by Prussian military imperialism and, as Barrington Moore reminds us, it proceeded in the absence of a successful bourgeois revolution.[6] Not surprisingly, in view of the economic and related problems facing German society at this time, Weber's attention turned to a consideration of the phenomenon of capitalism itself.

Moreover, as Weber himself acknowledges, speculation on the possible relationships between religion and the rise of capitalism had a long and distinguished pedigree. Thus, when a number of his early German critics attempted to deny the existence of any relationship whatsoever between ascetic Protestantism and modern capitalism, an exasperated Weber appended to the *Religionssoziologie* version of his essays a number of footnotes in which he listed past and present authorities who acknowledged this relationship, mentioning the poets Heine and Keats, the essayist Matthew Arnold, and historians such as Macaulay, Cunningham, Rogers, and Ashley. Indeed, some of the early Protestants themselves were clearly aware of the connection, and Weber triumphantly cites John Wesley and Thomas Manley to this effect, concluding that: 'It is really inexcusable to contest so lightly, as some of my critics have done, facts which are quite beyond dispute, and have hitherto never been disputed by anyone.'[7]

In his original essays Weber actually proceeds from the assumption that Protestantism and capitalism are related to each other, an assumption based on the frequently documented observation that Protestants were, and as far as the evidence could show always had been, economically more successful than Roman Catholics:

A glance at the occupational statistics of any country of mixed religious composition brings to light with remarkable frequency a situation which has several times provoked discussion in the Catholic press and literature, and in Catholic congresses in Germany, namely, the fact that business leaders and owners of capital, as well as the higher grades of skilled labour, and even more the higher technically and commercially trained personnel of modern enterprises, are overwhelmingly Protestant.[8]

The most recent study in this tradition to be cited by Weber is Martin Offenbacher's analysis of the religious, financial, and educational statistics of Baden. Offenbacher, a one-time student of Weber, in 1901 published a study which purported to show that Protestants were consistently over-represented in schools specializing in technical and scientific education, were more numerous and more successful in capitalistic enterprises, and in general were disproportionately to be found in the business world. Whether or not Offenbacher's statistics and his interpretation of them are accurate is beside the point. Their sole purpose in Weber's essays is simply to illustrate a relationship whose existence had become a platitude in his time and, at least until Weber's critics asserted themselves, had never been denied: 'It is thus not new that the existence of this relationship is maintained here. Lavelye, Matthew Arnold, and others already perceived it. . . . Our task here is to explain the relation.'[9] Weber's essays can be seen therefore as a logical extension of the literature represented by Offenbacher's study and summarized by Weber in the opening chapter ('Religious affiliation and social stratification') of the essays themselves. But to explain Weber's essays in terms of his personal inclinations, or his interest in an already formulated problem, begs the question of the origins of the concept which is central to the account that he subsequently offered of the Protestantism–capitalism relationship. Why, after all, should Weber choose to write about the *spirit* of capitalism?

There are essentially two perspectives that can be adopted in answering this question, and I have labelled these 'teleological' and 'genealogical' respectively. In essence, commentators adopting the former approach ignore the chronology of Weber's writings on religion and the rise of capitalism, ruthlessly systematize his contribution, and treat the assembled whole as a grandly conceived comparative history of the 'rationalization' of life in the West. This perspective on Weber's *Religionssoziologie* – which I have called 'teleological' because it presupposes that Weber had the general outline and objectives of his next fifteen years' work clearly in mind when he wrote *The Protestant Ethic and the Spirit of Capitalism* – has become increasingly fashionable in recent years and is well represented in the writings of, among others, Tenbruck, Schluchter, and Eisenstadt. For reasons which will later become obvious I shall postpone consideration of this interpretation of Weber's thesis until Chapter 6. In that chapter, I deal with the confusions that are likely to arise when it is mistakenly assumed that Weber's 'Author's introduction' of 1920 is the opening section of the original essays – and the teleological reading of Weber's argument actually *requires* this assumption.

The perspective that will be adopted here, by way of contrast, takes note of the chronology of Weber's writings on the economic ethics and consequences of the various world religions, and accords a specific historicity to his contribution by investigating its context and locating its origins in Weber's immediate intellectual surroundings. It is my contention that this 'genealogical' approach provides a better understanding of the structure and meaning of Weber's argument about the Protestant ethic and the spirit of capitalism than does the teleological alternative. In particular, the concept of 'the spirit of capitalism' can be analysed much better within the former, than the latter perspective. We can, in fact, locate the origins of Weber's discussion of this concept in four specific factors: first, in Weber's early substantive studies, in particular those of the conditions of rural labourers in East Elbia and of the workings of the Stock Exchange; second, in the writings of Georg Simmel; third, in those of Werner Sombart; and fourth, in Weber's essays on methodology, in particular his early discussions of the ideal-type and of the methodological principle of *Wertbeziehung* or 'value-relevance'. Each of these aspects will be taken up in turn in this chapter and, in the case of the principle of value-relevance, in Chapter 3, but before so doing we ought briefly to consider the intellectual backdrop to all four, namely, the method-ological controversy (*Methodenstreit*) which raged in German academic circles during the last decades of the nineteenth century. Here, ultimately, are to be found the origins of Weber's search for the spirit of modern capitalism.[10]

Political economy and the Methodenstreit

For some three decades prior to the outbreak of the First World War, German academic life was dominated and shaped by a number of identifiable controversies although, as Oberschall has observed, 'it is artificial to treat them independently of each other since one of the distinguishing marks of the period was precisely the way in which conflicting issues spilled over into neighbouring side-issues and expanded into personal polemics and rivalries'.[11] From our point of view, however, the two most important exchanges were those between the German Historical School of Economics and the Austrian marginal utility theorists – in particular that involving Gustav Schmoller and Carl Menger – and the associated but more general and philosophical controversy about the relationship between the natural and cultural-historical sciences and appropriate methodological strategies for each. These twin disputes are conventionally referred to as the *Methodenstreit*.[12] Weber's strictly methodological essays, in particular his discussions of concept formation in the social sciences, can be seen as a direct intervention in the wider of the two discussions. The origins of his concept of the spirit of capitalism are, however, more accurately to be found in the debate involving the economists.

When we realize that Weber's apparently peculiar concept of 'the spirit of modern capitalism', and his quotations from Franklin, are simply another way of talking about *homo oeconomicus* – man and woman as dominated by considerations of self-interest and completely absorbed in the pursuit of material gain – we lock Weber's essays on the Protestant ethic into a literature of political economy which encompasses the participants in the *Methodenstreit* itself, the whole tradition of German historical economics, the classical political economists, and, ultimately, the seventeenth-century theorists of mercantilism, contemporaries of the very businessmen and women to whom Weber accords the honour of being the first generation of modern capitalists. At this point it can become difficult to separate discussion of the origins of Weber's *concept* of the spirit of capitalism from a consideration of the origins of that spirit *itself*. At least one critic of Weber's thesis that the origins of the modern capitalist ethic are to be found in seventeenth-century ascetic Protestantism has suggested that these origins lie, instead, in contemporary reflections on the nature of economic action – in other words in mercantilist political economy.[13] It is difficult, however, to see how the proposal that the origins of *homo oeconomicus* are to be found in a body of literature which was concerned with the problem of describing and locating the sources of certain types of economic action, including that of the rational self-maximizing type, offers a serious challenge to Weber's thesis. Given that the alternative scenario accepts the Weberian idea of some sort of radical transformation in the economic consciousness and behaviour of significant proportions of the relevant populations during the sixteenth and seventeenth centuries, it is clear that here we are being asked to attribute this revolution to an ambiguous though sophisticated exchange involving only a limited number of literati. Weber was rightly sceptical of the mass revolutionary potential of intellectual discussions and theories such as these.[14] Let us take up the story of the possible origins of Weber's *concept*, therefore, with the Classical School of Political Economy, and in particular Adam Smith. It is Smithsian economics that are the target both of the *critiques* launched by the German Historical School and ultimately, through them, of Weber's Protestant ethic essays themselves.

Book 4 of Smith's *Wealth of Nations* actually contains a systematic exposition of the economic doctrines of mercantilism. Since Smith was essentially concerned with erecting a straw-man, in order to demolish it and thereby enhance his own analytical schema, the accuracy of his exposition is perhaps questionable. Nevertheless, it is clear that his framework and that of the mercantilists differ in important respects. Mercantilists operated with a zero-sum conception of wealth, and as a result were particularly concerned with the conditions under which the state might intervene in the economic sphere to secure a favourable balance of trade. Smith, on the other hand, emphasized real capital accumulation as the key to economic growth and was therefore more concerned about the systematic interrelationships between the primary agents in generating growth – labourers, landlords, and capitalists. Again, while the mercantilists debated the conditions under which economic actors might act according to the principles of rational self-interest and the maximization of returns, Smith, resting his case on a systematic theory of moral sentiments, tended to assume that economic actors actually behaved in this way. As he puts it in *The Wealth of Nations*:

The principal which prompts to save is the desire of bettering our condition, a desire which, though generally calm and dispassionate, comes with us from the womb, and never leaves us till we go into the grave. . . .
. . . there is scarce perhaps a single instant in which any man is so perfectly and completely satisfied with his situation, as to be without any wish of alteration or improvement of any kind.[15]

Finally, whereas the approach of the mercantilists was necessarily historical and empirical, dealing as they were with actual nation-states adopting 'begger-your-neighbour' policies, that of Smith was deductive, abstract, and system-building.

The extent to which Smith was ahistorical and the precise nature of his assumptions about human behaviour are, of course, matters of debate and these cannot be entered into here.[16] What is important from our point of view is that, whatever his intentions, Smith initiated a tradition of political economy which, as developed by Ricardo, Malthus, Nassau Senior, and Say, became more and more irrelevant to an understanding of the economic situation in Germany during the nineteenth century. By the mid nineteenth century the tradition of *Manchesterismus*, as the German historial economists were to label it, had become excessively abstract; increasingly predisposed to attempt a statement of the corpus of economic life in an ever-decreasing number of theoretical propositions; falsely universal at the expense of the particular; excessively materialistic; wholly indifferent to the demands of 'culture' and its effects on the economic sphere; insufficiently historical; too much committed to *laissez-faire* and too little interested in the rights and problems of the workers; and wholly dependent on a large number of empirically unverified assumptions about economic behaviour, notably that of the universal predominance of an income-maximizing and self-interested 'rational economic actor'.[17] Increasingly, in classical political economy,

The problems of international exchange, of the rate of profits, wages and rent, were treated simply as a number of [theoretical] propositions, expressed with almost mathematical precision. Admitting their exactness, we must also recognise that they are far from being adequate, and could not possibly afford an explanation of the different varieties of economic phenomena or help the solution of the many practical problems which the development of industry presents to the statesman.[18]

Conceivably there were two possible ways in which the gap between such theory and empirical reality might be narrowed. Towards the end of the nineteenth century the Austrian economist Carl Menger, with other neo-classical authors (especially Jevons in England and Walras in France), attempted a more comprehensive and precise theory. An alternative and more radical strategy was attempted earlier by the German Historical School, namely, to eschew abstract theory altogether and restrict economics to the description of concrete and historically specific economic phenomena.

The origins of German historical economics therefore are not difficult to identify since, as has been suggested, the realities of the German economy were markedly different from those that prevailed in England.[19] While England, in 1850, was already an industrialized nation, in Prussia at the same time, 65 per cent of the population were still employed in agriculture. Given the industrial predominance of England during the first half of the nineteenth century and protectionist policies that German states consequently felt obliged to pursue with respect to their own emerging industries, and considering also the fragmented political structure of the states themselves, the idea that the principle of natural self-interest could promote both economic growth and social welfare in the absence of governmental interference struck German political economists as wholly unrealistic. To contemporary statesmen and philosophers Germany was experiencing complicated labour and industrial problems that England had been spared and for which classical economics had therefore no solution. 'Capitalism' was viewed not as a natural economic order, as in the ahistorical classical tradition, but as an historically specific configuration. The question 'What is it that is unique about modern western capitalism?' came to the fore and demanded an answer in order that the historical emergence of the phenomenon might be understood and, in this way, an appropriate social and industrial strategy be implemented in the national interests of the German people. In fact, the question so dominated German intellectual and political life at the end of the nineteenth century, that by 1911 one of Weber's friends, the Christian social reform politician Friedrich

Naumann, was led to conclude: 'Just as the French have their theme: what was the great Revolution?, so our national destiny has given us our theme for a long time to come: what is capitalism?'[20]

In this way, then, the battle lines were drawn up for the *Methodenstreit* itself. Was economics to be an abstract, ahistorical discipline, based on a series of undemonstrated assumptions about economic phenomena and behaviour, notably that of the 'rational economic actor', or an historical, concrete, empirical, and particular science – inductive and descriptive rather than deductive and explanatory?

The German economists cannot be said to have held a unitary position with respect to these questions. Nevertheless, there is a certain unanimity displayed in the fact that each of the leading lights of the German tradition seems to disagree with the classical political economists at more or less the same points. Basing their conception of economics on a radical distinction between the natural and social sciences, the Historical School stressed that, unlike the subject matter of the former, society was in a continuous process of evolution and change and, therefore, that a social science based on the notion of timeless 'abstract' concepts was destined rapidly to lose touch with social and economic reality. One of the earliest critics of Smith and his followers and an acknowledged predecessor of the Historical School, Friedrich List, established the pattern in the early 1840s by arguing that economic life could readily be viewed as a series of economic stages. In examining the stages of development experienced and attained by different nations, List argued, we must recognize the relationships that exist between the social and political conditions of a society and its economic progress. Central to this conception of economics is an analysis of societies whose cultures, social and political structures, and therefore 'economies' are drastically different from our own. List's complaint about the Classical School was, of course, that because of its essentially deductive approach it failed to locate economic processes in the social frameworks which, in reality and in an empirically variable manner, affected them. List stressed, in particular, the important role that the state had to play in controlling the economic sphere and the processes of growth.[21]

Almost simultaneously Wilhelm Roscher, who is generally viewed as the founding father of the Historical School, expressed similar reservations when he attempted to reconceptualize German economics as essentially economic history:

Our aim is simply to describe what people have wished for and felt in matters economic, to describe the aims they have followed and the successes they achieved – as well as to give the reasons why such aims were chosen and such triumphs won. Such research can only be accomplished if we keep in close touch with the other sciences of national life, with legal and political history, as well as with the history of civilisation.[22]

Bruno Hildebrand, writing shortly after List and Roscher, pushed their ideas further by denying the existence of almost any economic generalizations whatsoever. He was, indeed, critical of Roscher for having recognized the existence of 'national economic laws', a position which, in his view, conceded too much to the Classical School. Elsewhere Hildebrand argued for a science of national economic development and a general evolutionary schema with three phases, namely, the periods of natural economy, money economy, and credit. (Whether or not it is possible to reconcile Hildebrand's denial of 'nationally specific economic laws' with his proposed 'general laws of economic development' is beyond the scope of this study.)[23]

The last of the members of the group that has become known as the 'Older Historical School', Karl Knies, carried the historical position to its logical conclusion by arguing that there were neither national economic laws nor laws of economic development. Economics, for Knies, is simply the history of ideas concerning the economic development of a nation at different periods of its history, an exercise that may allow us to draw analogies – nothing more – with the experiences of other countries.[24]

This short presentation of the position adopted by the Older Historical School is, of course, hopelessly superficial, but it can fairly be said from even such a brief exposition that the principals appear to share an agreement on certain essentials. They emphasize the relativity of institutions, the importance of the inductive method and of reasoning from concrete data, and the interrelations among human motives and among the social sciences. Hildebrand speaks for all when he writes:

Man as a social being is the child of civilisation and a product of history. His wants, his intellectual outlook, his relation to material objects, and his connection with other human beings have not always been the same. Geography influences them, history modifies them, while the progress of education may entirely transform them.[25]

There is, on the other hand, considerable disagreement with regard to the factors which make for change. Where it is assumed that there exist certain laws governing the development of national economies, there is no consensus on the nature of these laws, the methods to be used for their discovery, or the possibility that the laws themselves might be stated with any degree of precision.

The classical economists and the Older Historical School exchanged views on the nature of economic explanation at a distance; the views of the former being an independently developed alternative to, rather than a frontal assault on, those of the latter. In 1883, however, direct confrontation was initiated when the Austrian marginal utility theorist Carl Menger published what amounted to a defence of the underlying assumptions and premises of classical economic theory and offered certain measured criticisms of the historical tradition. The doyen of the second generation of historical economists (or 'Younger Historical School'), Gustav Schmoller, reviewed Menger's book acrimoniously and so began a polemical exchange of views which, especially when the controversy expanded into a full-blown methodological debate about the relationships between the sciences, dominated German intellectual life until the First World War.

The numerous dimensions and intricacies of the *Methodenstreit* need not concern us here. Just as the older generation of historical economists had failed to arrive at a common methodological position so the various members of the Younger School – Schmoller, Knapp, Brentano, Bucher, Sombart, and others – diverged on a number of important points both with respect to each other and their intellectual predecessors. The newer members of the school conceded that economic laws existed but denied that the methods of the Classical School could reveal them. Further, although Schmoller and his peers studied and classified the processes of economic evolution and development, they were sceptical as to the possibility of formulating Hildebrand's 'laws of development'. Indeed, the members of the Younger School as a whole tended to steer clear of theorizing about the possibilities of the Historical Method, preferring instead to put the method itself into practice, and so producing a stream of monographs describing the institutions of antiquity and the Middle Ages, contemporary economic organizations and practices, and the economic doctrines and policies pursued by specific communities at given periods in their history.[26]

Whatever their internal disagreements the members of the Younger School, following Schmoller, collectively diagnosed the failings of the Classical School to be principally three. First, they contested the assertion that social actors in their economic pursuits were driven exclusively by economic considerations, seeking always to maximize satisfaction of personal and especially economic interests. The narrow 'egoistic psychology' underpinning classical theory was deemed to be empirically at fault. It was argued that individuals, even in their economic activities, were influenced significantly by ethical and other non-economic factors that were historically variable. Relevant motives here, as elsewhere, might include a sense of duty, love, hatred, the desire for glory, pleasure afforded by the work itself, or the simple wish to conform with what was customary. Second, whereas classical theorists insisted that certain interrelationships between economic phenomena were valid independently of time and place, Schmoller and his followers argued that since the economic activities undertaken by a group or society were affected by the surrounding legal, political, religious, and other beliefs and institutions, and since these were changeable, then the relationships between economic phenomena must also be variable. Classical theorists made the mistake of assuming the economic system of a particular place and time (England during the period of industrialization) to be wholly indicative of economies generally. Third, for the Classical School's deductive approach, the Historical School substituted induction based on observation, arguing that it was only in this way that theoretical propositions could be constructed bearing an adequate relationship to empirical reality. This criticism is, of course, closely related to those concerning the underlying psychology and the universalism of the classical approach. Precisely because the classical theorists attempted to provide a one-sided and ahistorical representation of economic activities, their propositions failed to capture these activities in their concreteness, bound in as they were with a complex totality of non-economic factors.

Menger replied to Schmoller's criticisms much as we would expect. He argues that economic theory cannot provide a total picture of concrete reality and so elects consciously and for heuristic purposes to deal only with the 'economic' aspect of social reality, specifically with the interrelationships between human needs, available goods, and how these are matched, in the absence of any extraneous conditions which might or might not affect economic choices and decisions in reality.[27]

It is clear that these differences of approach represent alternative answers to the problems of concept formation or abstraction in the social sciences; this, indeed, explains why an exchange of views regarding issues germane to the discipline of economics so readily became a full-scale philosophical controversy. Both Schmoller and Menger conceived of scientific knowledge as a mental replica of the empirical phenomena in question. Their disagreement is essentially about what constitutes a satisfactory replica. Schmoller sought to capture a concrete historical moment in all its completeness and so favoured an 'individualizing' approach to abstraction. Menger felt that it was impossible to grasp the organic 'wholeness' of unique events as these were situated in an historical context and sought, instead, to discover what was recurrent in empirical phenomena by abstracting the regular relationships that could be identified throughout history. His was the completeness or replication of the one-sided picture rather than the historical moment. The charge against Menger, from the historical camp, was that the 'replication' of reality proposed by the classical theorists was unsatisfactory because it ignored the fact that economic behaviour is not motivated exclusively by economic considerations and, indeed, that the non-economic considerations affecting it are different in successive historical epochs.[28]

Against this background of the methodological controversy in German political economy we can place the immediate origins of Weber's essays on the Protestant ethic. Many have argued, with the advantage of hindsight, that the gap between the classical or neo-classical and the various historical authorities is by no means as large as was assumed at the time. The Historical School, in particular, seems ultimately to leave unresolved the issue of the status of 'economic generalizations', referring not only to economic stages, parallelisms and analogies, but also to the developmental and contemporary laws of economics themselves. Menger, on the other hand, consistently conceded the importance of historical studies.[29] From our point of view, this is neither here nor there. What is important is that it was in the context of a perceived controversy about the nature of modern capitalism and an appropriate framework within which to analyse it that Weber began to write about capitalism, about the principles of concept formation in the social sciences, and to study the writings of his colleagues Simmel and Sombart.

Weber's earlier studies

Weber's early writings on capitalist institutions bear the stamp of the

Historical School. His doctoral dissertation of 1889 and *Habilitations-schrift* of two years later investigate, respectively, the interrelation-ships between the legal institutions and economic forms of medieval capitalism, and between political interests and concepts of property in the Roman Empire. What is important about both of these early studies, from our point of view, is that in each Weber accords historical primacy to non-economic factors. Already he has denied an economistic approach to social evolution. In the former study, he insists that legal developments may follow a logic that is entirely extraneous to economic conditioning and, indeed, may shape develop-ments in the economic sphere. In the latter, historical primacy is given to political over economic factors in describing ancient Germanic and Roman forms of economic organization.[30]

A more obvious clue as to the origins of the concept of the spirit of modern capitalism and to the structure of Weber's essays on the Protestant ethic is provided in his studies of agrarian society in East Prussia.[31] On behalf of the *Verein für Sozialpolitik* (Society for Social Policy) Weber conducted a survey of the conditions of rural labourers east of the River Elbe in the early 1890s. Widespread concern was being expressed at this time about the steady erosion of the Germany peasantry on East Prussian *Junker* estates and their replacement by Russo-Polish seasonal labour. Weber concluded that the conflict between the fleeing peasantry and the new day labourers and landowning *Junkers* was more than simply an economic one. It was primarily a conflict between contrasting *Weltanschauungen* or 'world-views'. The indigenous labourers were no longer prepared to accept the contractual obligations of an ascribed and semi-servile status, personal subjection to the arbitrary will of a patriarchal employer, and the associated legacies of serfdom, in exchange for relatively long-term security and a fixed though modest standard of living. The material advantages of 'contractual subservience' could not compensate for the absence of personal freedom and lack of opportunity for upward social mobility, so many of the established German labourers chose to emigrate rather than remain in their subject position. Their new independence implied a more precarious existence, but it also opened up the possibility of satisfying aspirations for freedom and social mobility which could not be entertained under the traditional system of labour relations on the estates. Weber concluded therefore that, in the east Elbian situation, the 'bread and butter question' was less important than an understanding of the wider hopes and aspirations of the farm labourers. In explaining the labourers' 'break with traditionalism', ideological factors were as important as strictly economic considerations:

the question is not how high the income of the workers really is, but whether as a result of (the level of wages) an orderly economy is possible for the workers, whether he and his employer are satisfied according to their own subjective evaluation, or why they are not satisfied, what direction their wishes and aspirations are taking, for future development will depend upon these factors.[32]

From this period onwards, questions associated with possible alternative 'orientations to work', their origins and consequences, are a recurrent theme in Weber's writings.[33]

Weber was concerned with more than simply orientations to work. He was, as we would expect, more obviously interested in the behaviour and attitudes of capitalists. By observing the activities of businessmen and speculators on the Stock Exchange Weber was led to the conclusion that economic self-interest could take more than one form. Businessmen used the Exchange for the dual purposes of slowly but predictably generating regular though modest profits with a minimum of risk, and protecting themselves against unanticipated price fluctuations, whereas speculators risked all on marginal gains to make lucky windfalls: the rational strategist versus the bold gambler. Moreover, businessmen shared relationships of confidence with each other and displayed an ethic of mutual trust which was based on, but extended beyond, a common interest in 'rationalizing' the market and minimizing its uncertainties. (Speculators, on the other hand, remained individualists in competition with all others on the market.) In short, one of Weber's most important observations was that shared ideas about economic conduct could exert an influence on the economic sphere that went beyond the narrow requirements of common economic interest. The trading ethic of the businessmen was not simply an expression of mutual self-interest but was, Weber felt, at least in part the outcome of a shared conception of the meaning of economic activities that was rooted in the traditions of a merchant class.[34]

Weber was clearly impressed by the difference between the economic ethic of the businessman and that of the speculator. This distinction reappears in his discussion of the spirit of modern capitalism in the essays on the Protestant ethic, and it is one that he feels both Simmel and Sombart fail to appreciate; a failure which in Weber's eyes largely invalidates his colleagues' accounts of the nature and origins of modern capitalism.[35] As we shall see when, in Chapter 3, we come to look at Weber's argument in detail, the distinction between his concept of the spirit of modern capitalism and those employed by Simmel and Sombart emerges through Weber's use of the methodological principle of 'value-relevance' in conceptualizing his explanandum, a principle which Weber takes from the writings of the German neo-Kantian philosopher Heinrich Rickert. Weber, in fact, took up the works of Simmel, Sombart, and Rickert almost simultaneously. In 1897 he suffered a mental breakdown which resulted in his effectively ceasing to work for some four years. His recovery, from about 1902 onwards, was slow and in the end never more than partial. His ability to work fluctuated for years afterwards. Two of the first books he read while easing himself gently back into academic life were Simmel's *Philosophy of Money* (published in 1900) and Rickert's twin volumes on *The Limits of Concept Formation in the Natural Sciences*, which had appeared in 1896 and 1902 respectively.[36] Meanwhile, in 1902, Sombart had published the first edition of his *Modern Capitalism*, and in so doing appears to have provided the final provocation for Weber's argument. His essays on 'The Protestant ethic and the spirit of capitalism' are, therefore, an intervention in the *Methodenstreit*, a critical contribution to the German historical tradition of economics, and above all a reply to Sombart. Contrary to much popular opinion they were not conceived as a critique of historical materialism and the account of the development of capitalism there proposed. Weber is debating, not with the ghost of Marx, but – via German historical economics – with that of Adam Smith.

Simmel

The immediate origins of Weber's discussion of the spirit of modern capitalism can be seen clearly in the earlier contributions of Simmel and Sombart. Chapter 3 of Simmel's *Philosophy of Money*, entitled 'Money in the sequence of purposes', bears a striking similarity to Weber's discussion of 'economic ethics' in Chapter 2 ('The spirit of capitalism') of *The Protestant Ethic*.[37] Simmel offers the phenomenon of money as the most extreme example of a means becoming an end:

Money's value as a *means* increases with its *value* as a means right up to the point at which it is valid as an absolute value and the consciousness of purpose in it comes to an end. The inner polarity of the essence of money lies in its being the absolute means and thereby becoming psychologically the absolute purpose for most people. . . .[38]

How does such an attitude towards money arise? Certainly, for Simmel at least, it is not an ubiquitous phenomenon in human history. In antiquity the relatively stable technology of agricultural production focused people's economic consciousness on consumption rather than production, and political and moral debates centred on the organization of consumption rather than productive labour. What was important, from a moral standpoint, was how wealth was consumed and distributed, and since acquisition was frowned on, money was viewed as merely a necessary evil. Continuity of existence lay in the more substantial element of landed property. This, Simmel concedes, is not to deny the universal phenomenon of avarice:

There is no point of time in which individuals have not been greedy for money, yet one can certainly say that the greatest intensity and expansion of this desire occurred in those times in which the modest satisfaction of individual life-interests, such as the elevation of the religious absolute as the ultimate purpose of existence, had lost its power.[39]

Such an attitude towards money is however, as Simmel makes clear, at odds with religious and clerical values. Augustine's judgement on the businessman, that he may conduct himself without sin but cannot be pleasing to God, symbolizes the conflict between religious morality and money.

Simmel's general conclusion, then, is that the extent to which money becomes an end in itself depends on the 'cultural tendencies of an epoch'; or, as he puts it, 'distinction[s] in the meaning of money can be traced back to the ultimate decisions in the spirit of each epoch'. The origins of the Jewish attitude towards money, for example, are to be found in Judaism itself:

The specific ability and the interest of the Jews in the nature of money has certainly been related to their 'monotheistic schooling'. The temper of a people who for thousands of years became used to lifting their eyes up to a single supreme being, to finding in him – especially as he possessed only a very relative transcendence – the goal and intersection of all particular interests, would be suited to devoting itself to the economic sphere and especially to that value which presents itself as the encompassing unity and the common focal point of all sequences of purposes.[40]

Social and cultural marginality have a similar congruence with money: it rapidly becomes the centre of interest for diverse groups or classes of individuals who, because of their socially marginal position, are precluded from pursuing certain personal goals in specific spheres of life. The Huguenots in France, Armenians in Turkey, Quakers in England, and Jews universally 'applied themselves with the greatest intensity to money acquisition' because of their exposed position and restrictions on their status. 'Strangers' have everywhere taken up trading:

The significance of the stranger for the nature of money seems to me to be epitomised in miniature by the advice I once overheard: never have any financial dealings with two kinds of people – friends and enemies. In the first case, the indifferent objectivity of money transactions is in insurmountable conflict with the personal character of the relationship; in the other, the same condition provides a wide scope for hostile intentions which corresponds to the fact that our forms of law in a money economy are never precise enough to rule out wilful malice with certainty. The desirable party for financial transactions – in which, as it has been said quite correctly, business is business – is the person completely indifferent to us, engaged neither for nor against us.[41]

Such trading relationships were pure monetary transactions and their amorality sponsored the development of money as the expression of all values and an end in itself.

Indifference on the one hand and avarice on the other are, however, not the only attitudes towards money that are culturally possible. Simmel also mentions the cultural tendencies which sponsor extravagance, poverty as a virtue, cynicism, and 'the blasé attitude'. Each of these attitudes is typical of a certain 'money culture'. The last two, for example, find their expression in the modern market society. 'The nurseries of cynicism', according to Simmel, are

those places with huge turnovers, exemplified in stock exchange dealings, where money is available in huge quantities and changes owners easily. The more money becomes the sole centre of interest, the more one discovers that honour and conviction, talent and virtue, beauty and salvation of the soul, are exchanged against money and so the more a mocking and frivolous attitude will develop in relation to these higher values that are for sale for the same kind of value as groceries, and that also command a 'market price'.[42]

The blasé attitude towards money is the product of situations in which money can procure all the possibilities that life has to offer and is often accompanied by satiated enjoyment of these.

It should be obvious that none of these attitudes towards money is the equivalent of Weber's 'spirit of modern capitalism'. Franklin was neither cynical nor blasé about the accumulation and use of capital. Weber's concept is, however, identical with Simmel's general proposition that, in the modern market societies of the West, money has become an end in itself. Summing up his interest in the modern capitalist ethos Weber writes: 'The peculiarity of this philosophy of avarice appears to be the ideal of the honest man of recognised credit, and above all the idea of a duty of the individual toward the increase of his capital, which is assumed as an end in itself.'[43] It is perhaps not surprising, given this similarity, to learn that Weber considered Simmel's analysis of the spirit of capitalism to be 'brilliant'.

Weber did not, however, accept Simmel's account without reservation. In *The Protestant Ethic and the Spirit of Capitalism* he criticizes Simmel for his failure to draw an adequate distinction between the 'money economy' and 'capitalism'. Elsewhere his general charge was that Simmel's persistent attempts to uncover the essential 'meaning' of social phenomena resulted in an inadequately refined conceptualization of the concrete aspects of social life.[44] Certainly, in so far as *The Philosophy of Money* is concerned, Weber's criticism appears valid. Simmel's account is underpinned by a developing theory of the self. He is concerned not only to determine the effects of the money economy on social and cultural life, but also to establish a philosophy of culture and, ultimately, a metaphysics of life. Simmel's diverse purposes mean that, at the end of the day, we are unclear as to whether 'cultural tendencies' or strictly economic developments determine 'the meaning of money'. His attempt to distil 'essential forms' from historically specific appearances leaves the ontological status of the 'spirits of the ages' obscure. A much less metaphysical and more historical interpretation of the spirit of modern capitalism was offered shortly afterwards by Werner Sombart.

Sombart

The first edition of Sombart's *Modern Capitalism* appeared in 1902 and was immediately subjected to severe criticism. Sombart undertook to revise the work substantially and published a number of supplementary texts, including *The Jews and Modern Capitalism* (1911), *Luxury and Capitalism* (1912), *War and Capitalism* (1912) and *The Quintessence of Capitalism* (1913), before issuing a second edition of *Modern Capitalism* in two parts, published in 1916–17 and 1926–7 respectively.[45] The developments in Sombart's thought during the years between 1902 and 1927 make a systematic statement of his position somewhat difficult. In any case, what is important from our point of view is the position he outlines in his initial treatment of modern capitalism, since it is this position to which Weber addresses himself in his essays on the Protestant ethic.

In *Modern Capitalism* Sombart first investigates the self-sufficient and handicraft economic systems, then the early stages of the capitalistic system, and finally 'high capitalism' itself. Each of these systems is characterized by a particular combination of three elements: a set of economic values specifying the goals and rules of economic conduct; an economic order or procedure for organizing economic activity and in particular the various factors of production; and an economic technique involving methods, equipment, and the knowledge of how to use them. The first of these elements, 'economic value-attitudes', emerges from a balance between the principles of 'the satisfaction of relatively stable needs' and 'unlimited acquisition' on the one hand and 'traditionalism' or 'rationalism' on the other. Pre-capitalistic (self-sustaining and handicraft) economic systems are traditionalistic and oriented to the satisfaction of fixed needs. Although there are significant differences in the forms of economic organization characteristic of these systems, they both rest on traditional, empirical technologies, tied closely to the direct exploitation of natural resources.[46]

The capitalistic system that is peculiar to the modern western world not only introduces a battery of new techniques involving the exploitation of advanced technology, but also rests on a different economic order and spirit to its predecessors. On an organizational level it depends on an exchange in a market between those who own the means of production and organize the economic unit, and a stratum of propertyless workers. The most important factor in creating this new economic order is, however, the emergence of a spirit based on the principles of unlimited acquisition and economic rationality. The 'spirit of modern capitalism' therefore comprises two distinct elements, a spirit of enterprise or dynamism, and a bourgeois or rational spirit. This combination of unlimited material striving and calculating rationality first appeared in thirteenth-century Italy, began really to assert itself during the sixteenth century, and was finally triumphant by the beginning of the nineteenth century. A new economic ethos is, then, both a precondition for and a distinguishing characteristic of modern capitalism.

Certain other objective conditions are, of course, prerequisites of the capitalistic order. Among these, Sombart mentions the development of the modern state, the increase in liquid capital following the discovery of precious metals in the New World, the separation of business and household, and a number of important technological advances. In Sombart's sequence of events an inflow of precious metals permitted the accumulation of wealth in cities and expanded the demand for goods. At about this time a new spirit of enterprise or drive for profits, and a system of double-entry bookkeeping facilitating control over these profits, both made their appearance. Developments took on a momentum of their own; technical, technological, political, and religious obstacles to the maximization of profits were systematically dealt with and swept away. Eventually, by the period of high capitalism (commencing in the mid eighteenth century), the drive to unlimited acquisition had so established itself that the tendency for businessmen to retire on to the land, having made their fortunes, was undermined. The whole economic system has now become geared to the dictates of the capitalistic spirit.

Sombart's writings on modern capitalism are at least as voluminous as those of Weber himself, so we could not hope to enter into a full discussion of them in this context.[47] Detailed consideration of his studies is, in any case, unnecessary for an understanding of how they relate to Weber's essays. From our point of view, what is important about Sombart's argument is that it contains two principal assertions and two ambiguities.[48] Sombart maintains, first of all, that 'the spirit of capitalism' comprises two elements, namely, those of restless and ruthless acquisition and of calculating rationality. Following this assertion is, however, an ambiguity. Although this spirit stands at the centre of Sombart's entire contribution, its status is unclear. At times it seems to be a complex of value-elements – a world-view – which, given a number of situational conditions such as the development of rational capital accounting, certain forms of economic organization, and so forth, fosters capitalist development. The spirit of capitalism is, in other words, a necessary but not sufficient condition for the development of modern capitalism. Elsewhere, however, Sombart uses the term 'spirit of capitalism' with reference to the patterning of action in terms of a world-view. From this perspective the 'ethos' or complex of value-attitudes of a particular group or stratum in society appear as the prime mover generating the modern capitalist order: capitalism is, in neo-Hegelian fashion, simply the realization of an economic idea. Now, even if we suspend judgement on the question of the balance between value elements and situational conditions in Sombart's aetiology, there exists a related ambiguity deriving from the possibility that Sombart's account suggests a problematic tautology whereby 'the spirit of capitalism' is simultaneously the (or a) causal element in generating capitalism and a unique feature of capitalism itself. In other words, the capitalist spirit is both distinguishing characteristic of and important precondition for the capitalist system, a dualism which makes Sombart's version of events nigh unfalsifiable since the suggested consequence can never be found in the absence of the proposed cause, and vice versa.

Finally, and notwithstanding such ambiguities, the general thrust of Sombart's account is that the spirit of capitalism is the factor or one of the factors producing capitalism. This means that the spirit must have preceded the system. Where, then, are the origins of the spirit of capitalism itself? Sombart does not tackle this question in *Modern Capitalism*, but in his *The German Economy in the Nineteenth Century* published in the following year (1903), he attributes the changing orientation towards economic activity associated with the rise of capitalism to the influence of the Jews throughout Western Europe. Among Jews, according to Sombart, the spirit of capitalism was fostered by, among other things, the Deuteronomic injunction permitting different commercial dealings and specifying a different moral code in relations between Jews and Gentiles to that which governed transactions between Jews (permitting, for example, Jews to enter into usurious relationships with Gentiles but not other Jews); the legalism and rationalism of Judaism itself; a certain sobriety in the Jewish manner of living; and their being generally excluded from traditional means of advancement in church and state. Sombart maintains that Jewish merchants carried this economic ethic across Europe and propagated it (if only through being imitated) among indigenous business communities wherever they settled.

The relationships between these accounts of the origins of modern capitalism and Weber's essays on the Protestant ethic should by now be apparent. What I am suggesting is that we can most readily appreciate the structure of Weber's argument in terms of the whole intellectual tradition out of which it emerged. Weber followed the German Historical School in postulating the uniqueness of modern capitalism as an historical phenomenon. One aspect of this uniqueness lay in the particular economic ethic displayed by modern capitalists and labourers, namely, that of rational capital accumulation or the maximization of economic returns as an end in itself. Such an attitude is by no means an historical constant, as the Classical School of political economy would have us believe, for, as Simmel demonstrates, attitudes towards money and wealth are culturally specific and historically variable. Therefore, any explanation of the particular economic ethic that prevails in a given historical situation must take account of the interrelationships of human motives, and relate economic beliefs and action to the situational non-economic conditions in which these are located. Sombart's account of modern capitalism upholds the historical tradition in all of these respects. Finally, Weber's essays on the Protestant ethic can best be understood as a specific response to the details (but not the structure) of Sombart's argument, because what Weber's essays must obviously contest are Sombart's two assertions concerning, first of all, the dual elements of 'the spirit of modern capitalism' and, second, their Jewish origins. Moreover, as we shall now see, because Weber does not challenge the structure of Sombart's argument, his own account displays identical aetiological ambiguities and tautological leanings with respect to the effects and status of the spirit of capitalism itself.

3 The spirit of modern capitalism – 2

Weber's argument

As was observed in Chapter 2 Weber opens the argument of *The Protestant Ethic and the Spirit of Capitalism* by offering a provisional description of the phenomenon for which he seeks to provide a causal explanation – the spirit of modern capitalism. Sombart, in his studies of the origins of the same phenomenon, finds these largely in the ethical tenets of Judaism and the marginal social status of the Jewish people. Weber, as we know, will contest Sombart's explanation by suggesting that the source of the modern capitalist mentality is to be found, not in the doctrines of orthodox Judaism, but in those of the ascetic Protestantism of the sixteenth and seventeenth centuries. However, it is also Weber's belief that Sombart misinterprets the *origins* of the modern capitalist mentality largely because he is mistaken as to the *nature* of this mentality to begin with. In other words, Weber not only relocates the origins of the modern capitalist ethos, but also challenges Sombart's descriptions of that ethos itself. He does so for two reasons. The first of these may loosely be termed empirical. Weber argues that one of the two components of Sombart's 'spirit of modern capitalism', that of restless and ruthless acquisition, is not especially modern at all and can be identified in economic conduct throughout recorded history. Weber's second objection arises out of his methodological principle of 'value-relevance'. He suggests that Sombart's description of the modern capitalist mentality is not a particularly useful starting point for a causal explanation because the values underpinning its twin elements of adventurism and rationality are self-contradictory. Let us examine these objections in more detail.

Economic traditionalism and the capitalist mentality

Weber had no quarrel with Sombart's interpretation of the economic ethos of pre-capitalist ages. He agrees that

the most important opponent with which the spirit of capitalism, in the sense of a definite standard of life claiming ethical sanction, has had to struggle, was that type of attitude and reaction to new situations which we may designate as 'traditionalism'.[1]

'Economic traditionalism', like the spirit of modern capitalism itself, does not refer to a particular type of economic organization but rather to an ethos with which economic activities can be imbued. Weber illustrates such traditionalism and asserts its historical precedence over the spirit of capitalism in these terms:

At the beginning of all ethics and the economic relations which result, is traditionalism, the sanctity of tradition, the exclusive reliance upon such trade and industry as have come down from the fathers. This traditionalism survives far down into the present; only a human lifetime in the past it was futile to double the wages of an agricultural labourer in Silesia who mowed a tract of land on a contract, in the hope of inducing him to increase his exertions. He would simply have reduced by half the work expended because with this half he would have been able to earn . . . as much as before. This general incapacity and indisposition to depart from the beaten paths is the motive for the maintenance of tradition.[2]

In short, where economic traditionalism flourishes, all other things being equal, labourers prefer to work shorter hours and earn the same money, than to increase their exertions in exchange for extra wages. Traditionalistic labourers, treating 'everyday routine as an inviolable norm of conduct', do not ask 'How much can I earn in a day if I do as much work as possible?'; but 'How much must I work in order to earn the wage . . . which I earned before and which takes care of my traditional needs?'[3]

Similarly, among entrepreneurs economic traditionalism is expressed as a consistent preference for increased leisure over increased profit. Weber offers the life of the putter-out in the continental textile industry up to the mid nineteenth century as an example:

We may imagine its routine . . . as follows: the peasants came with their cloth . . . to the town in which the putter-out lived, and after a careful, often official appraisal of the quality, received the customary price for it. The putter-out's customers, for markets any appreciable distance away, were middlemen, who also came to him, generally not yet following samples, but seeking traditional qualities. . . . Personal canvassing of customers took place, if at all, only at long intervals. . . . The number of business hours was very moderate, perhaps five to six a day, sometimes considerably less; in the rush season, where there was one, more. Earnings were moderate; enough to lead a respectable life and in good times to put away a little. On the whole, relations among competitors were relatively good, with a large degree of agreement on the fundamentals of business. A long daily visit to the tavern, with often plenty to drink, and a congenial circle of friends, made life comfortable and leisurely.

The form of organisation was in every respect capitalistic: the entrepreneur's activity was of a purely business character; the use of capital, turned over in the business, was indispensable; and finally, the objective aspect of the economic process, the book-keeping, was rational. But it was traditionalistic business, if one considers the spirit which animated the entrepreneur: the traditional manner of life, the traditional rate of profit, the traditional amount of work, the traditional manner of regulating the relationships with labour, and the essentially traditional circle of customers and the manner of attracting new ones. All these dominated the conduct of the business, were at the basis, one may say, of the *ethos* of this group of business men.[4]

Economic traditionalism among entrepreneurs and labourers both precedes the spirit of modern capitalism and is the antithesis of it. The problem is then one of explaining how the latter comes to supersede the former as the norm of economic conduct. By what means is the shift accomplished between the attitude towards business activities implicit in the conduct of the continental putter-out and that preached in the writings of Benjamin Franklin?[5]

It is at this point that Weber and Sombart part company. Weber argues, contrary to Sombart, that a simple increase in 'the acquisitive impulse' is not sufficient to undermine the routine and sanctity of tradition:

The notion that our rationalistic and capitalistic age is characterised by a stronger economic interest than other periods is childish; the moving spirits of modern capitalism are not possessed of a stronger economic impulse than, for example, an oriental trader.[6]

Following Simmel, Weber acknowledges that avarice – the manifestation of a ruthless and restless acquisitive impulse – appears to be as old as civilization itself, and precisely for that reason cannot be unique to the modern capitalist mentality. But how does Weber reconcile this concession with his picture of economic traditionalism? Is not the conduct of the 'oriental trader' the antithesis of that of the continental putter-out and, indeed, the very epitome of 'the spirit of modern capitalism' itself?

Weber, unlike Sombart, answers this question in the negative. It is clear that, for Weber, there is more than one kind of economic traditionalism. The leisurely activities of the continental putter-out and the Silesian mower, representing capital and labour respectively, may be taken as exemplars of the world-view of traditionalism *stricto sensu*. But Weber is also aware that 'at all periods of history, wherever it was possible, there has been ruthless acquisition, bound to no ethical norms whatever'. The instinct of acquisition is universal:

> The greed of the Chinese Mandarin, the old Roman aristocrat, or the modern peasant, can stand up to any comparison. . . . The *auri sacra fames* is as old as the history of man. But we shall see that those who submitted to it without reserve as an uncontrolled impulse, such as the Dutch sea-captain who 'would go through hell for gain, even though he scorched his sails', were by no means the representatives of that attitude of mind from which the specifically modern capitalistic spirit as a mass phenomenon is derived. . . .[7]

Absolute ruthlessness in acquisition is itself a tradition:

> Capitalistic acquisition as an adventure has been at home in all types of economic society which have known trade with the use of money and have offered it opportunities, through *commenda*, farming of taxes, State loans, financing of wars, ducal courts and officeholders. Likewise the inner attitude of the adventurer, which laughs at all ethical limitations, has been universal.[8]

Traditionalism in economic activities therefore encompasses the world-view of the continental putter-out and that of 'dare-devil and unscrupulous speculators, economic adventurers such as we meet at all periods of economic history', for both of these types precede the spirit of modern capitalism and are to be contrasted with it. The peculiarity of the world-view of Franklin, by comparison, lies in its support for the idea of the honest person of recognized credit who, by means of rational capitalistic enterprise, increases his or her capital as a duty or end in itself.

In short, what Weber argues is that only one of the twin elements of Sombart's 'spirit of modern capitalism' is correctly placed, that of 'bourgeois rationality'. The element of ruthless acquisition is essentially an aspect of economic traditionalism and is, indeed, at odds with the characteristic ethos of modern capitalism. The modern capitalist mentality is not that of the bold adventurer, nor even the opportunist. Rather, it is the ethos of the risk-minimizing though relentlessly profit-maximizing strategist. Modern capitalists seek to maximize their return through rational calculation rather than by means of daring though potentially lucrative gambles. In a word, and in the terms of

Weber's earlier argument about the types of economic conduct to be observed on the Stock Exchange, modern capitalists are 'businessmen' rather than 'speculators'.[9]

All of this is, of course, empirically dubious. Weber documents his argument with an unconvincing mixture of fictitious illustrations, composite instances drawn from diverse times and places, and anecdotal empirical examples. As we shall see in Chapter 5, had Weber actually attempted to investigate empirically the economic conduct and motives of medieval businessmen and artisans, or those of early modern capitalists and labourers, he would have found the data difficult to unearth and ambiguous where it existed. A few generalizations based on 'what we all know' about the state of mind of pre-capitalist merchants, alongside the illustrative quotations from Franklin's texts, are scarcely sufficient documentation of Weber's argument. His insistence on separating Sombart's elements of 'bourgeois rationality' and 'limitless adventurism' is underwritten, however, not so much by his sketchy empirical data as by the Rickertian methodological principle of 'relevance to value'.

Rickert and value-relevance

Weber, it will be remembered, studied Rickert's epistemology while recovering from his mental breakdown in 1902. He was much impressed,[10] and it is now more or less generally accepted that his own theory of concept formation leans heavily on that of his philosophical mentor.[11] This is not the place to enter into a detailed discussion of Weber's complex essays on the methodology of the social sciences, far less a consideration of their diverse intellectual origins. My sole concern here will be with Weber's use of the principle of value-relevance as a method of concept formation in the social sciences, for it is through the application of this principle that he arrives at his concept of the spirit of modern capitalism. In order to understand Weber's use of this principle it is necessary to digress briefly and consider its Rickertian origins.[12]

Rickert was one of a number of eminent neo-Kantian philosophers who participated in epistemological discussions during the period of the *Methodenstreit*. As has been observed, the exchange between Menger and Schmoller concerning the appropriate methods for economics rapidly became part of a much wider controversy about the relationship between the natural and social sciences in general: what were their respective subject matters and which were the most appropriate methodological procedures for studying them? A number of Rickert's predecessors, notably Windelband, arguing from the premise that reality is indivisible, proposed an *a priori* logical distinction between natural and social sciences on the basis of their methods. Natural sciences, Windelband argued, utilize a 'nomothetic' or generalizing method since they seek to discover law-like and general relationships and properties, whereas social or cultural sciences employ an 'idiographic' or individualizing procedure, since it is their objective to explore the non-recurring events in reality and the particular or unique aspects of any phenomenon. Others, more obviously Dilthey, contrasted *Naturwissenschaften* and *Geisteswissenschaften* in terms of their subject matter, this criterion following logically from the alternative premise that reality can be divided into autonomous sectors – a fundamental distinction being that between the realms of 'nature' and of 'human spirit' – with each sector being the prerogative of a separate category of sciences. Rickert considers both of these criteria to be, by themselves, inadequate for describing the respective methodological bases of the natural and cultural sciences since the proposed formal and material divisions often cross-cut each other. Not all cultural sciences, for example, use an exclusively individualizing methodology: psychology might be an example here since psychologists are often concerned with what is constant about human behaviour. Rickert's contribution to epistemology is an attempt to combine logical and substantive criteria in order to arrive at an adequate description of the methods of concept formation employed by the different sciences.[13]

Starting from the axiom that reality is indivisible, infinitely complex, and conceptually unknowable in its completeness, Rickert proposes that the problem of attaining objective knowledge in any science is one of specifying a principle or principles by which we can reconstruct the data of direct experience, or abstract from reality, on a basis which is not arbitrary. How can scientific concepts be formulated objectively? Rickert accepts that there are two opposed methods of scientific cognition by which concepts of reality can be formed, namely, the generalizing and the individualizing. But these methods are simply polar extremes of a continuum along which are distributed the mixed forms of scientific conceptualization which, in reality, most sciences utilize. Moreover, to say that the purpose of concept formation in certain sciences is to represent the uniqueness of a given phenomenon is, ultimately, to claim at some point to be representing certain aspects of the phenomenon in all their concreteness and to be providing an exact copy of reality, which is, for Rickert, an impossibility. To the distinction between generalizing and individualizing sciences must be added a further distinction between the natural and the cultural. Natural phenomena are things which come into being independent of the existence of humanity. Nature is born of itself. The origins of cultural phenomena, on the other hand, lie specifically in their value to humanity. Cultural phenomena are aspects of reality to which attach values or complexes of meaning constituted by values. They possess or represent some value or values and are fostered intentionally with regard to values. Since natural phenomena come into being independent of human values, Rickert proposes to distinguish between the objects of natural science and those of cultural science on the basis of the criterion of 'relevance to value'; a criterion which reflects the fact that cultural objects, because of their relevance to values, acquire a meaning and can therefore be 'understood', whereas natural objects do not have meaning in an equivalent sense and are merely 'perceived'.

The uniqueness of Rickert's solution to the problem of the classification of the sciences, and to the clarification of the epistemological basis of the cultural sciences, lies in the combination of the substantive and formal criteria he has thus far outlined. In the historical and social sciences, which are concerned with the explanation of cultural phenomena, it is the particular values embodied in the cultural object which provide the principle whereby the formation of individual scientific concepts is made possible. A particular event, process, or personality is related to cultural values and in this way an individual concept is constructed which emphasizes the distinctive features of the phenomenon in question. In natural sciences, by comparison, the objects of study are indifferent to values, so concepts of these objects can be formed in terms of a universal or general point of view. Rickert offers a convenient summary of his research in epistemology – of which I have here offered only the briefest sketch – in these terms:

We can *conceptually* distinguish from each other two kinds of empirical scientific work without having to say that they are everywhere divergent *in fact*. Here I single out only the 'pure' forms.

On the one hand there are the *natural sciences*. The word 'nature' is applicable to them with respect to both their *subject matter* and their *method*. They view their objects as things and events that are devoid of any reference to values. Their interest is directed toward discovering the general conceptual relations and, if possible, the laws that hold good for these things and events.

For these sciences the particular is only a specimen. This holds true for *psychology* as well as for *physics*. Both make no distinction whatever among the various psyches and bodies with respect to values and valuations; both ignore the individual as unessential; and both ordinarily include in their concepts only what is *common* to a *plurality* of objects. Nor is there *any* object that is exempt, as a matter of principle, from being treated in this way, which is essentially the method of the natural sciences in the broadest sense of the term. *Nature* is the *whole* of psycho-physical reality conceived in a generalising manner and as indifferent to value.

On the other hand, there are the *historical sciences that deal with cultural phenomena*. We do not possess a single word for them which, corresponding to the term 'nature', could characterise them at the same time with respect to both their subject matter and their method. For that reason we must choose *two terms* ('historical' and 'cultural'), which correspond to the two meanings of the word 'nature'. As *cultural* sciences they are concerned with objects which are related to general cultural *values* and which can therefore be understood as meaningful; and as *historical* sciences they represent in its particularity and individuality the *non-recurring* development of cultural events. This is what, at the same time, provides their historical method with its principle of concept-formation, since what is essential for them is only what has significance, as a unique embodiment of meaning with its own distinctive individuality, in terms of the cultural values that serve as the guiding principle of selection. Hence what they select from reality with their *individualising* method – viz., 'culture' – is what the natural sciences are concerned with when they approach the *same* reality as 'nature' with their *generalising* method, because in most cases the significance of a cultural event depends precisely on the characteristic *peculiarity* that distinguishes it from other events. On the other hand, what it has in common with other events, ie., what constitutes it as an object of interest to the natural sciences, is unessential from the point of view of the cultural sciences.[14]

The important methodological principle to emerge from this epistemological position, from our point of view, is the principle of 'relevance to value' itself. This declares that when the values upon which an investigation is premised change, then that which is deemed to be significant for scientific conceptualization also changes. This is illustrated in Rickert's debate with Eduard Meyer over the historical significance of Fredrich Wilhelm IV's rejection of the German imperial crown relative to the actions of the king's tailor. Of course, the point is, that while the tailor may well be insignificant for political history he could be essential to an understanding of the history of fashion. Similarly, and of rather more contemporary concern, whether a person who robs a bank and kills the security staff is described as a 'terrorist' or a 'freedom fighter' will depend on the values relative to which one conceptualizes that person's activities.

Rickert insists that the theoretical principle of relevance to value is not to be confused with the question of practical evaluation. Concepts formed with reference to values are not value-judgements, since it is the scientist's task to describe and explain the world, not to pass sentence on it. As one of Rickert's disciples puts it:

The historian need not censure Theodore Roosevelt for calling the Portsmouth Conference, nor extol him, in fact, he should not do so, but the fact that he selects the Conference as part of his account and the manner in which he deals with it, reflect certain values with reference to politics, peace, etc., which determine his perspective.[15]

The exchange between Rickert and Meyer does, however, raise the issue of which (or whose) values are to determine concept formation in the cultural and historical sciences. Rickert suggests that the historian does not relate objects merely to arbitrary values. Rather, the cultural values, to which phenomena are related in order to facilitate the selection of significant data for their scientific conceptualization, are those values which are inherent in phenomena, as these are acknowledged by the intellectual community. He presupposes that the general values inherent in the state, religion, law, and so forth, are largely understood and acknowledged by those to whom his work is addressed. It follows that there will be a certain arbitrariness in concept formation in historical science. Historical knowledge will be culturally relative since objectivity will be confined to a group of scholars with a common cultural background. In an attempt to transcend this relativism, Rickert postulates that a universal cultural scientific knowledge would be possible if the values common to all cultures were established. Since universally acknowledged values would serve as the common basis for concept formation, a universally valid and objective history would result.

It is at this point – and only on this point – that Weber's theory of value diverges from that of Rickert. In his essays on the methodology of the social and cultural sciences Weber follows Rickert closely. He accepts the latter's propositions concerning the infinite complexity and conceptual inexhaustibility of reality; the typically generalizing and individualizing modes of concept formation employed by different sciences; and the distinguishing features of the objects of the natural and cultural sciences with respect to values, meaning, and understanding. In an essay on ' "Objectivity" in social science and social policy', published only one year prior to *The Protestant Ethic and the Spirit of Capitalism*, he lays bare the Rickertian foundations of his methodology and concludes:

In stating this, we arrive at the decisive feature of the method of the cultural sciences. We have designated as 'cultural sciences' those disciplines which analyse the phenomena of life in terms of their cultural significance. The *significance* of a configuration of cultural phenomena and the basis of this significance cannot however be derived and rendered intelligible by a system of analytical laws, however perfect it may be, since the significance of cultural events presupposes a *value-orientation* towards these events. The concept of culture is a *value-concept*. Empirical reality becomes 'culture' to us because and insofar as we relate it to value ideas. It includes those segments and only those segments of reality which have become significant to us because of this value-relevance. Only a small portion of existing concrete reality is colored by our value-conditioned interest and it alone is significant to us. It is significant because it reveals relationships which are important to us due to their connection with our values. Only because and to the extent that this is the case is it worthwhile for us to know it in its individual features. We cannot discover, however, what is meaningful to us by means of a 'presuppositionless' investigation of empirical data. Rather perception of its meaningfulness to us is the presupposition of its becoming an *object* of investigation. Meaningfulness naturally does not coincide with laws as such, and the more general the law the less the coincidence. For the specific meaning which a phenomenon has for us is naturally *not* to be found in those relationships which it shares with many other phenomena.

The focus of attention on reality under the guidance of values which lend it significance and the selection and ordering of the phenomena which are thus affected in the light of their cultural significance is entirely different from the analysis of reality in terms of laws and general concepts.[16]

For Weber, as for Rickert, it is the methodological principle of 'relevance to value' which is the distinguishing feature of the cultural as compared to the natural sciences.

In what ways does Weber's conception of value-relevance differ from that of Rickert? Weber rejects the possibility that Rickert forsees of a universally valid history because he denies the existence of a system of universal values commonly held by all regardless of ethical, aesthetic, and political persuasions. Weber sees as irresolvable the conflict between the competing sets of values to which people adhere, and he accepts, therefore, that the 'points of view' or values in terms of which we consider cultural phenomena, and by means of which they become the very objects of historical research, are forever changing.[17] Nevertheless, the historical sciences can be objective because the principle of value-relevance provides for historical investigations which are *intersubjectively testable*. Value-relevance is, as Rickert maintains, the principle which governs the selection of facts by clarifying the value inherent in a situation or phenomenon under analysis. Weber concedes that, of course, there are always several possible plausible interpretations of the values underlying any cultural phenomenon, and consequently several different points of view from which one might conceptualize the phenomenon (or 'historical individual') to be explained. However, once an historical individual is constructed for a particular inquiry, *objectively one-sided* social scientific knowledge becomes possible through the discovery of causal relationships between the value-relevant description of the object of inquiry and antecedent historical factors, because the formation of these relationships is governed by the rules of established scientific procedure.[18] If the particular value standpoint, according to which the object of the inquiry has been conceptualized, does not facilitate an explanation of the phenomenon which is both meaningfully and causally adequate (crudely, is both plausible in terms of what we know about social action in general, and can be upheld by comparative analysis), then there may be other values inherent in the phenomenon which permit a more satisfactory explanation to be constructed.[19]

Whether or not Weber's theory of concept formation in the social sciences is sound is, of course, a moot point.[20] Quite what his theory actually claims (and we have looked superficially at only a limited aspect of it) is itself a matter of some dispute.[21] The extent to which his methodology forms a coherent whole and the relationship between it and Weber's diverse empirical studies are further issues which cannot be considered systematically in the present context.[22] All that needs to be realized with respect to Weber's essays on the Protestant ethic is that his concept of 'the spirit of modern capitalism' is explicitly value-relevant.[23] This can be confirmed by looking again at the opening quotation in Chapter 2 in which Weber explains the explanandum of his study. The spirit of modern capitalism is, he tells us, an historical individual; an ideal-typical, one-sided accentuation of the mentality of modern capitalists. It is what the modern capitalist *Weltanschauung* would look like were it ruthlessly systematized in the direction of one underlying value, namely, that of seeing the accumulation of capital to be a duty and an end in itself. Franklin's texts are as good an example as Weber can provide of the empirical manifestation of such a view of the world. It is Weber's belief that this particular orientation to economic life is uniquely modern and that a meaningful and causally adequate explanation of the conduct of modern capitalists can be constructed upon this supposition or theoretical postulate. This, of course, remains to be seen, which is why he refers to his ideal-type of the spirit of modern capitalism as a 'provisional description' only.

Will this particular point of view ('value-relevant description') further our understanding of the capitalist mentality? For Weber, at least, it suggests a more promising starting point than Sombart's concept of the spirit of capitalism. Sombart offers, not a ruthlessly systematic one-sided accentuation of the phenomenon to be explained from a single point of view, but from two points of view, since the underlying values of that concept relate to ethics of bold adventurism and quiet rationalism which are, for Weber, both self-contradictory and an empirically unlikely combination. An internally inconsistent and two-sided ideal-type scarcely provides a sound basis from which to embark on a one-sided account of a social and historical phenomenon, such one-sidedness (as expressed in the methodology of ideal-types) being, for Weber, the only possible means by which to attain objective social scientific knowledge.

The puzzle: from Florence to Franklin

The problem being addressed by Weber in his essays on the Protestant ethic is therefore clear. He argues that the 'rational economic actor' has to be explained rather than assumed. The pursuit of profit-maximization itself is clearly not an ubiquitous phenomenon; it was preceded, as an orientation to economic life, by one which sought the customary income with a maximum of comfort and a minimum of exertion. The backward-sloping supply curve for labour and the traditional rate of return acceptable to many medieval and antiquarian capitalists bear witness to this argument. On the other hand, the attitude towards profits and wages characteristic of modern capitalists and labourers, and exemplified in the writings of Benjamin Franklin, is not simply an insatiable lust for wealth. The merchant princes of the Middle Ages also accumulated vast fortunes, often ruthlessly, and neither can the avarice that has been well documented among, for example, traditional peasantries be denied. However, such an ethic of 'adventurer capitalism' is to be distinguished from the spirit of modern capitalism because typically the bearers of the former are opportunistic and generally unscrupulous, whereas modern capitalists maximize profits rationally (basing their investments on extensive calculations in order to minimize the possibility of unpredictable outcomes) and claim an ethical basis to their activities. Moreover, capitalistic adventurers tend to consume much of their gain in luxuries, living spectacular and lavish life-styles. Modern capitalists, on the other hand, practise personal asceticism with respect to the use of material goods. Uniquely, among all known orientations towards economic activities, the modern capitalist mentality binds together, as a duty and an end in itself, both the pursuit of profit and forever renewed profit by means of continuous, rational, capitalistic enterprise, and extensive restrictions on personal consumption of capital once earned. Paradoxically, the moral teachings of Franklin upheld 'the conception of money-making as an end in itself to which people were bound, as a calling', such that one increased capital only to increase it further – not to consume it.[24]

Such an 'irrational' attitude towards wealth is, Weber argues, peculiarly modern. True, throughout the pre-capitalist ages each society has been possessed of its 'economic supermen', but such persons were few and far between and, in any case, their activities were viewed with moral scorn.[25] Similarly, the 'honest' earning of modest traditional profits may have been *tolerated* throughout most of recorded history, but 'only because of the unalterable necessities of life in the world'. Here again Weber echoes Simmel's earlier analysis:

The ethos of the classical economic morality is summed up in the old judgement passed on the merchant . . . he may conduct himself without sin but cannot be pleasing to God. This proposition was valid down to the fifteenth century, and the first attempt to modify it slowly matured in Florence under pressure of the shift in economic relations. . . .

. . . Some moralists of that time, especially of the nominalistic school, accepted developed capitalistic business forms as inevitable, and attempted to justify them, especially commerce, as necessary. . . . But the dominant doctrine rejected the spirit of capitalistic acquisition as *turpitudo*, or at least could not give it a positive ethical sanction. An ethical attitude like that of Benjamin Franklin would simply have been unthinkable.[26]

Weber's problem therefore can be stated concisely – although the rather unnecessary criticism of vulgar materialism in the following passage perhaps tends to obscure the remarkable simplicity of the issue to be resolved:

how could activity, which was at best ethically tolerated, turn into a calling in the sense of Benjamin Franklin? The fact to be explained historically is that in the most highly capitalistic centre of that time, in Florence in the fourteenth and fifteenth centuries, the money and capital market of all the great political

Powers, this attitude was considered ethically unjustifiable, or at best to be tolerated. But in the backwoods small bourgeois circumstances of Pennsylvania in the eighteenth century, where business threatened for simple lack of money to fall back into barter, where there was hardly a sign of a large enterprise, where only the earliest beginnings of banking were to be found, the same thing was considered the essence of moral conduct, even commanded in the name of duty. To speak here of a reflection of material conditions in the ideal superstructure would be patent nonsense. What was the background of ideas which could account for the sort of activity apparently directed toward profit alone as a calling toward which the individual feels himself to have an ethical obligation? For it was this idea which gave the way of life of the new entrepreneur its ethical foundation and justification. . . .

. . . In order that a manner of life so well adapted to the peculiarities of capitalism could be selected at all, i.e. should come to dominate others, it had to originate somewhere, and not in isolated individuals alone, but as a way of life common to whole groups of men. This origin is what really needs explanation.[27]

Weber, of course, finds the source of this ethic in ascetic Protestantism. We shall examine his account of the religious origins of the modern capitalist mentality in Chapter 4. Before doing so, however, it is necessary to pause and consider Weber's concept of the spirit of modern capitalism itself. It is by no means an unproblematic notion.

Some problems

In his essays on 'The Protestant ethic and the spirit of capitalism' Weber, as we have observed, clearly challenges Sombart's two principal assertions concerning the spirit of modern capitalism. He argues, first of all, that the modern capitalist mentality is not distinguished by the element of 'adventurism' which Sombart suggests. Second, the origins of this mentality can be located in ascetic Protestantism rather than Judaism, and we shall see how Weber sustains this argument against that of Sombart in Chapter 4. What Weber fails to do in his essays, however, is avoid those aetiological and tautological pitfalls which beset Sombart's account of the effects and status of the spirit of capitalism itself. These Sombartian derived errors arguably signal the weakest parts of Weber's argument and certainly ensure that any attempt to test empirically his propositions about the capitalist mentality will be an Herculean task.

We noted how Sombart, in *Modern Capitalism*, remains ambiguous with respect to the status of the key concept of 'the spirit of capitalism'. At times he sees this as a world-view: a set of values or an orientation towards economic activity which, given certain other conditions, results in capitalist enterprise. At other times he writes as if the spirit of modern capitalism is a pattern of action in terms of a certain world-view. It is almost as if, irrespective of situational constraints, the modern capitalist mentality will inevitably realize itself in a behavioural sequence which guarantees the development of modern capitalism; or, to introduce an additional problem, may even *be* modern capitalism itself, for this too is a matter of some ambiguity. The spirit of capitalism is then, variously, a unique and distinguishing feature of modern capitalism; a necessary but not sufficient cause of it; an attitudinal complex which may (depending on situational conditions) result in a certain pattern of economic behaviour; and, finally, that behaviour itself. Sombart's prevarications on these matters are simply echoed by Weber.

Weber's changing explanandum

We can see, for example, that Weber shares Sombart's tendency to tautologism with respect to the relationship between the spirit of modern capitalism and the modern capitalist economic complex. The former appears as both an important precondition for, and the distinguishing characteristic of, the latter. This means, of course, that the spirit of capitalism is, by definition, causally significant in explaining the development of modern capitalism: if the 'ethos' is not present then we are not talking about modern capitalism; if it is present then it must have been important for the development of the capitalist system because that ethos is, above all else, its distinguishing feature. The argument that a new spirit of capitalism was an important source of modern capitalism itself is thus made unassailable.

In his original essays, for example, Weber writes:

the *summum bonum* of this [modern capitalist] ethic, the earning of more and more money, combined with the strict avoidance of all spontaneous enjoyment of life, is above all completely devoid of any eudaemonistic, not to say hedonistic admixture. It is thought of so purely as an end in itself, that from the point of view of the happiness of, or utility to, the single individual, it appears entirely transcendental and absolutely irrational. Man is dominated by the making of money, by acquisition as the ultimate purpose of his life. Economic acquisition is no longer subordinated to man as the means for the satisfaction of his material needs. This reversal of what we should call the natural relationship, so irrational from a naive point of view, is evidently as definitely a leading principle of capitalism as it is foreign to all peoples not under capitalistic influence. . . . The earning of money within the modern economic order is, so long as it is done legally, the result and the expression of virtue and proficiency in a calling; and this virtue and proficiency are, as it is now not difficult to see, the real Alpha and Omega of Franklin's ethic. . . .

And in truth this peculiar idea, so familiar to us today, but in reality so little a matter of course . . . is what is most characteristic of the social ethic of capitalistic culture, and is in a sense the fundamental basis of it. . . .[28]

Here, as elsewhere throughout his essays, Weber takes the modern capitalist mentality to be the distinguishing *characteristic* of modern capitalism. On the other hand, and with equal force, he also argues that the capitalist spirit is one of the most important *causes* of modern capitalism: 'Today the spirit of religious asceticism – whether finally, who knows? – has escaped from the cage. But victorious capitalism, since it rests on mechanical foundations, needs its support no longer.'[29]

Weber never resolved this ambiguity in his writings on modern capitalism. As late as 1919–20 he could still argue:

Drawing together once more the distinguishing characteristics of western capitalism and its causes, we find the following factors. . . . Only the occident has known the state in the modern sense, with a professional administration, specialised officialdom, and law based on the concept of citizenship. . . . Only the occident knows rational law, made by jurists and rationally interpreted and applied, and only in the occident is found the concept of citizen because only in the occident again are there cities in the specific sense. . . . Only the occident possesses science in the present-day sense of the word. . . . Finally, western civilisation is further distinguished from every other by the presence of men with a rational ethic for the conduct of life. Magic and religion are found everywhere; but a religious basis for the ordering of life which consistently followed out must lead to explicit rationalism is again peculiar to western civilisation alone.[30]

On countless occasions Weber lists, as 'characteristics and prerequisites' of modern capitalism and modern capitalistic enterprise, the rational capitalistic organization of formally free labour; the separation of business and household capital; rational book-keeping; rational structures of law and administration; and 'the rationalization of economic life' (the spirit of modern capitalism). The 'distinguishing features' of modern capitalism are simultaneously the 'presuppositions for its existence' and its 'most important causes'.[31] Ultimately, Weber fails to specify whether the 'spirit of modern capitalism', rational book-keeping and the like, are attributes of the phenomenon of modern capitalism or empirical conditions which favoured or were necessary for its development.[32]

What explains this ambiguity in Weber's writings? In large part it arises precisely because his treatment of capitalism was a direct response to the earlier studies of Sombart, and both men, as it turns out, share an identical confusion about the explananda of their arguments.

Sombart's *Modern Capitalism* and *The German Economy in the Nineteenth Century* actually propose two major theses. In the former Sombart outlines a series of political, economic, and social factors that were important for the development of modern western capitalism. Among the numerous objective processes that are mentioned, Sombart includes the effects of colonial expansion on the organization and growth of markets in Europe; the transformation of the system of production from a handicraft to a factory basis; the effect of new technical processes and inventions as these were applied to commerce and industry; and changing patterns of demand related to the growth of urban centres. He argues, further, that one additional and important factor in explaining the development of modern capitalism was the transformation of the 'economic motive': the decline of traditionalism and the rise of the capitalist spirit. In *The German Economy in the Nineteenth Century* this development is attributed to Judaism and the influence of Jews in Western Europe. There are, in other words, two separate issues being posed by Sombart and he has a thesis about each: namely, that of identifying the diverse origins of the capitalist economic system (one causal factor in its development being a changed orientation towards economic activities); and, second, the problem of locating the origins of this new world-view itself (which Sombart finds in Judaism).

Weber's problems stem from the fact that, in *The Protestant Ethic and the Spirit of Capitalism* at least, he tends to conflate these two issues. His essays begin by posing *implicitly* the same initial question as Sombart, namely 'What is it that is unique about the modern capitalistic order?' Weber, like Sombart, sees its 'ethos' (the world-view of modern capitalists and labourers) as entirely unprecedented, although, as was observed, he disagrees with Sombart's characterization of the spirit of capitalism on the grounds that Sombart conflates several quite different types of economic motive and conduct under this rubric. Weber then poses *explicitly* an additional question: 'What are the origins of this unique orientation to economic activities?' It is to this second problem that his essays are addressed, and he argues that Sombart overemphasizes the role of the Jews in the development of the modern capitalist mentality, relative to the part played by ascetic Protestantism. But, of course, for Weber to address himself exclusively to the second question is to assume that his answer to the first is unproblematic. In other words, in *The Protestant Ethic and the Spirit of Capitalism*, Weber actually *assumes* that the spirit of modern capitalism is unique in those respects which he proposes and, further, that this particular world-view is an important causal element, alongside objective developments such as those associated with changes in technology, accounting practices, and other factors noted by Sombart, in explaining the development of the modern capitalist economy.

Weber's 'Protestant ethic thesis' is clearly two theses.[33] The foremost problem is one of specifying the origins of a particular orientation to economic activities. His proposed solution identifies these in the ethical and doctrinal principles of an earlier belief-system. However, behind the overt thesis about the relationship between Protestant ethic and spirit of capitalism lies a further thesis which is carried largely by assumption, namely the proposition that the spirit of modern capitalism was one of a number of factors that were causally effective in the development of modern western capitalism. The new 'spirit' was a necessary, though not sufficient, condition for the new economic system.

Weber's critics were not slow to translate this ambiguity in the original essays into the charge that he was proposing an idealistic interpretation of history in opposition to the approach of, for example, historical materialism. Fischer, Rachfahl, and somewhat later Brentano, all accused Weber of arguing to the effect that 'the Protestant ethic caused the development of modern capitalism', and in this way of ignoring the many additional political, economic and other structural preconditions for, and causes of, the modern capitalist economy.[34] Brentano, for example, argued that the Renaissance, Crusades, and extension and revival of Roman Law in the West, had all played a much larger part than Protestantism in the evolution of modern capitalism. Fischer actually accuses Weber of offering nothing less than a version of Hegelianism with the Protestant ethic substituting for Hegel's Absolute Spirit.

Weber was outraged at this charge of idealism. He conceded that other aspects of his argument may have been somewhat ambiguous, as originally formulated, but insisted that his critics had not troubled themselves to read his essays carefully.[35] In replying to their criticism he emphasizes the distinction between 'the spirit of capitalism' and 'capitalism as an economic form or system'.[36] The origins of the latter, he argues, are clearly diverse and are 'structural' as well as 'ideological'.[37] Nowhere does he claim that mere affiliation to a belief-system is sufficient to conjure up a particular economic form or order, and he adds sarcastically that despite what some of his critics might think he is not arguing that Siberian Baptists will inevitably become wholesalers and Calvinist nomadic Arabs inevitably manufacturers.[38]

Weber's self-righteous indignation at his critics' accusations of 'spiritualism' and 'Hegelianism' is not, however, entirely justifiable. His frequent though incidental references to Marxism throughout his original essays encourage a comparison with alternative accounts of the development of capitalism rather than the capitalist spirit.[39] It is also clear that, in his desire to challenge Sombart's thesis about the relationship between the Jewish ethic and the spirit of capitalism, Weber simply assumed his colleague's initial thesis about the significance of the spirit of capitalism for the development of Western capitalism to be valid. In later years Weber himself conceded that the argument of his essays on 'The Protestant ethic and the spirit of capitalism' *presupposes* that the modern capitalist mentality had a definite influence on the development of modern capitalism.[40] It seems that, at least at the outset, Weber does not distinguish adequately between the two theses that the Protestant ethic was responsible for the rise of the spirit of modern capitalism, and that this changed capitalist mentality was a necessary though not sufficient condition for the emergence of modern capitalism itself. Although this distinction becomes clear in Weber's immediate replies to his German critics,[41] the damage has been done, and the persistent conflation of the two arguments, usually culminating in a charge of idealism, has bedevilled discussion about his writings ever since.[42]

This whole problem has not been helped, of course, by the fact that the standard editions of *The Protestant Ethic and the Spirit of Capitalism* preface the original essays with the 'Author's introduction' of 1920, for it is clear that from the time of his early replies (1907–10) onwards, Weber's studies of religion and the rise of capitalism explicitly address both problems. In *The Religion of China*, for example, originally published in the *Archiv für Sozialwissenschaft und Sozialpolitik* in 1916 as part of his opening essay on 'The economic ethic of world religions', Weber discusses the diverse political, technical, material, and social-structural conditions that favoured the development of the Occidental type of capitalism in the

Chinese Empire. His conclusion is that, at different points in Chinese history, the country has been better placed with respect to the objective preconditions for modern capitalism than was seventeenth-century Europe. Nevertheless, it is clear that modern capitalism developed in Europe but not China, so the question must be posed as to why. Weber's answer is that the major belief-systems in China – Confucianism and Taoism – fostered orientations towards everyday life that were opposed to that represented by the ideal-type of the spirit of modern capitalism. It is possible, therefore, that what was 'missing' in China as compared to the West was an appropriate motivation on the part of the business classes to rational capitalistic acquisition as an end in itself, and it was for this reason that modern capitalism failed to appear in China. Weber's study of *The Religion of India* is similar in structure and arrives at similar conclusions regarding the development of modern rational capitalism in the Indian states.[43]

More noticeably, in the 'Author's introduction' itself, and in his lectures on *General Economic History*, Weber can be seen to be addressing the separate problems of the origins of the capitalist outlook and of the capitalist economy, and moreover, to have reversed the order of priority as compared to the original treatment in *The Protestant Ethic and the Spirit of Capitalism*. In that text Weber scarcely concerns himself with the second of these problems, being content to assume the causal efficacy of the capitalist spirit, alongside other (unstated) preconditions, for modern capitalist development. In the later pieces, however, Weber concerns himself explicitly with the diverse origins of modern capitalism as an economic order and only tangentially with the nature and source of the capitalist mentality. Nevertheless, the contrast between his two theses emerges clearly in his conclusion to *General Economic History*:

While capitalism of various forms is met with in all periods of history, the provision of the everyday wants by capitalistic methods is characteristic of the occident alone and even here has been the inevitable method only since the middle of the nineteenth century. . . .

The most general presupposition for the existence of this present-day capitalism is that of rational capital accounting as the norm for all large industrial undertakings which are concerned with provision for everyday wants. Such accounting involves, again, first, the appropriation of all physical means of production – land, apparatus, machinery, tools, etc., as disposable property of autonomous private industrial enterprises. . . . In the second place, it involves freedom of the market, that is, the absence of irrational limitations on trading in the market. . . . Third, capitalistic accounting presupposes rational technology, that is, one reduced to calculation to the largest possible degree, which implies mechanisation. . . .

The fourth characteristic is that of calculable law. The capitalistic form of industrial organisation, if it is to operate rationally, must be able to depend upon calculable adjudication and administration. . . . The fifth feature is free labor. Persons must be present who are not only legally in the position, but are also economically compelled, to sell their labor on the market without restriction. It is in contradiction to the essence of capitalism, and the development of capitalism is impossible, if such a propertyless stratum is absent, a class compelled to sell its labor services to live; and is likewise impossible if only unfree labor is at hand. . . . The sixth and final condition is the commercialisation of economic life. By this we mean the general use of commercial instruments to represent share rights in enterprise, and also in property ownership. . . .

It is a widespread error that the increase of population is to be included as a really crucial agent in the evolution of western capitalism. . . .

Nor can the inflow of precious metals be regarded, as Sombart suggests, as the primary cause of the appearance of capitalism. . . .

In the last resort the factor which produced capitalism is the rational permanent enterprise, rational accounting, rational technology and rational law, but again not these alone. Necessary complementary factors were the rational spirit, the rationalisation of the conduct of life in general, and a rationalistic economic ethic.[44]

But what is the nature of, and where lie the origins of this rationalistic economic ethic? At this juncture, of course, Weber simply offers a précis of the argument about the consequences of the doctrines of ascetic Protestantism, as this is spelled out in the original essays on the Protestant ethic.[45]

However, while the distinction between Weber's separate theses helps clarify the internal development of his writings on the subject of religion and the rise of capitalism, it leaves unresolved the problem of his tendency to define modern capitalism in terms of its preconditions, a predisposition which makes his argument that the modern capitalist mentality was an important cause of the development of capitalism both circular and unfalsifiable, since in the absence of the former the latter cannot be present, and vice versa. All that needs be said here is that Weber appears to have been a victim of intellectual circumstance. Given the several controversies of the *Methodenstreit* and Weber's involvement in these, especially his interest in the German Historical School of Economics and in particular the works of Roscher, Knies, Schmoller, and Sombart himself, Weber not surprisingly seems to have followed his intellectual predecessors in referring to the phenomenon of 'modern capitalism', when what he actually meant was 'economic development' or 'growth'. At the beginning of his original essays, in fact, he uses these terms interchangeably with reference to the particular characteristics of the modern West, speaking sometimes of the level of 'capitalist development' (*die kapitalistische Entwicklung*) it has experienced, and at other times of areas of high 'economic development' (*der ökonomische entwickeltsten Gebiete/wirtschaftlich entwickeltsten Gebiete*).[46]

More obviously, in his 'Author's introduction' to *Religionssoziologie*, he employs the term 'capitalism' when he is clearly referring to different levels of what economists nowadays call 'economic development' or 'growth'. 'Capitalism' is defined in these terms:

The impulse to acquisition, pursuit of gain, of money, of the greatest possible amount of money, has in itself nothing to do with capitalism. This impulse exists and has existed among waiters, physicians, coachmen, artists, prostitutes, dishonest officials, soldiers, nobles, crusaders, gamblers, and beggars. One may say that it has been common to all sorts and conditions of men at all times and in all countries of the earth, wherever the objective possibility of it is or has been given. . . . Unlimited greed for gain is not in the least identical with capitalism, and is still less its spirit. . . . But capitalism is identical with the pursuit of profit, and forever *renewed* profit, by means of continuous, rational, capitalistic enterprise. For it must be so: in a wholly capitalistic order of society, an individual capitalistic enterprise which did not take advantage of its opportunities for profit-making would be doomed to extinction. . . .
. . . a capitalistic economic action [is] one which rests on the expectation of profit by the utilisation of opportunities for exchange, that is on (formally) peaceful chances of profit. . . . The important fact is always that a calculation of capital in terms of money is made, whether by modern book-keeping methods or in any other way, however, primitive and crude. Everything is done in terms of balances: at the beginning of the enterprise an initial balance, before every individual decision a calculation to ascertain its probable profitableness, and at the end a final balance to ascertain how much profit has been made.[47]

Weber has to concede, however, that

in this sense capitalism and capitalistic enterprises, even with a considerable rationalisation of capitalistic calculation, have existed in all civilised countries of the earth, so far as economic documents permit us to judge . . . the capitalistic enterprise and the capitalistic entrepreneur, not only as occasional but as regular entrepreneurs, are very old and were very widespread.[48]

What then is peculiar about the capitalistic enterprises of the modern West? Weber's answer is that the level and type of economic development characteristic of the Occident has never been attained elsewhere:

the Occident has developed capitalism both to a quantitative extent, and (carrying this quantitative development) in types, forms, and directions which have never existed elsewhere. All over the world there have been merchants, wholesale and retail, local and engaged in foreign trade. Loans of all kinds have been made, and there have been banks with the most various functions, at least comparable to ours of, say, the sixteenth century. . . . Wherever money finances of public bodies have existed, money-lenders have appeared, as in Babylon, Hellas, India, China, Rome. They have financed wars and piracy, contracts and building operations of all sorts. In overseas policy they have functioned as colonial entrepreneurs, as planters with slaves, or directly or indirectly forced labour, and have farmed domains, offices, and, above all, taxes. They have financed party leaders in elections and *condottieri* in civil wars. And, finally, they have been speculators in chances for pecuniary gain of all kinds. This kind of entrepreneur, the capitalistic adventurer, has existed everywhere. . . .

The capitalism of promoters, large-scale speculators, concession hunters, and much modern financial capitalism even in peace time, but, above all, the capitalism especially concerned with exploiting wars, bears this stamp even in modern Western countries, and some, but only some, parts of large-scale international trade are closely related to it, today as always.

But in modern times the Occident has developed, in addition to this, a very different form of capitalism which has appeared nowhere else: the rational capitalistic organisation of (formally) free labour. Only suggestions of it are found elsewhere. . . . The frequent use of day labourers led in a very few cases – especially State monopolies, which are, however, very different from modern industrial organisation – to manufacturing organisations, but never to a rational organisation of apprenticeship in the handicrafts like that of our Middle Ages.

Rational industrial organisation, attuned to a regular market, and neither to political nor irrationally speculative opportunities for profit, is not, however, the only peculiarity of Western capitalism. The modern rational organisation of the capitalistic enterprise would not have been possible without two other important factors in its development: the separation of business from the household, which completely dominates modern economic life, and closely connected with it, rational book-keeping. . . .

However, all these peculiarities of Western capitalism have derived their significance in the last analysis only from their association with the capitalistic organisation of labour.[49]

Weber's initial question: 'What is it that is unique about modern western capitalism?' is therefore more accurately to be understood as: 'What are the causes of economic development in the West?' To this question the reply can then be the argument which is put in *General Economic History*. Economic growth and development in the West over the long term has been due to the institutionalized separation of business and household capital; the widespread adoption of rational book-keeping and accounting techniques; the creation of a formally free labour-force which has been forced to sell its labour openly on the market; the development of rational structures of law and administration; of industrial processes and technology; and, importantly, óf a business orientation that valued the accumulation of capital as an end in itself – the spirit of modern capitalism as defined by Weber.

Whether or not this interpretation of Weber's writings is accurate (although I am suggesting it is), it is certainly sociologically fruitful, for it at least enables us to open up the argument of the comparative studies, of the 'Author's introduction', and *General Economic History* to meaningful discussion and empirical test, two possibilities which are specifically precluded if we retain the procedure of defining modern western capitalism in terms of its particular causes.

The relationship of 'form' to 'ethos'

Turning now to the concept of 'the spirit of modern capitalism', again it soon becomes apparent that Weber is no less ambiguous than Sombart as to the precise nature of this phenomenon. In describing his 'historical individual', or ideal-type of the modern capitalist mentality, Weber concludes his précis of the teachings of Benjamin Franklin with the words:

Truly what is here preached is not simply a means of making one's way in the world, but a peculiar ethic. The infraction of its rules is treated not as foolishness but as forgetfulness of duty. That is the essence of the matter. It is not mere business astuteness, that sort of thing is common enough, it is an ethos. This is the quality which interests us.[50]

The spirit of modern capitalism is an idea; a social ethic; a particular set of moral attitudes; a complex of motives; an ethically coloured set of maxims for the conduct of life. It is, in short, an attitude of mind. Similarly, economic traditionalism is a type of world-view; a state of mind; a 'psychic attitude-set'. On the other hand, the spirit of modern capitalism is also a description of a particular type of action; a manner of behaviour; a definite form of conduct. Traditionalism, too, is 'expressed in the practical action of the average man of pre-capitalistic times'. In other words 'the spirit of modern capitalism' and 'economic traditionalism' are both sets of attitudes and patterns of behaviour.[51] Weber, like Sombart, seems unsure as to whether the spirit of capitalism is a complex of values which, given appropriate situational conditions, fosters capitalist activity; or, alternatively, is a patterning of economic and social action in terms of a particular set of values. Is the spirit of capitalism a world-view or the realization of a world-view; an attitude or a pattern of conduct?

This is an important question from an aetiological point of view because it is by no means the case that values or attitudes are mechanically translated into actions with which they are consistent. The relationship between beliefs and action is complex and in each instance a matter for empirical investigation. For example, individuals may act in a manner that accords with normative expectations, without themselves subscribing to the values and beliefs which underlie the norms. This will be, in part, a function of how strongly anchored are both the norms and the actor to a significant reference group. Situational constraints of one kind or another – subjugation to a form of power relationship, lack of material resources, the desire to create or necessity of maintaining a favourable image of self – may effectively specify 'conditions of action' which prevent the realization of a particular value-complex as a pattern of action oriented towards the realization of these valued ends. Empirical studies have shown that the influence of a wide range of such 'conditions of action' prevent the researcher from legitimately drawing conclusions about attitudes or motives from observed behaviour alone – and vice versa. There is no necessary correlation between symbolic and non-symbolic behaviour; between speech and action; intention and actuality; motives or purposes and institutionalized social arrangements or social behaviour.[52] This means that a satisfactory motivational explanation of action must rest upon independent evidence as to *both* the action and the motives that allegedly precipitated it. Otherwise our explanations become unacceptably circular: we observe behaviour, impute motives, and then 'verify' the attribution of motives by the existence of the behaviour that is supposedly consistent with them; or, conversely, document motives, assume action consistent with them, and then 'verify' the reality of the action by referring to the motives that allegedly generated it.[53]

Alasdair MacIntyre, almost alone among Weber's critics, has noted Weber's problems in this department:

what he [Weber] specifically relates causally to Protestantism is what he calls 'the spirit of capitalism', a concept by means of which capitalist attitudes appear to be contrasted with capitalist activities. In fact, of course, an attitude can never be identified except in terms of the activities in which it is manifested. An attitude is precisely a propensity to do certain things, perhaps in a certain style. So that to talk about 'the spirit of capitalism' and its causes is to talk about the causes of a set of activities, viewed in a certain way, and not about something else.[54]

MacIntyre seems to be guilty of overstating his case, for the distinction between 'attitudes' and 'actions' is conceptually sound and the relationship between the two can be investigated empirically in a contemporary setting where the results of attitude surveys can be checked against observed behaviour, and the intervening 'conditions of action', which in part may determine whether the former are translated into the latter, can be similarly explored.[55] In the particular case of Weber's Protestant ethic thesis, however, MacIntyre is correct in his assertion that the limitations of the available data concerning the attitudes and actions of seventeenth-century capitalists and labourers mean that, in practice, it is often the case that the only evidence as to the presence and nature of the attitudes is the presence and nature of the actions. The fact that Weber and his followers may be reduced to implying outlook from behaviour, as indeed mostly they are, clearly weakens their case, for just as they assert the logical priority of capitalist spirit over capitalist action, critics are entitled to assert the opposite. Where we are compelled empirically to deduce attitudes from action, it is as plausible to argue that changes in the former follow changing circumstances affecting the latter as it is to suggest that these attitudinal changes caused the changing pattern of action.[56] We are, in short, left with no *empirical* means by which to arbitrate between Weber and his critics as to whether ideas exert an independent influence on social conduct or are simply epiphenomena which reflect and are more or less determined by changes in other spheres, such as shifting class interests. All that remains are two opposing declarations of theoretical preference.[57]

Weber is not unaware of this problem but his discussion of how to surmount it is not particularly helpful. He does not talk about the relationship between attitudes and actions but addresses himself instead to the problem of specifying the relationship between the *form* of a capitalist enterprise ('capitalist actions') and the *ethos* with which it is imbued ('capitalist attitudes'). He appears to accept the principle that these vary independently of each other:

> To be sure the capitalistic form of an enterprise and the spirit in which it is run generally stand in some sort of adequate relationship to each other, but not in one of necessary interdependence. . . .
> . . . the two may very well occur separately. Benjamin Franklin was filled with the spirit of capitalism at a time when his printing business did not differ in form from any handicraft enterprise. . . .
> The management, for instance, of a bank, a wholesale export business, a large retail establishment, or of a large putting-out enterprise dealing with goods produced in homes, is certainly only possible in the form of a capitalistic enterprise. Nevertheless, they may all be carried on in a traditionalistic spirit.[58]

Weber repeatedly affirmed this principle of the interdependence of forms of economic organization and types of economic ethics, and indicated that he chose Franklin specifically as an example in his original essay precisely because, in North America, the modern capitalist 'spirit' appeared independently of and prior to the modern capitalist economic 'system'. He insisted, indeed, that because the various possible economic 'ethics' could exist independently of their objective manifestations in economic 'forms' or 'orders', and in certain cases (such as that of North America) had done so, their respective origins must be investigated separately.[59] Nevertheless, he is inclined throughout to assume that, in practice, economic 'spirit' and economic 'form' tend to develop an 'adequacy' for each other. Where they do not share an 'elective affinity', where spirit and form collide, then one or other (or both) will change accordingly.[60] This assumption conveniently allows Weber to deduce motives from observable behaviour, on the one hand, and presuppose that documented attitudes were translated into appropriate action, on the other. The assumption of symmetry between economic 'form' and 'ethos' is

> justified by the historical fact that that attitude of mind [the spirit of modern capitalism] has on the one hand found its most suitable expression in capitalistic enterprise, while on the other the enterprise has derived its most suitable force from the spirit of capitalism.[61]

But, as MacIntyre has reminded us, this is not so much an 'historical fact' as an unwarranted methodological assumption.

The simple truth is that Weber offers little or no independent evidence concerning the motives and world-view of either modern or medieval businessmen and labourers. His evidence concerning the former, apart from the 'provisional description' offered by Franklin's advice, is drawn exclusively from Protestant teaching. This, of course, suggests a further tautology whereby the Protestant ethic and the spirit of modern capitalism are defined in terms of each other. More on this problem in Chapter 5. His evidence for the latter is taken from casual observations of the forms of economic 'adventuring' in which medieval merchants participated: financing of colonial enterprises, wars, and of office-holders; farming of taxes; money-lending; and the formation of *commenda* or ad hoc trading associations between exporters and shippers for carrying out specific sea-voyages. Thus we return to Sombart's problem: an economic ethos is simultaneously an attitude-set and the patterning of action in terms of that attitude-set. The only proof Weber can offer as to the motives and world-views of medieval businessmen is to point to the nature of their activities. But, of course, this is no proof at all.

What is the importance of this long documentation of the way in which Weber fails to avoid the ambiguities of Sombart's earlier argument? Quite simply, it leads us to one of the most telling objections to Weber's essays on the Protestant ethic; namely, that his 'provisional descriptions' of 'economic traditionalism' and the 'spirit of modern capitalism' are empirically unverified and possibly, in practice, unverifiable. *Homo capitalisticus* seems always to be just beyond the data which the researcher can unearth. Some examples of this problem, and a discussion of the general difficulties that emerge from the attempt to subject Weber's argument to empirical scrutiny, are the subject of much of Chapter 5. However, since a consideration of these questions will involve us in looking not only at Weber's central concept, but also at the relationships which he posits as existing between the spirit of capitalism and ascetic Protestantism, it is necessary first to introduce into our discussion the other important concept in Weber's essays – the 'Protestant ethic'.

4 The Protestant ethic

Of the several aspects of Weber's thesis that have been the object of critical scrutiny it is his interpretation of the doctrines and pastoral theology of Calvinist and neo-Calvinist Churches, denominations, and sects that has received most attention. His apparently complex argument about the psychological consequences of certain Calvinist teachings, as compared to the effects on the everyday life of the average believer engendered by corresponding aspects in Roman Catholic and Lutheran theology, has been criticized repeatedly at almost every point and from nearly all conceivable angles. Faced with such a copious critical literature the lay observer will in all probability conclude that Weber's interpretation of Protestant doctrine is erroneous, or, more charitably, that the whole question of how we interpret Church teachings is simply so complicated that it is best left to theologians and to the faithful themselves. However, we should be neither so misled nor discouraged, for it is in fact the case that Weber's argument about the nature and consequences of Calvinist beliefs is both the most straightforward and demonstrably the strongest part of his thesis as a whole. In other words, the succession of critics who have sought to deal a death-blow to Weber's thesis by challenging his interpretation of Protestantism have missed their mark. In this chapter I shall attempt to sustain such an assessment of Weber's argument by offering both an outline of the central tenets of the argument itself and some suggestions as to why much of the criticism that has been levelled against it is misdirected.

Weber's argument

What Weber is seeking to identify, it will be remembered, are the origins of an orientation towards everyday and especially economic life which he sees as unique to the modern era – the spirit of modern capitalism. This ethos is exemplified in the teachings of Benjamin Franklin which eulogize the accumulation of capital as an end in itself and as a duty of the individual. Weber's seemingly complicated attempt to trace the origins of such a world-view to the teachings of certain versions of Protestant theology, with his prolific and wide-ranging references to diverse Protestant divines and movements and to religious doctrines (such as that of predestination) which are no longer of relevance to the majority even of contemporary Christians, tends to obscure the fact that his argument is both unambiguous and breathtakingly simple.

His interpretation of Protestantism can most easily be comprehended if it is treated as being concerned with essentially two elements; namely, a code of ethics for the conduct of everyday life, and a sanction which operates to compel the faithful to adhere to these ethical maxims. These twin elements are closely related to each other and in the following exposition they are necessarily intertwined. We begin, however, with the prescriptions for conduct itself.

Ascetic Protestantism and the calling

It appears to Weber that a number of seventeenth-century Reformed Churches subscribed to a common code of conduct according to which believers were expected to organize their daily lives. He focuses specifically on four such religious groupings: the various neo-Calvinist Churches and denominations of Western Europe and North America; Continental Pietism; Anglo-American Methodism; and the sects associated with and developing out of Anabaptism. Collectively these movements comprise 'ascetic Protestantism'. He accepts that these labels are merely heuristic. Empirically there is a certain overlap among these Churches and even the boundary between the groupings as a whole and other non-ascetic Protestant Churches is at various times indistinct. For example, one of the neo-Calvinist movements in which Weber is particularly interested is English Puritanism, but as every student of the civil war period knows there is a good deal of controversy as to the definition of a Puritan and about the relationship of the movement to Anglicanism as a whole.[1] Nevertheless, notwithstanding the simplicity of the typology, the four aforementioned Reformed Churches may be fairly grouped together under the rubric of 'ascetic Protestantism' on the basis of their shared conception of what constitutes 'a godly life'.[2] Their respective doctrines may diverge in other ways (for example, Baptists were unambiguously opposed to the doctrine of predestination which was central to Calvinism), but the ethical maxims pertaining to mundane activities that are preached by each of the four are very similar and constitute an ethos which Weber refers to as 'worldly (or inner-worldly) asceticism'. The ethical tenets which they have in common are, in fact, principally three: diligence in worldly callings or vocations; strict asceticism with respect to the use of material goods and the indulgence of worldly pleasures; and systematic use of time.[3]

The doctrine of callings originates in the teachings of Luther. Whether it is Weber or his critics who are correct as to the etymology of the term itself is not particularly important.[4] Weber's argument really commences with the observation that Luther rejected the Roman Catholic dualism of ethical precepts into *praecepta* and *consilia*; the former pertaining to the majority of humankind, and the latter being those of the minority, the religious orders, who interceded between the worldly and sinful masses and the deity on their behalf. The distinction between the higher morality of the monastery and the ethics appropriate to those living in the everyday world was discarded. The central achievement of the Reformation, from the point of view of Weber's thesis, was the acceptance of secular life as of equal moral significance to that of the religious order. Henceforth, the 'godly life' was the prerogative of all believers, whatever their station. In Lutheranism, then,

at least one thing was unquestionably new: the valuation of the fulfilment of duty in worldly affairs as the highest form which the moral activity of the individual could assume. This it was which inevitably gave every-day worldly activity a religious significance and which first created the conception of the calling in this sense. . . . The only way of living acceptably to God was not to surpass worldly morality in monastic asceticism, but solely through the fulfilment of the obligations imposed upon the individual by his position in the world. That was his calling.[5]

The implications of the religious concept of 'calling' for secular conduct can, however, be subject to several different interpretations:

The effect of the Reformation as such was only that, as compared with the Catholic attitude, the moral emphasis on and the religious sanction of, organised worldly labour in a calling was mightily increased. The way in which the concept of the calling, which expressed this change, should develop further depended upon the religious evolution which now took place in the different Protestant Churches.[6]

Luther himself, according to Weber, offered a 'traditionalistic' interpretation of the doctrine. He placed great emphasis on the doctrine of justification by faith. Above all else the Lutheran strove to achieve *unio mystica* with God. While recognizing his or her sin-stained unworthiness the believer is encouraged to secure a state of grace through feeling himself or herself to be the vessel of the Holy Spirit: the Spirit enters the soul and the believer is simultaneously absorbed in the deity. In one sense, then, Lutheranism tends to devalue worldly activity in favour of inward emotional piety.[7] On the other hand, Luther increasingly moved towards the idea that God had placed each person in a station in life in order that all might labour for their material necessities, and so be a burden to none other. So that, whilst acceptance of one's station and calling in life is a divine ordinance which all must abide by, Luther places no particular value on labour in callings beyond that which is required for one's 'daily bread'. Indeed, it is specifically the godless who pursue material gain, since excess profits are usually secured at the expense of the needs of others. In short, according to Luther,

The individual should remain once and for all in the station and calling in which God had placed him, and should restrain his worldly activity within the limits imposed by his established station in life. While his economic traditionalism was originally the result of Pauline indifference, it later became that of a more and more intense belief in divine providence, which identified absolute obedience to God's will, with absolute acceptance of things as they were. Starting from this background, it was impossible for Luther to establish a new or in any way fundamental connection between worldly activities and religious principles.[8]

Luther's conception of the calling is therefore of little significance for Weber's argument and serves merely as an introduction to the concept itself. The really decisive religious figure in Weber's eyes is not Martin Luther but is, rather, John Calvin. It is Calvinism that is the true opponent of Catholicism.[9]

Calvinism and predestination

The entry of Calvin into the picture raises the question of the so-called 'psychological sanction' and thus the controversial issue of Weber's interpretation of the doctrine of predestination. All of the great world religions are, to some extent, predestinarian. The *raison d'être* of a systematic theology is to lend purpose and meaning to the world so that the life of the individual can be read as a moment in some wider design, and thus may be said to be – to a greater or lesser extent – 'predetermined', rather than simply being a spontaneous happening with no consequences beyond the grave. The question arises, of course, of how one may intercede with the deity or deities to ascertain the purpose of one's life on earth and procure either grace itself or knowledge that one has already secured it. Luther, for example, held that God's secret decrees were the ultimate and sole source of religious grace but, brushing logical consistency aside, allowed the notion of predestination to recede in his teachings in favour of the idea that grace could be lost by the individual but regained through true faith and trust in the Word of God and his sacraments.[10] Calvin, on the other hand, was increasingly and ruthlessly consistent in his systematic theology and, as a result, pushed the doctrine of predestination to its logical and, Weber felt, terrifying conclusion: namely, that God has so predestined all things that none may know whether they are saved or damned; and, moreover, has denied all means of attaining grace on earth and so of altering his eternal decrees. How does Calvin arrive at such a conclusion and what are the implications of his position for the practical conduct of the average believer?

The broad outline of the Calvinist doctrine of predestination itself seems relatively non-controversial. The world exists only for the sake and glory of God. All things contained therein are governed by his providence, to his glory, and for purposes which he alone perceives. We cannot understand his decrees (except in so far as he graciously reveals such knowledge to us) nor can we apply earthly standards of justice to them. Any attempt to question or comprehend his sovereign will is, in fact, an insult to God's majesty. Now, although by the Fall all persons are inherently sinful, nevertheless God has, of mere mercy alone, predestined some to be saved through faith in Christ as their Saviour. The rest of humanity is destined for damnation.[11]

The important point about this doctrine of predestination is that God's decree of election or damnation is eternal. One has been, is, and forever shall be either a child of God or a sinner, to the glory of God and irrespective of one's wishes and intentions in the matter:

For the damned to complain of their lot would be much the same as for animals to bemoan the fact they were not born as men. For everything of the flesh is separated from God by an unbridgeable gulf and deserves of Him only eternal death, in so far as He has not decreed otherwise for the glorification of His majesty. We know only that a part of humanity is saved, the rest damned. To assume that human merit or guilt play a part in determining this destiny would be to think of God's absolutely free decrees, which have been settled from eternity, as subject to change by human influence, an impossible contradiction. . . . God's grace is, since His decrees cannot change, as impossible for those to whom He has granted it to lose as it is unattainable for those to whom He has denied it.[12]

All must observe the laws of the Church, participate in the sacraments, and attempt to live the godly life, for we are all upon the earth only to testify to the glory of God. But observation of these precepts provides no guarantee of salvation. The true Christian cannot stay away from church but the visible Church also encompasses the reprobate who must participate, not in order to attain salvation, but simply in observance of God's commandments which all must obey to his glory. The sacraments too, must be observed as an external manifestation of faith by the elect and as a declaration of God's glory by all, but, as with all forms of works on earth, they do not offer a means of attaining grace. Salvation cannot be earned in life for one's whole existence is simply a predetermined realization of the will of God.

Weber felt that the psychological consequences of such a doctrine for the individual Calvinist were little short of horrific:

In its extreme inhumanity this doctrine must above all have had one consequence for the life of a generation which surrendered to its magnificent consistency. That was a feeling of unprecedented inner loneliness of the single individual. In what was for the man of the age of the Reformation the most important thing in life, his eternal salvation, he was forced to follow his path alone to meet a destiny which had been decreed for him from eternity. No one could help him. No priest . . . no sacraments. . . . There was not only no magical means of attaining the grace of God for those to whom God had decided to deny it, but no means whatsoever.[13]

At a time when salvation was a matter of real importance for the average person the question must have been posed sooner or later by the faithful Calvinist as to whether or not he or she was of the elect. Certainty of grace was no problem to Calvin who was assured of his own salvation as a prophet of God. Correspondingly he taught that, in the last resort, the single distinguishing feature of the elect is that they trust to the end in God's mercy through wholehearted faith in Christ. Theirs is a *true* faith. This aside, all other subjective experiences and external conduct can be shared by elect and reprobate alike, up to and including the living out on earth of a life filled with apparently godly behaviour and good works.

Such an answer was scarcely calculated to satisfy the psychological crisis generated by the doctrine of predestination among ordinary believers, and, recognizing this fact, Calvinist theologians from Beza onwards began to elaborate more concrete means by which the faithful could resolve the question of their unknown and predetermined status, at least for pragmatic purposes if not in any ultimate sense. At the level of pastoral advice, later Calvinist theologians taught the 'terrible' decree of predestination but also suggested, by way of averting the crisis of salvation generated by this doctrine, that it was the absolute duty of the individual to assume himself or herself to be chosen (since any doubts about this were a sign of imperfect faith and therefore of imperfect grace), and that in order to attain such self-assurance intense worldly activity – living the godly life – was commended.[14]

In short, Calvinists were encouraged to *prove* their election by identifying the fruits of true faith in appropriate everyday conduct. Such conduct served also, of course, to increase the glory of God. This is not to say that Calvinists were encouraged to accumulate good works and earn salvation, as in Roman Catholicism. The godly life does not procure salvation so much as eliminate the fear of damnation. Works cannot purchase salvation: they demonstrate it.[15] In this way, Weber maintains, the Calvinist belief-system arrives at a practical result which is wholly opposite to its own logical consequences. The only logical consequence of the doctrine of predestination is fatalism. (Live as one will, the reprobate can neither earn salvation, nor the elect fall from grace.) However, by tying works to faith such that only the systematic and relentless practice of appropriate worldly activity can permit the individual to draw the conclusion that his or her faith is true and therefore saving, the psychological consequences of Calvinism are made dynamic rather than passive.[16]

Of what does the Calvinist code of ethics for the conduct of everyday life consist? What sort of 'intense worldly activity' did pastors encourage by way of attaining assurance of grace? For Weber at least, a study of neo-Calvinist texts shows that they commended, above all else, those three interrelated ethical maxims which, it was suggested above, were shared by all forms of ascetic Protestantism; namely, diligence in lawful callings; asceticism with respect to material satisfactions; and constructive utilization of one's time.

Since one has only a limited time on earth in which to give glory to God, and to make sure of one's election by attaining that quiet self-confidence of salvation which is the fruit of true faith and of proving one's regeneration in the conduct of one's daily life, then every moment spent in idleness, leisure, gaming, idle talk, excessive sleep, unnecessary recreation, and enjoying luxury is literally a waste of time, is worthy of moral condemnation, and is a sign of imperfect grace. How, then, ought the faithful to employ their time? That first of all they must fulfil their spiritual duties – prayer, attendance at church and sacraments, Sabbath observance, and the like – goes without saying. But equally they must work hard in their lawful callings. Hard, methodical, continuous, manual and mental labour in a legitimate calling is required of all: it is God's commandment that they who shall not work shall not eat. Idleness, like time-wasting, is the mark of a reprobate. Finally, we must guard against the dangers and temptations of wealth, which are principally idleness itself and hedonism. We are put on earth to glorify God, not to enjoy a carefree and comfortable life. Social drinking, delicate foods, fine clothes, excessive decorating of the home, sexual pleasures, and material comforts in general encourage the unprofitable use of time and turn people from the diligent pursuit of their lawful callings.[17]

Pietism, Baptism, and the importance of 'proof'

These three tenets of everyday conduct – diligence in lawful callings, asceticism, and accounting for the use of time – stand at the centre of the ethical codes of a number of Reformed Churches. Not only are they fundamental to the teachings of seventeenth-century Calvinist groupings (such as the English Puritans), but they are also readily identifiable as the foundation of the prescribed form of everyday conduct in Pietism, Methodism, and in the sects associated with the Baptist movement.[18] It is important to realize, however, that Weber nowhere suggests that this code of everyday conduct is unique to seventeenth-century ascetic Protestantism. A number of medieval scholastics, for example, had upheld the social desirability of work over idleness and condemned many of the hedonistic practices outlawed by Calvinists. With the exception of the particular interpretation placed upon the idea of the calling, the ethical maxims of ascetic Protestantism were not especially original.[19] What was unprecedented, however, was the provision in a theology of a psychological sanction which effectively enforced adherence to these maxims among all of the faithful and thus led to the disappearance of the Catholic *consilia evangelica*. Calvinist pastors were not commending worldly asceticism to their flocks as something which might be desirable in an ideal world. Rather, their exhortations can be reduced to the simple declaration that if one does not behave according to the strict observances of the Calvinist precepts for daily living, then one can take it for granted that this is a sure sign that one is of the damned. It was, indeed, his discovery of the psychological sanction arising out of the combination of the doctrine of predestination with the idea of proof that Weber considered to be his distinctive contribution to the discussion about the relationship between Protestantism and capitalism:

The essential point . . . is . . . that an ethic based on religion places certain psychological sanctions (not of an economic character) on the maintenance of the attitude prescribed by it, sanctions which, so long as the religious belief remains alive, are highly effective. . . . Only in so far as these sanctions work, and, above all, in the direction in which they work, which is often very different from the doctrine of the theologians, does such an ethic gain an independent influence on the conduct of life and thus on the economic order. This is, to speak frankly, the point of this whole essay. . . .[20]

But does this sanction originate only in the doctrine of predestination as this was formulated by neo-Calvinist Churches and denominations? The Pietist, Methodist, and Baptist movements, for example, may have shared the Calvinist conception of the godly life but they by no means subscribed uniformly to the idea of predestination. Where, then, lie the origins of the psychological sanction in these Churches? Weber's reply to this question is twofold. First, he concedes that his essays offer only an exploratory sketch rather than a complete analysis and that empirically the picture is very complicated, but insists, nevertheless, that some variant of the idea of proof remains central to the teachings of these Churches. Second, and especially where the Baptist sects are concerned, an entirely separate sanction is created by the organizational structure of the sects themselves.

Pietism offers an illustration of the first of these arguments. The movement itself is extremely diverse and appears in both Calvinist and non-Calvinist forms. Certain versions emphasized the importance of a saving faith (the attainment of *certitudo salutis*) to such an extent that believers pursued, above all else, a state of blissful community with God which was not unlike the Lutheran *unio mystica*. Such emotionalism, where it occurred, tended to undermine the insistence on searching for assurance of election within the everyday routine of life in a worldly calling. Broadly speaking, however, most versions of Pietism retained the idea that striving for certainty of grace was a sign of grace, and where they retreated from the Calvinist version of the doctrine of predestination they emphasized a relationship between faith and works which had the same practical consequences. Thus, it was important to attain assurance of a saving faith; true faith inevitably manifests itself in appropriate everyday conduct; good works are therefore a sign of grace but only if the believer seeks constantly to further assurance of grace through a more secure faith, which necessitates yet further diligence in one's calling, more systematic use of one's time – and so the spiral continues ever upwards in pursuit of increasing sanctification in this world as proof of eventual salvation in the next. Rarely, if at all, did Pietism fall back on the traditionalistic faith of Lutheranism, with its exclusive reliance on the use of word and sacraments, and only minimal performance of the duties of one's calling.

Weber concludes that in so far as Pietism can be distinguished from neo-Calvinist movements which subscribed to the version of the doctrine of predestination found in, for example, the famous *Westminster Confession of Faith* of 1647, it nevertheless provided a 'functional equivalent' to this doctrine by binding together genuine faith and everyday conduct such that assurance of the former depended on methodical performance of the latter. Such a sanction may not have been able to provide so powerful a motive to rationalize mundane activity as the Calvinist doctrine of predestination but it was certainly more favourable to it than were the teachings of orthodox Lutheranism. The idea of proof remained central to the theology itself.[21]

The Baptist movement shares the Calvinist ethical maxims for everyday conduct but offers an example of an independently originating sanction compelling adherence to these. Calvinist doctrine states that the glory of God requires the Church to bring all – elect and reprobate alike – under God's law and into the body of the visible Church. Where this doctrine was outweighed by the conviction that it was an insult to God to admit the unregenerate into his house, and to partake of his sacraments, the resulting insistence on preserving a pure Church led to the formation of exclusive communities of those acknowledged as being reborn. The Calvinist insistence upon proof occasionally led to the development of such a Donatist conception of the Church inside Calvinism itself as, for example, in the case of the Independent sects of the seventeenth century.[22] However, the most significant of the sectarian movements originates outside Calvinism in Anabaptism. Here, too, the sects are considered to be

the true blameless Church of Christ; like the apostolic community, consisting entirely of those personally awakened, and called by God. Those who have been born again, and they alone, are brethren of Christ, because they, like Him, have been created in spirit directly by God.[23]

Those who have not yet received the inner light remain creatures of the flesh and pursue worldly and godless ends. The new person, however, having his or her heart opened by the Holy Spirit is so much the subject of divine grace that he or she can pursue only the ordinances of the saint – worldly asceticism. A relapse into sinful ways scarcely becomes possible. But here the very organizational structure of the sect itself comes into play. The sectarian, unlike the member of the authoritarian state Calvinist Churches, submitted voluntarily to the discipline of the sect having once declared his or her regeneration. Henceforth that person's conduct would be publicly judged by those with whom they had freely entered into association. One had to prove oneself continuously, not only before God, but also before one's fellow sectarians.[24]

In the case of the sects then, as in Calvinism itself, we return at the end of the day to the importance to the individual of proving himself or herself to be of the regenerate in the practice of his or her daily life:

To repeat, it is not the ethical *doctrine* of a religion, but that form of ethical conduct upon which premiums are placed that matters. Such premiums operate through the form and the condition of the respective goods of salvation. And such conduct constitutes 'one's' specific 'ethos' in the sociological sense of the word. For Puritanism, that conduct was a certain methodical, rational way of life which – given certain conditions – paved the way for the 'spirit' of modern capitalism. The premiums were placed upon 'proving' oneself before God in the sense of attaining salvation – which is found in *all* Puritan denominations – and 'proving' oneself before men in the sense of socially holding one's own within the Puritan sects. Both aspects were mutually supplementary and operated in the same direction: they helped to deliver the 'spirit' of modern capitalism, its specific ethos: the ethos of the modern *bourgeois middle classes*.[25]

The submission about the consequences of the organizational structure of the voluntary sects, however, is not fully elaborated in Weber's original essays. The complete version of his argument is to be found in his related essay on 'The Protestant sects and the spirit of capitalism'.

Worldly asceticism

Weber's general argument therefore seems unambiguous. The average medieval Catholic layperson could live ethically, as Weber puts it, 'from hand to mouth'. He or she was obliged conscientiously to fulfil traditional duties, but beyond this each separate good work could be treated as a single act which might atone for a sin committed, better his or her chances of salvation, or serve as an insurance premium against damnation. (It was in pursuit of the last of these that, for example, so many Catholic merchants bequeathed the fortunes which they had accumulated during their lifetime to religious charities.) The Catholic sacrament of absolution symbolizes the idea of the values accredited to individual acts and the doctrine of salvation by works. Periodic remission of sin was, however, a luxury denied to ascetic Protestants, for the doctrine of predestination eliminated 'magical' means (the sacraments, ritual atonement, works in general) to salvation:

To the Catholic the absolution of his Church was a compensation for his own imperfection. The priest was a magician who performed the miracle of transubstantiation, and who held the key to eternal life in his hand. One could turn to him in grief and penitence. He dispensed atonement, hope of grace, certainty of forgiveness, and thereby granted release from that tremendous tension to which the Calvinist was doomed by an inexorable fate, admitting of no mitigation. For him such friendly and human comforts did not exist. He could not hope to atone for hours of weakness or of thoughtlessness by increased good-will at other times, as the Catholic or even the Lutheran could. The God of Calvinism demanded of his believers not single good works, but a life of good works combined into a unified system. There was no place for the very human Catholic cycle of sin, repentance, atonement, release, followed by renewed sin. Nor was there any balance of merit for a life as a whole which could be adjusted by temporal punishments or the Churches' means of grace.[26]

The average neo-Calvinist was required continuously, methodically, and relentlessly to prove his or her election by diligence in a lawful calling, asceticism, and accounting for the use of his or her time. In this way the moral conduct of the layperson was deprived of its unsystematic or planless character: it was rationalized in the direction of, and dominated entirely by the aim of, adding to God's glory on earth.[27] Spontaneous enjoyment of life and of material possessions was eliminated. All actions were carefully considered in terms of their ethical consequences. Ethical conduct was systematized and under the constant supervision of the individual believer and, often, of fellow Church members and sectarians.

Weber acknowledges that such a conception of the godly life finds its predecessor in Western monasticism. The monks, too, were ascetics dedicated to freeing themselves from 'irrational' impulses and dependence on the world and nature. But theirs was a methodical asceticism which withdrew from the world. The Reformation, as we have seen, carried Christian asceticism into it. Now each of the faithful had to be a monk throughout his or her life for it was only through such rational asceticism in daily living that one could prove one's faith and hence one's election. All must live as saints.[28]

To Weber, the consequences of such a revolution in the conduct of the daily lives of whole populations appeared self-evident. Protestant asceticism restricted consumption of luxuries and prohibited spontaneous enjoyment of the world. On the other hand, it insisted upon relentless efforts in one's lawful vocation as the duty of all Christians. This unique combination, Weber felt, was almost certain, *ceteris paribus*, to lead to the accumulation and reinvestment of capital by those involved in business activities:

When the limitation of consumption is combined with the release of acquisitive activity, the inevitable practical result is obvious: accumulation of capital through ascetic compulsion to save. The restraints which were imposed upon the consumption of wealth naturally served to increase it by making possible the productive investment of capital.[29]

Thus, through the entirely unintended consequences of the double injunctions to diligence in lawful callings and asceticism in the world, ascetic Protestantism created the modern capitalist mentality:

the religious valuation of restless, continuous, systematic work in a worldly calling, as the highest means of asceticism, and at the same time the surest and most evident proof of rebirth and genuine faith, must have been the most powerful conceivable lever for the expansion of that attitude toward life which we have here called the spirit of capitalism. . . .

. . . One of the fundamental elements of the spirit of modern capitalism, and not only of that but of all modern culture: rational conduct on the basis of the idea of the calling, was born – that is what this discussion has sought to demonstrate – from the spirit of Christian asceticism. One has only to re-read . . . Franklin . . . in order to see that the essential elements of the attitude which was there called the spirit of capitalism are the same as what we have just shown to be the content of the Puritan worldly asceticism, only without the religious basis, which by Franklin's time had died away.[30]

Ascetic Protestantism was opposed to ostentation, spontaneous enjoyment of life, elegance: it was opposed, in short, to the magnificence of the feudal way of living. Against it was set the Puritan ideal of sober simplicity, the 'clean and solid comfort of the middle-class home'. In sum,

As far as the influence of the Puritan outlook extended, under all circumstances – and this is, of course, much more important than the mere encouragement of capital accumulation – it favoured the development of a rational bourgeois economic life; it was the most important, and above all the only consistent influence in the development of that life. It stood at the cradle of the modern economic man.[31]

This particular implication of Protestant asceticism may have seemed obvious to Weber but, as we shall now see, commentators since have been inclined to paint an entirely more complicated picture of the Reformation and its consequences for economic life.

Some critics criticized

Weber's interpretation of Protestant theology, as was stated above, is that part of his thesis which has most often been the object of strong criticism, indeed, occasionally of ridicule. A number of such criticisms have been recurrent in the literature from the time of Weber's own exchanges with his early German critics up to the present day. For example, the arguments have repeatedly been put that Weber overemphasizes the importance of the idea of predestination and misrepresents the doctrine of callings in Calvinist theology; that all of the elements of the 'Protestant ethic' are also to be found in medieval Catholic theology; that Calvinism, Lutheranism, and Roman Catholicism are indistinguishable with respect to their attitudes towards wealth and its accumulation; and that Weber's selection of Puritan divines is so unrepresentative even of the Puritan movement as a whole that it casts doubt upon his entire characterization of ascetic Protestantism.

There are two ways of looking at this phenomenon. It may be assumed, on the one hand, that these criticisms are recurrent because they are the most forceful and damning objections that can be raised against Weber's thesis and that they therefore remain unanswered by Weber or his followers. It is also possible, however, to take entirely the opposite view and argue that, repetitious though these objections might be, they have been adequately countered by Weber or those who subscribe to his thesis, and the frequency with which they recur simply testifies to the failure among critics to read Weber's argument carefully or to line up their target properly.

My own inclinations are towards the latter viewpoint. This is not to say that Weber's comparative presentations of Roman Catholic and Reformed theologies are entirely unproblematic. It is merely to suggest that much previous criticism fails to approach Weber's argument at points where it is genuinely weak. Any attempt to demonstrate the accuracy of this interpretation of the controversy, however, is rendered difficult by two factors. First, many of the points that Weber wishes to make concerning the relevant theologies are best presented, indeed sometimes only fully developed, in the untranslated replies to his critics. Second, much of the detailed evidence concerning the theologies of the various Churches is acknowledged by Weber to lie in the independent studies carried out by Ernst Troeltsch into the complex history of the relationships between the development of Christian theologies, and their social and material settings. Troeltsch's *The Social Teachings of the Christian Churches*, for example, so decisively confirms Weber's interpretation of the social ethics of the major Western Churches that a reading of it ought really to be mandatory for all prospective critics of Weber's account of Protestantism. Weber acknowledged that he was no theologian, but insisted that since he was interested primarily in the practical results of religious doctrines, rather than the nuances of the doctrines themselves, his own ideal-typical approach served to establish sufficiently the overall thrust of pastoral teaching, the brevity of his sketch notwithstanding. The documentation of theological subtleties he ceded to professional theologians such as Troeltsch.[32] Nevertheless, even if Weber's critics are given the benefit of the doubt with respect to these omissions in his presentation, it seems to me, there is still sufficient evidence in Weber's original text to give the lie to many of their objections. When we go on to consider the 1920 version of the essays which are the basis of subsequent translations, with their footnoted replies by Weber to his critics, the weight of the evidence seems convincingly to be in Weber's favour.

Logical errors

A number of criticisms would seem to be questionable on prior logical grounds. Clearly mistaken, for example, are the many commentators who criticize Weber's presentation of the ethos of 'ascetic Protestantism' for being an inaccurate representation of the teachings of John Calvin.[33] At its most perverse this line of criticism is expressed in W. S. Reid's complaint that Weber is unjustified in looking to seventeenth-century Puritans as 'trustworthy exponents of Calvin's economic views'.[34] Those familiar with Weber's text will recognize that Weber makes no such claim since, of course, his argument turns on the very distinction between the teachings of Calvin and those of the pastoral theologians of the seventeenth-century neo-Calvinist

Churches into which Calvinism evolved. Weber is wholly unambiguous on this point:

> I may here say definitely that we are not studying the personal views of Calvin, but Calvinism, and that in the form to which it had evolved by the end of the sixteenth and in the seventeenth centuries in the great areas where it had a decisive influence and which were at the same time the home of capitalistic culture.[35]

Therefore, to complain, as Biéler does, that Puritanism 'deforms' and 'secularizes' the original teachings of Calvin and that it is unfair to hold Calvin responsible for what later so-called 'Calvinists' made of his teachings, may well be true but it is as much to vindicate Weber's argument as to refute it. Indeed, Biéler himself concedes that Weber's description of the practical ethics of later Protestantism may be entirely accurate, although he insists, again, that these are not an adequate representation of the original teachings of Calvin, a judgement which Weber could readily have accepted without in any way weakening his own argument.[36]

Critics have also made much, over the years, of the hostile attitude of neo-Calvinist theologians towards wealth and its accumulation. Weber, it is argued, appears to have overlooked the elementary fact that even those Puritan divines from whose teachings so much of his evidence derives denounced avarice and materialism with a vehemence scarcely equalled by their Roman Catholic counterparts. Hudson, for example, has concluded that

> If any one thing is clear in the writings of Richard Baxter, it is his intensely anti-Mammon spirit. He constantly insists that God and Mammon are antithetical, and lashes out against the hypocrisy of those who think they can be reconciled.[37]

A great deal of evidence has therefore been marshalled to testify to the near universal opposition among Calvinist divines to rack-renting, enclosures, economic exploitation or oppression, unrestrained seeking for gold, dishonest business practices, and the like. Calvin's not entirely unambiguous attitude towards the taking of interest is similarly invoked. Samuelsson speaks for generations of critics when he insists that no Reformed theologian (of any hue) from Calvin to Wesley preached 'free-for-all capitalism'. Neither Calvin (as Lecerf reminds us) nor his followers can anywhere be quoted as having said: 'You doubt your election? Enrich yourself, and you will be sure of the love of God.'[38]

Nor, of course, would Weber expect this to be the case. His thesis does not require such crass materialism either among lay Calvinists or their ministry and he is fully aware of the anti-Mammonistic stream in Calvinist theology. 'Examples of the condemnation of the pursuit of money and goods', he writes, 'may be gathered without end from Puritan writings, and may be contrasted with the late medieval ethical literature, which was much more open-minded on this point.'[39] His argument is not that Calvinist preachers consciously fostered the accumulation and reinvestment of capital; rather, it is that this phenomenon, and the bourgeois world-view in general, arose as the entirely *unintentional* consequences of their injunctions to diligence in lawful callings and worldly asceticism. To reduce Weber's thesis to the assertion that he, Weber, maintains that Calvinist pastors taught 'God grants material and business success to the elect', so that those who fail to prosper are clearly of the damned, is therefore to distort the arguments of both parties.[40] Similarly, irrespective of what the material results of the direct intervention of either the Roman Catholic or Reformed Churches as institutions into economic life may or may not have been, discussions of Church wealth, tithes, patronage, and the effects of Church building programmes on economic development are of no consequence whatsoever for Weber's argument about the religious origins of the spirit of modern capitalism.[41]

Weber's argument, though unambiguous, is rather more subtle. Again and again he emphasizes the distinction which he wishes to draw between the ethical doctrine of a religion and those forms of ethical conduct upon which, as he puts it, 'premiums are placed'. For example, in reply to Brentano and Sombart, two early critics who repeatedly point to the ethically 'traditionalistic' aspects of Puritan theology, a frustrated Weber declares that against their 'selective presentation' he has attempted

to show how, in spite of its anti-mammonistic doctrines the spirit of this ascetic religion nevertheless, just as in the monastic communities, gave birth to economic rationalism because it placed a premium on what was important for it: the fundamentally ascetic rational motives. That fact alone is under discussion and is the point of this whole essay.[42]

The formal and abstract theology of Calvin and his disciples is one thing. Calvinism – a theological system which arises from the needs of religious practice and, like all great world religions, addressed the layperson's question 'How can I become certain of my salvation?' – is quite another. Weber's critics, as he legitimately complains, seem incapable of grasping this distinction between formal ethical codes, on the one hand, and 'motives to practical action, dependent on the desire for salvation', on the other. They 'continually cite the ethical writers ... as codifications of rules of conduct without ever asking which of them were supported by psychologically effective religious sanctions'.[43]

In any case, Weber adds (and this is a point of empirical substance), it is clear from a careful reading of the appropriate literature that ascetic Protestantism does not condemn wealth as such, only the impulsive pursuit of it. Wealth and even its acquisition are not seen as necessarily evil, although they do contain certain inherent temptations which must be guarded against. Thus, as Weber rightly concludes,

The real moral objection is to relaxation in the security of possession, the enjoyment of wealth with the consequence of idleness and the temptations of the flesh, above all of distraction from the pursuit of a righteous life. In fact, it is only because possession involves this danger of relaxation that it is objectionable at all.[44]

Certainly, Calvinism was entirely opposed to spontaneous enjoyment of material possessions, and to luxury itself. But it was also obsessive in its insistence on diligence in lawful callings as a means of proving one's election and glorifying God, an obsession which, according to Weber,

had the psychological effect of freeing the acquisition of goods from the inhibitions of traditionalistic ethics. It broke the bonds of the impulse to acquisition in that it not only legalized it, but (in the sense discussed) looked upon it as directly willed by God. The campaign against the temptations of the flesh, and the dependence on external things, was, as besides the Puritans the great Quaker apologist Barclay expressly says, not a struggle against the rational acquisition, but against the irrational use of wealth.[45]

The correct use of wealth then, according to Weber's interpretation of Protestant sermons, was to 'improve' it to the glory of God. (This point will also be considered when we come to investigate those aspects of Weber's argument about Protestant theology which can best be judged on empirical, as opposed to theoretical grounds.)

A number of eminent contributors to the debate about Weber's interpretation of theologies have offered criticism from a somewhat different angle. Rather than (or in some cases in addition to) suggesting weaknesses in Weber's understanding of the doctrines of the new Reformed Churches, they have taken the argument a step further back and questioned his conception of Roman Catholicism itself. The argument here is that there is little or nothing to choose between the ethical teachings of sixteenth- and seventeenth-century Catholic and Reformed faiths and, therefore, that the former was as conducive to the modern capitalist mentality as the latter.[46] Some, such as H. M. Robertson, have even gone so far as to suggest that certain branches of Roman Catholicism were more favourably disposed to the spirit of capitalism than were the Reformed faiths themselves. Robertson argues that Catholic and Calvinist theologies are indistinguishable with respect to their ethical teachings concerning the dangers of riches and the desirability of orderly and hard work, and that 'Catholics employed doctrines cognate with that of the "calling" with the same practical effect'.[47] So, when we take into account the definite hindrances to the capitalist mentality resulting from Calvinist attempts to subject all aspects of economic life to strict regulation by the Church, it is not unreasonable to conclude that

The Protestants as well as the Catholics spoke with an ambiguous voice. But as a rule the Calvinistic contribution to the capitalist spirit was the same as that of the Jansenists or stricter school of Catholics, consisting of the encouragement of industry, thrift, order and honesty; while the Jesuits went further and favoured enterprise, freedom from speculation and the expansion of trade as a social benefit. It would not be difficult to claim that the religion which favoured the spirit of capitalism was Jesuitry, not Calvinism.[48]

In reply to this assertion Tawney has suggested that Robertson's attempts to find parallels to the Protestant idea of the 'calling' in Catholic writings 'have not been very happy', while Parsons maintains that Robertson so misrepresents Weber's argument, especially his conception of the spirit of capitalism and his use of ideal-types, that his entire *critique* fails to engage Weber's thesis at any point.[49] To these objections might be added Weber's repeated insistence that, whatever the similarities between the ethical doctrines of the various theologies, his critics have nowhere shown that Catholicism (or any other religion) places a psychological sanction on certain standards of ethical and practical conduct such that it enforces adherence to them. Whatever ethics Roman Catholic laypersons may or may not have been taught at the pastoral level, they were certainly *not* required consistently to prove themselves of the regenerate in the way that ascetic Protestants were.

However, a more thorough refutation of Robertson's conclusions about the 'modern capitalistic' characteristics of Roman Catholicism, and in particular of the Jesuits, has been provided by James Brodrick, a Catholic writer who was so angered by Robertson's text that he set about a methodical critique of his entire argument, accusing him, in the process, of selectively using unreliable sources, of quoting out of context, and of systematically distorting Jesuit teaching on economic matters.[50] Brodrick's particular reservations have been introduced at this juncture because they lead us in to the problem of dealing with those criticisms of Weber's argument which are of an empirical rather than a logical or discursive nature. And it is, in fact, the case that the majority of the objections that have been voiced with respect to Weber's account of religious doctrines can, like Brodrick's rejection of Robertson's ideas about Jesuit casuistry, be decided only on empirical grounds.

Empirical issues

The general accusation that Weber's interpretation of ascetic Protestantism is empirically at fault has most often taken the form of a claim that his argument rests on an unrepresentative selection of Protestant texts and, in particular, lends too much weight to the pastoral theology of one English divine, namely, Richard Baxter. A number of related criticisms arise from this conclusion. The alleged bias in his choice of texts and, equally serious, the unjustifiable and misleading attention which he accords to only selected themes from the texts themselves, reputedly lead Weber to oversimplify the Protestant conception of the calling, substantially overemphasize the importance of the doctrine of predestination in neo-Calvinism, and to ignore the differences between the various branches of Calvinism such that certain ideas peculiar to English Puritanism are read as being typical of the movement as a whole.[51]

Again on empirical grounds there have been forwarded a number of significant amendments to Weber's thesis, including the argument that it is not ascetic Protestantism *per se* but the presence of and discrimination against an ethnic or religious minority that fosters the capitalist mentality, and a related suggestion of 'negative causality' – the contention that the Reformation was less an encouragement to the rise of capitalism than the Counter-Reformation was an obstacle. The first of these is essentially a restatement of Simmel's argument (noted on page 35) about the significance of socially and culturally marginal groups ('strangers') for economic development. English Puritans were disproportionately to be found in the business world, and unusually successful in their business activities, not for reasons relating to the content of their theology but simply because, as Nonconformists, they were excluded from public office, state honours, the liberal professions, and all other traditionalistic and respectable avenues to power. By default they entered the business world and, unable to escape from it having made their fortunes, stayed there and reinvested instead of retiring into the state bureaucracy or on to the land. Weber's critics maintain that this same behavioural pattern, with similar consequences for economic conduct and success, can be found among all such persecuted minorities at this time, irrespective of the religious creeds and geographical locations involved. Thus the Jews of Central and Eastern Europe, Protestant sectaries in Western Europe, and the religious minorities of the Near East and India, all achieved greater economic success than the relevant host populations, and precisely because of their minority status.[52]

The 'negative causality' hypothesis, independently and simultaneously developed by Hugh Trevor-Roper and Herbert Luethy, is really a variation on the same theme. Both authors maintain that an analysis of the outlook and background of the Protestant business communities of the seventeenth century shows that many such groups were not Calvinist or, at best, only nominally so. What is significant about these people – the business communities of the Dutch Republic for example – is that, by and large, they are first generation immigrants from hitherto capitalistically developed areas; in the case in point, from the declining Southern Netherlands in the last quarter of the sixteenth century. The relationship between religion and economic development then turns largely on the actions of the Southern European Catholic powers – Spain, the Spanish Netherlands, Italy and, somewhat later, France – who, in the course of the Counter-Reformation, directly or indirectly (through harassment) expelled their critical and often anti-clerical business classes and townspeople, with the exception only of certain indispensable court monopolists and financiers.[53]

It would be a simple enough matter for Weber's followers to argue polemically against the above charges. Some of Weber's critics, for example, are themselves guilty of grossly oversimplifying Protestant and Catholic belief-systems: treating Protestantism as if it were a unitary phenomenon is one of their most common errors.[54] Similarly, as Besnard has rightly suggested, the negative causality thesis does not preclude Weber's own argument since it fails to explain why the (expelled) business classes were so often Protestant in the first place.[55] But such an exchange as this carries the discussion forward very little at the end of the day. Questions pertaining to Weber's alleged misrepresentation of ascetic Protestant teachings raise largely empirical issues and may only be resolved, in the last resort, by reference to appropriate theological data. Sociologists seeking to assess the relative merits of theological and historical criticism of Weber's accounts of Church doctrine have failed to come to terms with this fact. Weber's defence cannot rest exclusively on the charge that his critics have misunderstood his methodology or the logic of his explanation.[56]

Can Weber's interpretation of the various neo-Calvinist and related Protestant belief-systems be corroborated empirically? A number of his critics have argued, on the basis of empirical research of varying degrees of thoroughness, that it cannot. Albert Hyma, for example, has consistently maintained that the ideal-type of 'ascetic Protestantism' does not reflect accurately the nature of Dutch Calvinism. English Puritanism and Dutch Calvinism, Hyma argues, are not the same thing, and whatever interpretation the Puritans may or may not have placed upon the doctrine of predestination, the fact is that the Calvinist position on this question (which was, in any case, more complex than Weber suggests) is indistinguishable from that of Arminians and of Anglicans in general.[57] Similarly, and with respect to the Puritan conception of the calling, Charles and Katherine George argue that, although Weber is correct to point to the break which this doctrine represents with the social theory of medieval Catholicism, the doctrine itself is 'broadly Protestant' – Lutheran as much as Calvinist – and, they imply, its quiescent practical consequences are the same in both cases:

Weber himself defines the spirit of capitalism as consisting essentially in the rational pursuit of profit. What is farthest from the English Protestant doctrine of the calling, what is specifically contrary to it, in fact, is this very rational pursuit of profit. The Christian pursues nothing in the calling except, through the proper performance of the duties it involves, the service of God and his fellow men. Even the Christian's simple maintenance . . . is to be seen as an incidental consequence of diligence in the calling rather than as an object of endeavour. Profit entails enriching, furthermore – an increase of wealth in the hands of the person undertaking the profitable enterprise. The English Protestant divine . . . attacks from many angles any orientation of life toward the increase of wealth. Through exhortations to constancy in the calling and other related arguments, he encourages and sponsors, just as does his Roman Catholic forebear, a stable rather than a mobile society.[58]

The Georges' argument is somewhat complicated and obscured by the fact that they argue both that Puritanism is 'traditionalistic' in respect of its attitude towards economics and politics, and that, as a 'modernising agent', its 'transformative capacities' are enormous.[59] Less ambiguous have been the lengthy and detailed studies of Puritan theology conducted by Michael Walzer and David Little. While disagreeing as to the doctrinal and related mechanisms by which Puritanism became a 'revolutionary ideology', both authors maintain that the Puritan belief-system acted as an agent of modernization by transforming peoples' views of the political and social order as a whole, rather than simply their attitude towards capital or even economic life in general. Little, for example, while not denying Weber's argument concerning the significance of personal anxiety about salvation in encouraging activity in the world, suggests that a more thoroughgoing rationalization of life can be traced, above all, to the new conception of social order which was implicit in Puritan theology and which revolutionized popular conceptions of the nature and meaning of social relationships:

Puritanism may be ranged along a spectrum that moves from the Presbyterian emphasis upon regimentation and uniformity on one side to the sectarian inclination for liberty and pluralism on the other. . . . But what is fundamentally important is that all groups on the spectrum engendered the principles of voluntary choice, self-initiated behaviour and consensuality, while all took up arms against the old order that the rule of freedom might replace the rule of necessity.[60]

Walzer, by comparison, sees Puritanism as the retreat of persons experiencing social dislocation, and so personal anxiety, during a period of rapid social change. The Puritan texts convey the authoritarian ideas of groups of 'political entrepreneurs' pursuing collective control both of the rapidly changing socio-economic order and of themselves – and not, as Weber would have it, personal wealth and individualistic solutions to their anxieties:

Puritan zeal was not a private passion; it was instead a highly collective emotion and it imposed upon the saints a new and impersonal discipline. Conscience freed the saints from medieval passivity and feudal loyalty, but it did not encourage the individualist, Italianate politics of faction and intrigue. Puritan ministers campaigned against the personal extravagance of the great Renaissance courtiers and deplored the role of 'private interest' in politics. The conscientious activity that they favoured is perhaps best revealed in Cromwell's New Model Army, with its rigid camp discipline, its elaborate rules against every imaginable sin from looting and raping to blasphemy and

card-playing and finally its workmanlike and efficient military tactics. . . .
Indeed, the new spirit of the Puritans can be defined as a kind of military and
political work-ethic, directly analogous to the 'worldly asceticism' which
Max Weber has described in economic life, but oriented not toward
acquisition so much as toward contention, struggle, destruction, and
rebuilding. Calvinist conscience gave to war and to politics (and if Weber is
right to business as well) a new sense of method and purpose. It is this above
all that distinguishes the activity of the saints from that of medieval men,
caught up in the unchanging world of tradition, fixed in their social place and
loyal to their relatives; and also from that of Renaissance men, pursuing a
purely personal ambition.[61]

It is argued by all of these authors then, that because Weber
misreads or distorts Puritan theology, he fails to identify correctly the
principal consequences of Puritan doctrines in terms of their effects
on practical conduct and the 'modernization' process as a whole.
Clearly, however, such extensive empirical refutations and recastings
of Weber's interpretation of Protestant theology cannot be considered
in any detail in the present context. To evaluate the empirical
accuracy of even one conflicting account of the doctrines of ascetic
Protestantism, as compared to Weber's own, would be an enormous
(and inevitably tedious) task. One can, at this juncture, simply draw
the reader's attention to the fact that alternative readings of appropriate
Calvinist and neo-Calvinist literature have confirmed Weber's interpretation of the general thrust of pastoral theology as being correct in
essentials.[62]

For example, on the matter of the 'psychological sanction' arising
out of the doctrine of predestination and the idea of proof, it has been
demonstrated that Calvinist pastors insisted that only the reprobate
could draw fatalistic conclusions from predestinarian premises.
Again and again they emphasized that God inevitably forces an
assurance of salvation into his elect through having them prove their
faith in methodical everyday conduct and especially through diligence
in their respective callings or vocations. This sanction can be shown to
be reinforced by a number of related aspects of pastoral theology. The
'golden chain of salvation' (those whom God elects he inevitably
calls, justifies, and sanctifies) relates faith (justification) to works
(sanctification) in such a manner that it becomes impossible for the
Calvinist to sustain the belief that his or her faith is genuine in the
absence of 'fruits' or proof – appropriate everyday conduct. Since the
visible Church (those who partake of the sacraments) includes both
the elect and the reprobate, one must seek an assurance that one's

apparent faith is truly a saving faith, a faith which 'bursts forth in fruits'. But hypocrites, who are of the damned, may also conduct themselves 'honourably' in everyday life. So, to avoid the dangers of hypocrisy, one must incessantly seek the assurance of a knowledge that one's faith is true by persevering, never lapsing, in the renewal of one's faith through diligence in a lawful calling. A picture is painted in sermons of each person's conscience as an ever-seeing accountant who records every slip, each transgression, the slightest falter in our faith or conduct, in order that these may be cast before us at the Day of Judgement. The reprobate will then have to acknowledge the righteousness of God's justice in condemning them from the beginning of all time. The message of ascetic Protestant divines is, in short, 'no fruits, no true faith'. There is simply no means by which the faithful can retain their faith without reforming their lives.[63]

Moreover, as regards everyday conduct itself, the ethical maxims on which these 'premiums' are placed are, for the literatures which are the subjects of the studies in question, exactly as Weber describes them for ascetic Protestantism as a whole. Pastors explicitly distinguish the 'calling in general' (to be of the elect) from the 'calling in particular' (to practise a specific vocation in the world itself). They insist, as Weber suggests, upon striving for assurance of the former by systematic, methodical, diligent pursuit of the latter. Vocations which involve hard, bodily labour, and those requiring only mental effort and calculation, are seen to be equally legitimate. Although unambiguously opposed to idleness (the mark of a reprobate), all insist that teachings such as 'earn thy bread with the sweat of thy brow' and 'he who will not work neither shall he eat' are to be taken figuratively, and as applying to any faculty of body or mind employed in a lawful calling. The injunction to 'labour in a calling' is explicitly taken to govern all legitimate callings, including those of craftworkers, merchants, and even princes. Ministers sought diligence in a lawful calling for all: not manual labour for all. For this reason wealth, and even its incessant accumulation, is not seen as inherently evil. It carries with it, of course, the dangers of sloth, avarice, materialism, laziness, luxury, and carelessness in pursuit of a lawful vocation. But it is only the reprobate among the wealthy who fall prey to these temptations. The elect treat material blessings as a trial to test their faith, and persevere in testifying to their election by renewed efforts in practising a godly life, despite their riches. Many Calvinist pastors go further and, commending the example of the good steward in Christ's parable, arrive at the clear conclusion that the proper use of wealth is neither to consume it in luxuries nor waste it in excessive charity (thus encouraging idleness) but is, rather, to 'improve it to the glory of God'.

Finally, according to Calvinist teachings, in pursuing one's vocation all forms of time-wasting are to be eliminated. It is clear from the studies in question that a wide spectrum of Calvinist and neo-Calvinist teachers were, in fact, obsessed with the dangers of wasting time. Sermons abound with references to the despicable example set by the reprobate who testify to their damnation by losing time in 'idle chatter', gaming, carding, excessive recreation, 'idle strolling around', tippling in ale-houses, laughing and jesting, dancing, and (even) excessive sleeping. The elect, on the other hand, are ruthlessly methodical. They prove the sincerity of their faith by 'redeeming time', passing not a moment in idleness or 'unprofitable' activities, and by their ascetic practices: they eat, sleep, drink, and decorate themselves and their houses modestly; they are not inclined to extravagance or spontaneity in any way, such as socializing merely for enjoyment; they desire no jewellery or other luxuries; and they practise sexual abstinence and modesty. In short, the elect must inevitably and methodically practise an inner-worldly asceticism in order to prove their election. Weber is vindicated.

Weighing up the evidence on both sides it seems not unreasonable to conclude that there are as good grounds for maintaining Weber's interpretation of the overall thrust of ascetic Protestant teachings to be empirically sound as have been offered by way of challenging it. Certainly, his summary of certain of the doctrines of ascetic Protestantism is not the unrealistic and distorted account that many of his critics have claimed it to be. To the extent that they have focused exclusively on, for example, Calvinist condemnations of avarice and materialism, and have ignored the way in which pastors explicitly reconciled this idea with the acceptability of improving one's wealth, to the glory of God, through an insistence on diligence in lawful callings as a duty and means of proving one's faith, then it is reasonable to argue that certain of Weber's critics are more guilty of telling only selected parts of the story, and of presenting aspects of Calvinist theology out of context, than Weber is himself. The fact of the matter is, as Christopher Hill and others have pointed out, that Calvinist texts and doctrines, no less than those of any other developed theology, can be interpreted in several different directions. Weber's interpretation of the consequences of the Calvinist idea of proof is certainly *plausible*. However, by carefully selecting one's evidence from elsewhere in the vast and often internally inconsistent literature, it may well be possible to offer a contradictory and equally feasible interpretation. Ultimately, therefore, having demonstrated that Weber's thesis about the consequences for everyday conduct arising from certain Calvinist doctrines is acceptable in principle because his interpretation of Protestant doctrine is empirically plausible, we must return to the 'spirit of capitalism' side of his argument in order to determine whether or not the thesis is sound in practice. If it can be demonstrated empirically that pre-Reformation capitalists and labourers behaved in an economically 'traditionalistic' manner, whereas conversely the economic activities of seventeenth-century ascetic Protestants are consistent with the dictates of the spirit of modern capitalism as these are outlined by Weber, then his argument about the practical consequences of Calvinist teachings will be vindicated.

Was the 'psychological sanction' effective in changing peoples' orientation towards economic activities? This question may be answered only by investigating empirically the attitudes and everyday conduct of the Protestant business and labouring classes. Unfortunately this is something which Weber fails to do. For someone who is so explicitly interested in the practical consequences of theology, rather than theology itself, he is strangely unconcerned about documenting these consequences empirically as opposed simply to arguing them by assertion. As was noted in Chapter 3, all of Weber's data derive from Protestant theology. He provides no evidence whatsoever to substantiate his claim that the orientation towards economic conduct allegedly induced by the belief-systems of ascetic Protestantism was, in fact, subscribed to by the Protestant business community. His ideal-type of the spirit of modern capitalism, based entirely on the teachings of Franklin, remains but a 'provisional description'. It is therefore legitimate to claim, as several critics have, that Weber nowhere demonstrates that the average Protestant internalized and acted upon the ideas which he describes in his essays. Bendix puts this objection succinctly when he observes that

he [Weber] shows in a brilliant fashion, that the religious beliefs of the Puritans contained incentives encouraging a personal conduct of 'innerworldly asceticism' *to the extent that these beliefs were internalised* – clearly a conditional assertion. Yet his whole analysis rests on the thesis that Puritan believers differed from Catholics in their greater internalisation of religious precepts, their anxious concern with the uncertainty of salvation unrelieved by indulgences or the confessional, each man facing the stern and inscrutable majesty of God alone and unaided. In his responses to critics Weber declared that this intensified motivation had been a causal factor of great, but uncertain, magnitude, because men of that day were more deeply affected by abstract religious dogmas than a more secular age can readily understand.

This reply, it seems to me, does not resolve the issue. . . .[64]

What would resolve the issue, as was suggested above, would be empirical documentation of a prevalent economic 'traditionalism' among pre-Reformation capitalists and labourers, and a 'salvation panic' among ascetic Protestants such that they changed their attitudes towards economic conduct in the direction of Weber's ideal-typical 'modern capitalist'. This raises two general themes: first, the question of the relationship between Protestant ethic and spirit of capitalism; and, second, the problems associated with investigating this relationship empirically. These closely related issues form the substance of Chapter 5. Between them they raise almost all of the genuine difficulties in Weber's argument.

5 The heart of the matter

Ideas, interests, and action

How does Weber conceptualize the relationship between Protestant ethic and spirit of capitalism? Here we must investigate the precise manner in which Protestants came to adopt a new and, as it turned out, revolutionary attitude towards everyday activities. How did they come to conclude that they must practise a methodical, systematic, 'modern capitalistic' manner of life?

Generally speaking, Weber conceives of the motives that mobilized the new Protestant capitalists as 'internal states', indeed he consistently refers in his essays to the psychological 'impulses' or 'inducements' (*Antrieben*) evoked by the theological doctrines and necessity of proof. The 'economic ethic' of a theology, he tells us, 'points to the practical impulses for action which are founded in the psychological and pragmatic contexts of religions'.[1] The important point here is that the interest in rationalizing everyday conduct is seen to be a novel development arising out of Protestant doctrine. Weber's exchanges with Sombart, Keller, and others about the significance of the writings of the literati and moralists of the late Middle Ages illustrates this point clearly. In *The Quintessence of Capitalism*, for example, Sombart challenges Weber's argument that Protestantism was important for the development of the spirit of capitalism on the grounds that evidence can be found of the secular ethic which Weber calls 'the spirit of capitalism' long before the Reformation. He cites a number of North Italian, Spanish, and French authors of the fifteenth and sixteenth centuries, some of whom predate Franklin by almost 400 years, yet wholly anticipate his writings. One of these in particular, the Florentine author and architect Leon Battista Alberti (1404–72), wrote a number of books on household management in which are commended nearly all of the 'bourgeois' virtues that Weber identifies in the writings of Franklin, including those of thrift, balancing income against expenditure, careful planning and proper co-ordination of economic activities, and the profitable and constructive utilization of one's time. Much of Weber's reply straightforwardly challenges Sombart's interpretation of Alberti's work and is, therefore, essentially a dispute about the details and nuances of the texts themselves. Weber argues, for example, that Alberti's extensive recommendations concerning the 'rational' organization of the household and business are intended simply to ensure that expenditure is limited to income, and are thus 'a principle of maintenance, a given standard of life, and not of acquisition'. Similarly, his condemnation of laziness and dishonest practices and his commendation of business and trading ventures are aimed at sustaining the ideal of the 'country villa', and the 'honourable' life of a nobleman. They are nothing more than an 'insurance policy' against changes of fortune and the possible loss of social honour. In these and other respects the writings of Alberti (and his peers) and those of Franklin are wholly dissimilar.[2]

But this is not the main thrust of Weber's reply, for even if it were the case that Alberti and Franklin demonstrably shared a common ideal as regards economic activities, there remains one essential difference between the 'worldly wisdom' of Alberti's texts and the ethical qualities evident in those of Franklin:

Alberti's discussions . . . form an excellent example of the sort of economic rationalism which really existed as a reflection of economic conditions, in the work of authors interested purely in 'the thing for its own sake' everywhere and at all times; in the Chinese classicism and in Greece and Rome no less than in the Renaissance and the age of the Enlightenment. There is no doubt that just as in ancient times with Cato, Varro, and Columella, also here with Alberti and others of the same type, especially in the doctrine of *industria*, a sort of economic rationality is highly developed. But how can anyone believe that such a literary *theory* could develop into a revolutionary force at all comparable to the way in which a religious belief was able to set the sanctions of salvation and damnation on the fulfilment of a particular (in this case methodically rationalised) manner of life?[3]

In like vein, irrespective of the extent to which the Catholic moralists of the late Middle Ages may or may not have conceded the ethical acceptability of the productive investment of capital and of honest business endeavours generally, the fact remains that their tortuous casuistry represents, at best, only a difficult and not unambiguous compromise with regard to the taking of certain types of profit and the performance of a limited number of socially necessary economic transactions and activities. Even the most subtle of schoolmen, San Bernardino of Siena and Sant' Antonino of Florence (who were, as

Weber puts it, 'relatively friendly to capital'), attempted only to justify certain types of profit as legitimate reward to the merchant for his or her *industria*. In other words,

what is for us the most important thing is entirely lacking both here and in the case of Alberti . . . the characteristic Protestant conception of the proof of one's own salvation, the *certitudo salutis* in a calling, provided the psychological sanctions which this religious belief put behind the *industria*. But that Catholicism could not supply, because its means to salvation were different. In effect these authors are concerned with an ethical doctrine, not with motives to practical action, dependent on the desire for salvation. Furthermore, they are, as is very easy to see, concerned with concessions to practical necessity, not, as was worldly asceticism, with deductions from fundamental religious postulates. . . . And even these concessions have remained an object of controversy down to the present.[4]

The fact is that, no matter how conciliatory the rhetoric of the medieval moralists may have been as regards the investment of capital, only ascetic Protestantism could induce a change in the individual's economic conduct, because it alone levied a 'sanction' (in this case the necessity of proof) which systematically channelled the religious interest of the faithful in salvation in the direction of rationalizing their everyday conduct. In this way the religiously derived idea of proof directs the religious interest in salvation into a new material interest, namely, that of being methodical, diligent, and sober in the performance of everyday affairs. Material interests and economic conduct were thus transformed. Economic traditionalism gave way to the spirit of modern capitalism.

In summary, then, we can see that in this (fairly conventional) account of the motivational complex leading from Protestant ethic to spirit of capitalism, particular emphasis is placed upon the 'psychological sanction' arising out of, on the one hand, the neo-Calvinist interpretation of the doctrine of predestination and, on the other, the public scrutiny of everyday conduct practised within the Protestant sects. In both of these cases, as has been shown, the sanction can be reduced to the necessity of providing systematic proof of election. Weber's reasoning here, despite acknowledged problems deriving from the translation of his argument into English, is more or less unambiguous. An interest in methodical, ascetic, 'modern capitalistic' action was created by the ideas of ascetic Protestantism. In particular, the religious concept of proof so altered a person's view of the world and of the significance of certain types of behaviour within it, that everyday conduct itself took on an entirely new meaning and form.

Calvinist theology gave the faithful an interest in a systematic 'worldly asceticism' sufficient to undermine the prevailing traditionalism in economic activities. Weber offers a summary of this model of social action in a well-known passage in his essay on 'The social psychology of the world religions':

> Not ideas, but material and ideal interests, directly govern men's conduct. Yet very frequently the 'world images' that have been created by 'ideas' have, like switchmen, determined the tracks along which action has been pushed by the dynamic of interest. 'From what' and 'for what' one wished to be redeemed and, let us not forget, 'could be' redeemed, depended upon one's image of the world.[5]

The Protestant business classes now had an interest in 'capitalistic' activity which, in as much as it was shaped by the unique sanctions arising out of the doctrines of Calvinism, was an entirely new interest in methodical conduct and diligence in business activities.

Obviously our next step must be to investigate the activities of the pre- and post-Reformation business classes in order to determine whether or not Weber's hypothesis about the practical consequences of Protestant teaching can be corroborated by empirical data. Unfortunately, however, we shall discover, in our attempt to carry out such a programme, a number of features about Weber's argument itself which, while they do not render it empirically untestable in principle, certainly make empirical investigation extremely difficult in practice.

Capitalists and profits

What would count as evidence for or against Weber's argument about the practical consequences of ascetic Protestant theology? The neo-Calvinist and Protestant sectarian business communities ought, according to Weber's thesis, to display an unambiguously 'modern capitalistic' orientation towards economic activity. Presumably here we are looking for such traits as the systematic use of available time so that as long as possible is spent in the pursuit of an honest 'vocation' and as little as possible 'wasted' in useless recreation and pastimes. Since the domestic life of the faithful would be limited to the duties associated with the family and home-centred religious obligations (such as family prayer), and since a general asceticism would prevail in life-styles, limited consumption and a deliberately modest standard of living would help the incidental accumulation of capital which, by default, would be channelled back into the economy. In the productive sphere itself the individual would continuously be seeking to 'improve' his or her performance: rational expansion would be pursued; less profitable lines of economic activity would be abandoned in favour of more profitable ones; a continual balance of costs against returns would be kept so that policies could be adopted which increased productivity and utilized resources in the most efficient manner. Investments would result from careful costings and informed predictions as to the profitability of projected enterprises. Transactions offering relatively secure, steady, and calculable, if somewhat modest returns, would always be preferred to high-risk, unpredictable, though potentially lucrative investments which could result in a total loss as readily as a spectacular gain. The ascetic Protestant would be up early and about his or her craft or business, accepting few distractions from the tasks in hand, and, above all else, treat his or her performance in the productive sphere as a duty or obligation. The 'job', or means by which material needs were fulfilled, would be experienced as a 'vocation'.

Prior to the Reformation it ought not to be possible to detect such beliefs and practices among the business classes in any part of the globe. Rather, economic traditionalism would be the norm, both as ideal and practice. Individuals would seek either to reproduce only that material standard of living to which they had become accustomed (and might well 'rationally' organize their book-keeping, supervisory, and productive activities towards this end), this goal being reflected in an easygoing attitude towards the business, the frequent taking of holidays, the pursuit of traditional markets, profits, standards, and the like; or, conversely, being motivated by the desire to secure a fortune, they would invest in all forms of business activity including colonial adventures, moneylending, and tax-farming, and (in all probability) having earned a fortune would consume their profits in the spontaneous enjoyment of the 'good things' in life (delicate foods, the fine arts, sporting and recreational pastimes, and so forth). By comparison with ascetic Protestants, pre-Reformation capitalists would view their activities in a number of ways – as ethically neutral, as a means of becoming powerful, as socially necessary and therefore 'justifiable', or even as mere 'fun' – but none of these would be equivalent to the modern idea of diligence in one's economic tasks as an obligation or 'calling'. Just as 'the spirit of modern capitalism' ought not to characterize the beliefs and conduct of pre-Reformation capitalists, it would be possible, indeed it seems likely, that non-Protestant business communities after the Reformation would continue to subscribe to the norms of economic traditionalism, at least until such times as the increasingly 'capitalistic' nature of their economic environment and the economic threat posed by Protestant competitors forced them to fall in with the logic of capitalist developments.

The empirical implications of Weber's account are therefore clear. Where ascetic Protestantism flourished we should also find the rational, systematic pursuit of honest profits, by means of diligence in a 'vocation'. By comparison, both prior to the Reformation itself and for some generations afterwards in those areas which did not experience neo-Calvinism or Protestant sectarianism, economic tasks would be informed by the search for the 'traditional' rate of profit or, at the other extreme, by an insatiable appetite for wealth and enjoyment of it which finds outlets in all manner of economic ventures, irrespective of legality.

The case for the defence

On investigation the relevant historical materials reveal a good deal that, at least intuitively, seems entirely consistent with the contrast which Weber draws between pre-Reformation and Roman Catholic 'traditionalism' and the 'modern capitalist' mentality of ascetic Protestants. Supporters of Weber's argument can therefore point to a wealth of data to illustrate his interpretation of the history of the 'economic ethic' in the West. For example, it appears that both variants of 'traditionalism' can readily be located among pre-Reformation capitalists. Consider the following description of the activities of one famous sixteenth-century merchant:

Wealth's power to transform is evident in the history of the Fuggers. Before his marriage in 1498, Jakob the Rich spent little on his person; afterwards, his style of living became ostentatious. Many a princess might have envied his wife's finery and jewels. The receptions he gave in his spacious home (one of several houses he owned in Augsburg) to honor illustrious guests, were incomparable in their splendor. For him, such extravagance was almost always connected with some important business deal. He was not indifferent to considerations of prestige. His gifts to churches were motivated as much by the desire to display his munificence as by piety. When the older Fuggers had a chapel or altar erected or a stained-glass window designed, they were never close-fisted. They called on the finest workmen, always. But at the same time, they insisted on having their coat of arms emblazoned on every work. These benefactors did not seek anonymity; rather they felt that their gifts should enhance the glory of their family name, as well as promote the salvation of their souls. For the deserving poor of Augsburg, Jakob the Rich founded not a traditional almshouse, but a miniature city within a city . . . although the fortunate inmates were obliged to recite, each day, a *Pater*, an *Ave*, and a *Credo* for the souls of the founders and their family.

One cannot deny the religious sentiment that inspired these acts of charity. . . . But this religiosity had very little, if anything, to do with intellectual disquietude. . . . His life was geared for action; there was no place in it for art or culture. When someone suggested to Jakob that, in view of certain difficulties it might be best to wind up his commercial activities in Hungary, his reply was unequivocal: 'I want to make as much money as I can.' . . .[6]

The desire to make money is undeniable, but arises out of motives which are bound in with the search for honour, prestige, and a magnificent style of life. Moreover, this desire is tempered by guilt, evident in Fugger's ongoing attempt to safeguard his salvation from his profit-making activities through various atonement rituals associated with Roman Catholic beliefs.

Jakob the Rich was by no means atypical. The evidence for the pre-Reformation era, some of it brought forward by Weber's critics themselves, shows merchants both great and small pursuing profits by almost any means which come to hand. The larger international merchants were as ready to finance wars and political *coups d'état*, to misappropriate public funds, speculate in mines and precious metals, and to buy and bribe their way into political office in order to gain control of certain state finances, as they were willing to involve themselves in legitimate and honest trading transactions. Smaller national and local merchants may have lacked equivalent resources but were the equal of wealthier peers in their ability to mislead, short-measure, and generally defraud as many of their customers and competitors as possible on the way to earning their living. Summing up this picture, one reviewer concludes that

There is little doubt that at almost every level above that of the smallest, strictly mercantile activity was mixed with financial operations, whether speculation on the exchanges, tax-farming, loans to local or central government, or to local landowners or peasants. The merchants of the sixteenth century were important accumulators of liquid capital, to whom society naturally turned for credit. . . .

It is often difficult from the surviving evidence to estimate the relative importance in the construction of a fortune between trade and other activities, but it might be on balance likely that these ancilliary operations were in the long term more profitable. The least scrupulous were often the most notorious. The example of Lionel Cranfield reveals the worst side of the business world and its ambitions. A London cloth merchant in the German trade who burnt his fingers with unsaleably poor quality kersies, and mixed wet and dry pepper for sale even to King James I, he graduated via tax-farming, land deals and bribery to the Earldom of Middlesex, and a career as Lord Treasurer of England which saw an attempt to impose higher ethical standards and tight budgetary control on a court from whose corruption he had profited so much, but which finally engineered his downfall.[7]

Pre-Reformation capitalists may well have employed precise accounting procedures, modern financial institutions, double-entry book-keeping,[8] indeed all the devices of the large, sophisticated, capitalist organization, but theirs was a 'rampant individualism' which knew few scruples. In England, for example,

The borough courts were kept pretty busy with trade offences, for there were few ways of earning a dishonest penny that the medieval tradesman did not try. The prize for perverse ingenuity may perhaps be awarded to certain London bakers; when their customers brought dough in to be baked they would put it down on the counter before making it into loaves, and a small boy hidden under the counter would open a little trap-door and remove a quantity of dough before the customer's very eyes. Compared with such a trick the use of false weights and bad materials, passing off a gilded copper as gold and selling shoddy goods at night by the dim light of flickering tapers, were clumsy devices.[9]

The 'capitalist mentality' of the medieval business classes rested on the dictum: 'A profit is a profit, however it is acquired.' The end always justified the means.[10]

Moreover, having earned their profits, there is a similar consensus among commentators as to how such businessmen and women employed them. A substantial proportion was reinvested in further business transactions, of course, but profits were to be enjoyed as well as reinvested. Those who were fortunate enough, whether by chance or diligence, to acquire large profits were quick to indulge their penchant for ostentation:

The well-to-do were confident of their dignity but did not stand on ceremony: they displayed their wealth with pride – in their homes, their luxurious attire, their jewelry. Posthumous inventories of their possessions have provided us with detailed information concerning all these items, but more systematic studies will have to be made before we can determine the subtle gradations of opulence.[11]

Carus-Wilson records how the overseas trading merchants of Bristol in the fifteenth century spent vast sums of money on erecting splendid houses, equipping them luxuriously, and on wining, dining, and dressing like monarchs.[12] The splendour of the North Italian merchant princes is, of course, legendary, but even their less wealthy peers displayed an appetite for the material comforts of life. We know that the palatial, sumptuously decorated dwellings, and lavish entertainments of families such as the Medici and Strozzi were emulated by lesser merchants such as Francesco Datini (*c.* 1335–1410), merchant of Prato, and many like him throughout Europe. Profits not only bought jewellery, silks and furs, fine wines, servants, and land: they also brought leisure. The businessman or woman need no longer devote all their energies to the making of money. There was time enough now to enjoy life, to entertain, plan grand new houses and gardens, to relax and appreciate the arts.[13]

Of course, not every member of the pre-Reformation business community was as personally ambitious as the great financiers like Jacques Coeur or Pierre Rémy. The majority of merchants, traders, and small craft manufacturers were content to make only a comfortable profit and, similarly, to enjoy the benefits of a comfortable standard of living. In other words, just as Weber's picture of the avarice and decadence of one type of traditionalism has been corroborated by later commentators and can be illustrated by examples throughout medieval Europe, so his description of the 'traditionalism' exemplified in the conduct of the nineteenth-century German putter-out, whom we discussed in Chapter 3, has also found widespread support. Numerous commentators, as far apart in time and perspective as Adam Ferguson and Fernand Braudel, have depicted the orientation towards economic activities among the majority of pre-Reformation capitalists in almost identical terms to those employed by Weber. Ferguson's social theory may not have been particularly well documented, but even with the benefit of subsequent empirical research behind them, many would agree with his conclusion (if not his moral sentiments) about the economic beliefs and practices of pre-modern capitalist peoples:

It might be apprehended, that among rude nations, where the means of subsistence are procured with so much difficulty, the mind could never raise itself above the consideration of this subject; and that man would, in this condition, give examples of the meanest and most mercenary spirit. The reverse, however, is true. Directed in this particular by the desires of nature, men, in their simplest state, attend to the objects of appetite no further than the meal which gratifies their hunger: they apprehend no superiority of rank in the possession of wealth, such as might inspire any habitual principle of covetousness, vanity, or ambition: they can apply to no task that engages no immediate passion, and take pleasure in no occupation that affords no dangers to be braved and honours to be won.

It was not among the ancient Romans alone that commercial arts, or a sordid mind, were held in contempt. A like spirit prevails in every rude and independent society. . . .[14]

In modern phraseology, 'an attitude of resignation, involving under-consumption of goods and services combined with overconsumption of leisure . . . seems to have been the "natural" attitude of man in most societies over long stretches of history'.[15]

The leisurely tempo of a business community imbued with such a 'traditionalistic' attitude towards work and profits is not to be taken as an argument that people were uninterested in acquiring wealth. Chance opportunities for personal gain were quick to be exploited, but the systematic creation of wealth through ceaseless efforts in the marketplace was seen to be the prerogative only of ambitious and greedy persons who were personally inclined to such pursuits, and was certainly not considered to be an obligation incumbent upon the individual. Again it is Ferguson who best summarizes this view of economic activity:

Mankind, in the very early ages of society, learn to covet riches, and to admire distinction: they have avarice and ambition, and are occasionally led by them to depredation and conquest: but in their ordinary conduct, these motives are balanced or restrained by other habits and other pursuits; by sloth, or intemperance; by personal attachments, or personal animosities; which mislead from attention to interest.[16]

Where financiers, traders, and craftworkers did devote themselves wholeheartedly to the acquisition of wealth, whether by speculation, banking, or financing political authorities, they soon encountered a profoundly suspicious Church. The telling point in Weber's favour here is that even those pre-Reformation capitalists and manufacturers who generated honest profits by means of entirely legitimate trans-actions which were adjudged to be 'socially necessary', and therefore not immoral, or by sheer hard work, were unable to escape the social stigma and personal guilt attached to the concept of the business or trading profit itself. Here again, we see Weber's interpretation of the pre-Reformation situation amply illustrated by such phenomena as the widespread renunciation of accumulated fortunes by merchants nearing old age. The aforementioned merchant of Prato, Francesco Datini, was so troubled by the obvious sin of avarice which (in his view and that of his peers) he must have been possessed of to have acquired his huge business fortune, that he dreamed of his damnation. Eventually, in fear for his salvation, he bequeathed his entire fortune to religious charities. We have previously observed the attempts of Jakob Fugger to insure his soul against a similar fate. These men are not atypical. Ritual gestures of remorse and penance were widely employed by pre-Reformation merchants and manufacturers as restitution for a lifetime spent in the pursuit of profits. In a great many cases an attempt was made to escape from the suspect world of business into that of the landed gentry or court aristocracy. The pre-Reformation capitalist sought respectability on the land or in the service of the state. Certain business profits may have been legitimate in the sense that they were a 'fair return' to the capitalist for his or her risks, and for performing a socially necessary service, but this merely neutralized such profits, it did not make the pursuit of them ethically commendable.[17]

Compare this with the attitudes and practices of the ascetic Protestant business communities of the North Atlantic in the centuries after the Reformation. There were no self-doubts about the morality of business and profits here. Providing the latter were accrued by means either of honest business practices or hard work they were not only legitimate but were the very pinnacle of morality itself since they testified to the bourgeois virtues of thrift, diligence, hard work, dedication, and persistence. Profits were the result, not of personal greed, but of application in a profession or vocation. The life-styles and business successes of the English Nonconformists have long been cited as offering striking confirmation of Weber's argument about the economic outlook and everyday conduct of ascetic Protestants and it seems unnecessary at this late stage in the debate to do little more than record this in passing.[18] The contrast between the world-view of the 'modern' capitalist and that of his or her 'medieval' or 'traditionalistic' counterpart is posed clearly in Hill's observation that

Successful mediaeval business men died with feelings of guilt and left money to the Church to be put to unproductive uses. Successful protestant business men were no longer ashamed of their productive activities whilst alive, and at death left money to help others to imitate them. . . .[19]

And, of course, the Protestant and profit-seeking Elizabethan, Stuart, and early Georgian financiers, speculators, and businessmen of the interregnum, unscrupulous heroes of sixteenth- and seventeenth-century *Frühkapitalismus* such as Lionel Cranfield and Sir John Banks, can readily be dismissed by Weber's followers on the grounds that, although they may have been Protestants, these men were only nominally so and were certainly not ascetic Protestants in the Weberian mould; so their unambiguous traditionalism (selling goods which they knew to be faulty, employing bribery and blackmail, using public office to further personal interests, and a generally spectacular and lavish life-style) provides no refutation of Weber's thesis.[20]

Having brought forward empirical materials of the kind, and in the manner outlined above, are not Weber's supporters justified therefore in resting their case? The answer, at least in this author's opinion, is that they are not. Patterns of economic activity in pre- and post-Reformation Europe may appear, at first glance, to substantiate Weber's thesis. On further examination, however, it becomes clear that the interpretation of this evidence is rendered problematic by a number of factors which Weber and his followers have persistently ignored. There are, broadly speaking, three closely related areas of difficulty that emerge from Weber's construction of the Protestant ethic–spirit of capitalism relationship and which make his thesis empirically problematic. These concern his ideas about value-relevant concept formation in the social sciences and the associated definitional problems involved in identifying the twin elements of 'enterprise' or 'adventurism' and 'bourgeois rationality' in economic activities; the problems of determining the meaning of economic behaviour for social actors; and, finally, the possibility that Weber's principal variables are defined in terms of each other and that his argument is therefore tautological. I shall examine each of these in turn.

The prosecution: 'adventurism' and 'rationality'

First, then, the definitional issues. Weber, as we have observed, employs a 'value-relevant' conceptualization of 'the spirit of modern capitalism'. His account of this phenomenon is an 'ideal-type', an explicitly one-sided depiction of an attitude towards economic activities, accentuated and ruthlessly systematized in the direction of one underlying variable, namely, that of accumulating capital as a duty and end in itself. It is this particular value that Weber hypothesizes to be a novel element in the capitalist's world-view from the Reformation onwards. Hitherto, businessmen and women had conducted economic transactions in accordance with objectives such as the pursuit of social honour or political office, providing for themselves and their kin in the time-honoured manner of their ancestors, or – simply – for the love of money and all that it might buy. Weber accepts that motives such as these have prompted economic activity at all times and in all societies with developed money economies. His argument is merely that, because of the influence of ascetic Protestantism, an additional and uniquely 'modern' motivation was added to this picture during the late sixteenth and the seventeenth centuries in societies in which such a religious development occurred. For the first time ever, a section of the population began to practise a mode of conduct and style of life which (Weber alleges) reflected an interest in the dutiful and satisfactory performance of worldly tasks simply for the psychological satisfaction of seeing them well done.

At this point, we begin to get an inkling of just how tightly circumscribed Weber's argument really is. 'We have no intention whatever', he writes,

of maintaining such a foolish and doctrinaire thesis as that the spirit of capitalism (in the provisional sense of the term explained above) could only have arisen as the result of certain effects of the Reformation, or even that capitalism as an economic system is a creation of the Reformation. In itself, the fact that certain important forms of capitalistic business organisation are known to be considerably older than the Reformation is a sufficient refutation of such a claim. On the contrary, we only wish to ascertain whether and to what extent religious forces have taken part in the qualitative formation and the quantitative expansion of that spirit over the world. Furthermore, what concrete aspects of our capitalistic culture can be traced to them. In view of the tremendous confusion of interdependent influences between the material basis, the forms of social and political organisation, and the ideas current in the time of the Reformation, we can only proceed by investigating whether and at what points certain correlations between forms of religious belief and practical ethics can be worked out. At the same time we shall as far as possible clarify the manner and the general *direction* in which, by virtue of those relationships, the religious movements have influenced the development of material culture. Only when this has been determined with reasonable accuracy can the attempt be made to estimate to what extent the historical development of modern culture can be attributed to those religious forces and to what extent to others.[21]

Weber is interested solely in the orientation towards economic activity that is represented by Franklin's ethical maxims. He concedes freely that diverse 'capitalistic' (but not 'modern capitalistic') world-views existed before, after, and alongside that which viewed diligence in one's economic activities as an obligation. Business transactions motivated by straightforward avarice are no less infrequent in the era of bourgeois capitalism than prior to it. Indeed, according to Weber, the two great obstacles against which the ethos of modern capitalism to this day has had to struggle have been the strict traditionalism of persons desiring only to earn as much as is necessary for living in the manner to which they have been accustomed, and 'the reign of absolute unscrupulousness in the pursuit of selfish interests by the making of money'.[22]

Translating this into the terms of reference of empirical investigation, the clear implication is that any attempt to test the validity of Weber's argument will be concerned only with identifying and documenting the history of the particular value of diligence in economic activity as a duty. Does this motive exist before the Reformation or only after it? For Weber, the presence of alternative 'traditionalistic' attitudes towards capital and work after the Reformation does not constitute evidence against his thesis since such attitudes persist up to the present and, at least during the formative period of early modern capitalism, were the prerogative of an entirely different stratum of the population to that from which the modern bourgeoisie emerged. The different economic world-views, he maintains, can unambiguously be distinguished as the separate properties of distinctive social groupings and strata. In seventeenth-century England, for example,

Calvinism opposed organic social organization in the fiscal-monopolistic form which it assumed in Anglicanism under the Stuarts, especially in the conceptions of Laud, this alliance of Church and State with the monopolists on the basis of a Christian-social ethical foundation. Its leaders were universally among the most passionate opponents of this type of politically privileged commercial, putting-out, and colonial capitalism. Over against it they placed the individualistic motives of rational legal acquisition by virtue of one's own ability and initiative. And, while the politically privileged monopoly industries in England all disappeared in short order, this attitude played a large and decisive part in the development of the industries which grew up in spite of and against the authority of the State. The Puritans . . . repudiated all connection with the large-scale capitalistic courtiers and projectors as an ethically suspicious class. On the other hand, they took pride in their own superior middle-class business morality, which formed the true reason for the persecutions to which they were subjected on the part of those circles. Defoe proposed to win the battle against dissent by boycotting bank credit and withdrawing deposits. The difference of the two types of capitalistic attitude went to a very large extent hand in hand with religious differences. The opponents of the Nonconformists, even in the eighteenth century, again and again ridiculed them for personifying the spirit of shopkeepers, and for having ruined the ideals of old England. Here also lay the difference of the Puritan economic ethic from the Jewish; and contemporaries . . . knew well that the former and not the latter was the bourgeois capitalistic ethic.[23]

A similar identification of religious affiliations with economic practices is said by Weber to have existed in North America and Holland. Everywhere the contrast is between the small, bourgeois and petty bourgeois Puritan business classes, concerned with the rational capitalistic organization of private property and free labour and motivated by the desire to perform the duties of a vocation, and the great merchant aristocracy and financial adventurers, the classes of magnates, monopolists, Government contractors, financiers of the state, colonial entrepreneurs, moneylenders, landed estate seekers, and promoters of various speculative monetary schemes, none of whom are characteristically supposed to have been ascetic Protestants of the type with which Weber's thesis is concerned.[24]

It is at this point that Weber's argument begins to run into serious difficulties which, arguably, remain to this day unresolved and indeed largely ignored by contributors to the debate about the spirit of capitalism. It is certainly the case, as Weber suggests, that larger European merchants throughout not only the Middle Ages, but also the sixteenth and seventeenth centuries (the formative era of modern capitalism) and well into the period of the industrial revolutions, held portfolios which involved them in a 'traditionalistic' pattern of economic activities. Merchant aristocrats of diverse Protestant and Catholic affiliations seem at all times and in all places to have been involved in a simultaneity of careers including those of private merchants and public financiers, officers of central or local government, landed gentry, rentiers and landlords, occasionally even diplomats and military personnel. Their business activities encompassed the conquest, robbery, and enslavement of comparatively defenceless non-European peoples; private and joint-stock voyages of exploration in search both of an El Dorado and of more modest trading opportunities; financing the state and exploiting state finances; war profiteering and peacetime merchandising; moneylending, speculation in exchange, insurance, and precious metals; and buying up real estate and land.[25]

These men and women appear to display few, if any, of the

characteristic traits of the ascetic Protestant-capitalist: no regard for the systematic use of time here; no careful balance of costs and profits. This class embraces a traditionalistic spirit of adventure, daring, enterprise, and unscrupulous opportunism, rather than one of diligence, honesty, sobriety, thrift, and rational calculation.

Or does it? Merchant adventuring, as the term itself implies, involved risks. Merchants trading abroad hazarded their goods and sometimes their lives to a long sea voyage or overland journey. Often the business transactions themselves took place at a distance and involved external parties and markets of which the merchant had limited knowledge and little control. The whole process left a great deal to chance. Therefore, so long as alternative outlets for capital could be found it made sound economic sense for merchants to utilize these also, rather than commit their total reinvestments to further trading ventures. Weber, like many subsequent commentators, appears to be guilty of viewing the term 'adventurer' as a reference to a psychological trait rather than the way in which merchants necessarily confronted the market. Given the economic and political instability of the Middle Ages it was perfectly 'rational' for the business classes of Western Europe to diversify investments into a number of economic sectors. Why gamble everything on a highly speculative and risky overseas venture when capital could more safely be put into land or property, advanced to the state, converted into household effects and plate, or loaned to private individuals and companies? Where and how the medieval merchant classes invested their money can as readily be seen to be a function of the relevant markets as of any prior commitment arising out of an attitude towards specific types of economic transactions.[26] Thus, to take a specific example, land in the Netherlands in the seventeenth century was scarce, expensive, and highly taxed, so a relatively high proportion of money found its way back into the merchant trading company. In England, by contrast, the greater availability of land resulted in capital being continually withdrawn from more speculative trading and industrial enterprises to the less risky opportunity of a landed estate.

It is possible, in this light, to read what Weber would call conspicuous ('traditionalistic') consumption – the accumulation of jewels, buildings, household goods, and land – simply as conspicuous investment.[27] Commercial capital being altogether too vulnerable, the medieval businessman and woman could better secure the fortune of future generations of the family by acquiring permanent and self-regulating assets – land, urban property, governmental holdings, and personal effects. Far from being imbued with a spirit of reckless 'adventure' these activities can be interpreted as a testimony to sober economic 'rationality'. Moreover, in so far as it was possible, merchants 'adventuring' their stock attempted to control the outcome of business, to make it calculable and predictable, by adopting such safeguarding and protecting devices as were available at the time: insurance, sharing risks through the use of *commenda* associations, diversifying cargoes, and the like. Was the management of such enterprises any less rational, calculating, or sober than that of the Puritan-controlled shop or small manufactory? It can be argued that what emerges from the comparison of the activities of medieval and modern capitalists is not a demonstrable contrast in the underlying 'spirit' of enterprise so much as a contrast in the outlets for enterprise. The spirit remains the same: it is the fields of capitalist endeavour which have expanded.[28]

The prosecution: the meaning of profits

In equating the activities of the merchant aristocracy with economic traditionalism Weber and his followers are guilty of imputing motives to conduct in a naive and rather simplistic way. Weber, as was observed in Chapter 3, is somewhat inconsistent in this matter. On the one hand he warns us against deducing motives from conduct (or vice versa) by noting the independence in principle of 'economic ethos' from 'economic form'. Identical forms of putting-out enterprise, for example, can be imbued with entirely different economic spirits. However, as was also observed, Weber tends in practice to deduce 'ethos' from 'form' on an entirely *a priori* basis. Despite his lack of independent evidence concerning the *meaning* of economic activity to the individuals concerned (that is, direct evidence as to economic beliefs or motives), he is nevertheless prepared to equate specific forms of economic activity and commercial enterprise with certain world-views, on the assumption that 'ethos' and 'form' will develop an 'elective affinity' or adequacy for each other. Thus tax-farming, moneylending, merchant adventuring, colonial expansion, and the financing of State agencies unambiguously signal an ethos of tradition-alism, while centralised manufacturing industry is always associated with the spirit of modern capitalism.[29]

Weber's argument here is wholly lacking in any empirical foundation. His attempt to impute specific motives to certain types of economic conduct on the basis of observed behaviour alone ignores the objective and empirically variable conditions of action which provide the setting for all types of social interaction. If, as is rightly claimed, 'the capitalist spirit is a point of view, a state of mind, and is not associated with any particular stage of industrial technique',[30] then what can we conclude about the 'ethos' that informs an economic transaction from an observation of conduct alone, especially when that conduct is clearly influenced by a number of factors of which the world-view of the economic actor is only one? Eileen Power, for example, has pointed to the importance of the local market as a factor which may restrict the business opportunities of the petty bourgeoisie and so shape their conduct. It is worth quoting her account at some length since the contrasting market situations of the 'local' and 'international' capitalists whom she describes provide the setting for what is effectively Weber's two types of economic traditionalism. In considering the medieval class system, and in particular what is loosely known as the 'bourgeoisie', she observes that

It is quite clear that the middle class which is typical of the period is a *petit bourgeoisie* serving an inelastic town market and grouped into the professional associations proper to such a market. The typical and average craft gild of the middle ages is inegalitarian in its policy and democratic in its government, just because it is working for a local urban market, in which demand and supply are alike known and inelastic. In such a town there is no room or need for individual businesses to expand, and it must never be forgotten that the majority of the towns of the middle ages were of this type. The whole egalitarian social policy of urban governments and town crafts and the whole body of canonist doctrine on such subjects as usury, the just price, and the fair wage rest upon the fact that the typical *milieu* of the urban middle class is one in which individuals cannot extend their share of that market beyond a certain limit without impinging on the standard of life of other individuals.

. . . The typical picture of the medieval bourgeoisie as one in which an inelastic market holds the acquisitive instinct in check, damps down speculation, and limits the scale of production, is broken in certain localities and by certain forms of production. There emerge at certain points of time individuals who are very different from the little local tradesmen. . . . This *haute bourgeoisie* . . . emerges, in the first place, among men engaged in the great export trades whether as exporters or as industrialists. Here the market is neither circumscribed nor inelastic, and therefore no check is placed by authority upon the enterprising individual. . . .

The other element out of which the *haute bourgeoisie* was formed was the financiers. If great bourgeois fortunes were made in trade the greatest merchant fortunes were made in finance, and above all in state finance. Where trade was so important as to play a role in royal finance and the traders were so rich as to be able to assist the crown, a still larger role in royal finance and a further increase in merchant riches were achieved by involving the merchant in the raising of revenues and loans, and by directing into his possession or into his control that part of the national wealth which the state succeeded in converting to its purposes.[31]

Thrupp, in almost identical terms, observes the same distinction between the conservative character of locally oriented businesses and the 'individualism' or 'familism' of trade at the non-local level, but explains this dichotomy as a function of 'distance' or freedom from local agencies of social control. Where business transactions took place on the non-local plane they escaped the influence of the Church, public opinion, and especially of the guilds, all of whom held a 'zero-sum' conception of available opportunities and were able, at the local level, to operate sanctions 'to the public good' (that is, to prevent any individual from benefiting at the expense of any others).[32] Given the widely different economic and political circumstances surrounding the activities of the seventeenth-century international merchants and financiers on the one hand, and 'yeoman, artisans and small and middling merchants' on the other, the fact that the former did not share the same economic outlook as the latter should not, as Kitch observes drily, cause undue surprise.[33] Here again the implication is that any particular structure and pattern of economic conduct is – at least in part – a function of a number of objective circumstances and is therefore no mere application of a consistent set of abstract principles which the capitalist brings to the transaction at the outset.

Without accepting the implicit determinism of some of these accounts, it is nevertheless hard to deny the general point that economic conduct is the negotiated outcome of social action which is subject to political, economic, and social, as well as ideological influences and constraints. Thus, for example, the attempts of certain glassmasters in Germany during the second half of the sixteenth century to increase productivity by taking advantage of a number of significant technical advances were frustrated by a shortage of available credit and want of a local skilled and free labour-force, both of these being restricted by a resident feudal aristocracy who succeeded in prolonging traditional handicraft production, in their own interests, for a further century.[34] The simple fact is that the issue of the basis on which capitalists make economic judgements – to save or not to save, where and how much to reinvest, and such like – is an empirical question. It cannot be said *a priori* that certain conservative patterns of conduct are the result either of a traditionalist mentality or are a simple function of the local market; or, similarly, that conduct indicative of the modern capitalist world-view is the straightforward result of the application of that world-view or of a change in the local market situation. There are good grounds for maintaining that the elements of 'enterprise' and 'rationality' which Weber wishes to distinguish as separate, prior, and absolute orientations towards economic activity are, in fact, situationally relative. As we have observed, it is as 'rational' for the merchant of the Middle Ages to diversify his or her portfolio and even to 'consume' (or 'invest' in?) luxuries, as it is for the 'modern' manufacturer regularly to reinvest in the productive enterprise. Consequently, it is difficult to corroborate empirically Weber's picture of the precise fit between the religious orientation of groups of capitalists and the form of economic conduct (monopolistic, 'speculative', or whatever) in which they participated. Would that it were empirically so neat and tidy! Seventeenth-century businessmen and women seem, however, to have been less troubled about the internal consistency of their lives than Weber proposes that they ought to have been. A discomfortingly large number both of ascetic Protestants and others seem to have been content to involve themselves simultaneously in 'modern rational' petty bourgeois and bourgeois retailing and manufacturing enterprises, and in more 'traditionalistic' pursuits such as tax-farming, war-profiteering, colonial expeditions, and speculation in land, precious metals, and currency.[35] However, by itself, this information tells us little or nothing about the (possibly differing) motivations of the various participants in question.

The truth of the matter is that Weber's account of the history of the meaning of economic practices is carried largely by assertion and his failure to provide empirical substantiation of his argument is disguised only by his continual prevarications as to the ontological status of 'the spirit of modern capitalism'. At times this is an attitude towards economic conduct and at other times it is a pattern of conduct itself. Thus he argues that the really distinguishing feature of the spirit of modern capitalism is the idea of economic activity being performed as a 'calling'; but also that a whole range of economic practices and types of transaction (tax-farming, colonial expeditions, and the like) are testimony to the absence of this attitude whereas, conversely, small petty bourgeois enterprises (retailing? small manufacturing shops?) are indicative of it. Why must this be so? True, there are certain organizational imperatives inherent in the working of a centralized manufacturing establishment which 'call forth', as it were, aspects of the modern capitalist mentality. The division of labour, horizontal and vertical integration of complex technical processes such as those involved in, for example, the manufacture of cloth, may require the capitalist to plan ahead, develop strict accounting and book-keeping procedures, and calculate costs, expenses, and profits in a systematic way. In order to control productivity he or she will want the labour-force to work predictable and hence calculable hours and to produce in a regular and equally calculable manner. It would probably be difficult then, in the long term, to run an integrated manufacturing enterprise with no regard for balancing the books, no thought given to planning and organizing supplies of raw materials and labour, and without channelling a significant proportion of one's profits back into the enterprise. Even the putting-out type of manufacturing concern itself demands that the merchant at the centre adopt fairly sophisticated accounting, book-keeping, and supervisory techniques in an attempt to prevent wastage and theft and to maintain some control over productivity and the turn-over of the labour-force.[36] Similarly, it is hard to describe merchant adventuring, colonial expeditions, and mining for precious metals in terms other than those of speculation, enterprise, daring, and adventure, so lending weight to Weber's idea that 'merchant adventurers' exemplified only the 'dare-devil' mentality of the traditionalistic capitalist. 'A venture was [after all] a risk. To venture was to take a chance, to hazard one's life or one's goods in an enterprise that might bring a worthwhile reward.'[37]

However, whatever the 'elective affinities' between 'form' and 'ethos' at the rhetorical level, there is nothing in the organizational basis of any form of economic transaction which automatically calls forth a specific meaning for the profits that are accrued and so permits us to conclude that the practitioners are or are not interpreting their conduct as the diligent application of a calling. The meaning of economic activities is rarely – if ever – self-evident from the pattern of economic conduct itself. When capitalists make a profit do they do so as a means to a lawful end or as an end in itself? Do they trade *at* a profit or *for* a profit? The Catholic schoolmen whom Weber criticizes for their casuistry seem to have been more sophisticated in addressing these questions than Weber himself, since they explicitly allowed for the possibility that the same external patterns of economic conduct could be prompted by entirely different motives, and it was, for them, the intentions of the trader – not the simple technique of the trading itself (providing, of course, that it was honestly done) – that determined whether or not it was morally acceptable.[38] Weber and his supporters, by contrast, continually and mechanically impute motives to economic conduct from an observation of behaviour itself.[39] The dangers of this procedure have been pointed to above and by critics such as MacIntyre. Businessmen and businesswomen may 'over-consume' leisure because they lack, or think they lack, alternative 'investment opportunities'.[40] Weber makes no allowance for this. Such conduct would, for him, be the unambiguous and inevitable consequence of economic 'traditionalism' and the prevalence of a 'natural attitude' towards profit – a conclusion which is mere speculation given the empirical data upon which it is based.

The absence of a simple one-to-one correspondence between economic 'ethos' or motives and economic conduct, of the type which Weber implies, can be observed in the widely varying motives of the entrepreneurial Elizabethan 'gentry' of the century before the English civil war. Notwithstanding the many methodological, conceptual, and theoretical difficulties, and polemical obfuscations that have dogged that particular debate, it has become apparent that substantially the same types of entrepreneurial conduct were being pursued by individual peers and groups of peers for wholly different reasons. Some were genuinely interested in profit 'for profit's sake'; many sought only to preserve a style of life based on conspicuous consumption from the encroachments of rising prices and of a *nouveaux riches* based upon non-agricultural sources of wealth; some seem merely to have been seeking relief from boredom. For example, it has been argued, by way of illustrating the last-mentioned of these categories, that one of the main reasons why the Earl of Shrewsbury became a leading industrialist was that he was exiled on his estates through being charged with responsibility for the imprisonment of Mary, Queen of Scots.[41]

If specific motives cannot be equated with given forms of economic conduct or types of business where does this leave Weber's argument? This brings us to the third and final criticism that we shall make of Weber's attempt to relate the Protestant ethic to the spirit of capitalism. In the last resort, as has been suggested, the really distinguishing feature of the modern capitalist mentality, according to Weber, is the idea of diligence in economic pursuits as a vocation, calling, or duty. It is this motive alone which distinguishes the 'spirit of modern capitalism' from all other orientations towards economic activity. But how are we to identify this motive from evidence pertaining only to organizational techniques and economic conduct, given the widely documented proof that there were no significant commercial institutions, business devices, or patterns of economic activity known and in use in ascetic Protestant lands during the seventeenth century which had not been equally common centuries earlier among the business communities in Lyons, Augsburg, the North Italian States, and other great capitalistic centres of the Middle Ages?[42] At the end of the day, all other empirical data being shown to be inappropriate and of dubious validity, Weber's argument rests on a methodological device which comes dangerously close to making his argument tautologous. The only real evidence which he offers for the change in the economic orientation of the ascetic Protestant business classes is taken, not from capitalists' declarations as to their motives, but from Puritan religious texts. This raises the damaging possibility that he may have defined the Protestant ethic and the spirit of modern capitalism in terms of each other and that his argument is therefore unfalsifiable.

The prosecution: the thesis as a tautology?

The argument that the crucial, unique, and distinguishing feature of 'the spirit of modern capitalism', namely, a motivation to pursue economic activity as a 'calling', is actually a trait which Weber defines into the capitalist mentality having first identified it in the alleged consequences of Protestant doctrine, is one which critics have levelled against his thesis almost from the outset. It certainly underlies Brentano's objection that Weber's explanandum is so constructed as to include in its assumptions a link with ascetic Protestantism which the argument itself is supposed to be demonstrating (a criticism which Weber claims to find 'incomprehensible').[43] Similarly, and more recently, it has been argued that Weber *a priori* builds the same terms – in particular the notion of the 'calling' – into his two major variables (Protestant ethic and spirit of capitalism) so that these inevitably appear to be interlocking and mutually reinforcing. The argument here is that Weber provides no independent evidence as to capitalists' substantive orientations towards economic activities and, further, that their alleged motivation is so defined in (and restricted by) Weber's value-relevant and ideal-typical presentation of the modern capitalist mentality that it can only be located in the religious sphere and, in particular, cannot be found in the absence of ascetic Protestant teachings. His argument is therefore tautologous and, as it stands, unfalsifiable.[44]

This is generally held to be one of the most damaging criticisms of

Weber's thesis. It is certainly symptomatic of a fundamental weakness in his presentation which has been considered (see pages 113–19), namely, Weber's failure to offer any empirical evidence whatsoever as to the motivations of particular capitalists or groups of capitalists. All of his data, as has been observed, are taken from Protestant texts. He is really *alleging* certain motivational (and behavioural) consequences to follow from an adherence to these. It does not follow from this, however, that Weber's argument is necessarily tautological. In practice, certainly, Weber reads into Franklin's texts tendencies which may or may not be there, but which certainly draw his maxims close to those of ascetic Protestantism. For example, whereas the recommendations of Alberti and other pre-Reformation proponents of business astuteness are mere 'worldly wisdom', Franklin is supposedly teaching an 'ethic', indeed a 'calling':

the ethical quality of the sermon to young business men is impossible to mistake, and that is the characteristic thing. A lack of care in the handling of money means to him that one so to speak murders capital embryos, and hence it is an ethical defect. . . .

The earning of money within the modern economic order is, so long as it is done legally, the result and the expression of virtue and proficiency in a calling; and this virtue and proficiency are, as it is now not difficult to see, the real Alpha and Omega of Franklin's ethic. . . .[45]

Really? Weber nowhere actually cites Franklin (or, more importantly, any Protestant businessmen and businesswomen) to the effect that certain economic practices were important to them since diligence in business was a duty, vocation, or *calling* – far less one that had its origins in religious precepts. And Weber does tend, in practice, to slip to and fro between the capitalist mentality and Puritan doctrine, using concepts like that of the 'calling', as if he had already demonstrated the importance of this concept as an aspect of the motivational make-up of modern capitalists, rather than (as is in fact the case) simply having hypothesized this. Passages such as the following are all too common in his essays:

It must . . . be noted that the accumulation of wealth springs from two quite distinct psychological sources. One reaches into the dimmest antiquity and is expressed in foundations, family fortunes, and trusts, as well as much more purely and clearly in the desire to die weighted down with a great burden of material goods. . . . That is not the case with that bourgeois motive with which we are here dealing. There the motto of asceticism is 'Entsagen sollst du, sollst entsagen' in the positive capitalistic sense of 'Erwerben sollst du, sollst erwerben'. In its pure and simple non-rationality it is a sort of categorical imperative. Only the glory of God and one's own duty, not human vanity, is the motive for the Puritans; and to-day only the duty to one's calling.[46]

Moreover, Weber's use even of the theological material itself is suspect, in that this is often cited as if it constituted evidence of the world-views of pre- and post-Reformation business communities. Contrary to his own precept, which we observed in Chapter 4, that it is inadmissible to present the formal teachings of the Reformed Churches on the subjects of wealth, avarice, or any other matter as evidence of the possible economic attitudes of Calvinist businessmen and business-women since this procedure fails to observe the vital distinction between ethical teaching *per se* and that form of conduct on which psychological premiums are placed (that is, it confuses the logical consequences of Church doctrines and their psychological conse-quences); nevertheless, where Weber's argument requires him to offer evidence as to the world-views of pre-Reformation capitalists he himself employs precisely such a procedure. Ignoring his own methodological prescription, he offers the formal canonical doctrines of the medieval Catholic Church as evidence of the genuine motivation of medieval businessmen and businesswomen, thus making the assumption that the practical consequences of these doctrines for everyday conduct were self-evident and universally adhered to. Medieval capitalists simply practised what was preached in the official ethical compendia of the Church at the time.

On the one hand, then, the 'gap' between formal ethical doctrine and practical economic conduct in the Reformation era is all-important: the content of the former can tell us little (in fact, according to Weber, can be positively misleading) as to practice in the latter. On the other hand, however, Weber fails entirely to consider the possible gap between canonist teaching and the mentality and practices of medieval capitalists. He is thus able to deduce the latter from the former – a device for the production of evidence which he explicitly withholds from those who challenge his description of modern capitalist practices and motives. Weber is clearly operating here with a methodological double standard whereby 'the spirit of modern capitalism' cannot be a simple logical deduction from Calvinist theology but, in documenting the ethos of economic 'traditionalism', we can point straight to canonical teaching since it can be assumed that the relationship between formal theology and everyday practice was non-problematic.[47]

Whatever the weaknesses of Weber's practice, however, it is not the case that his argument is in principle circular and unfalsifiable. The problem is not that Weber defines his variables in terms of each other but that he displays a marked tendency to offer as evidence of one (the spirit of capitalism) data which, in fact, pertain to the other (the Protestant ethic). He repeatedly cites religious texts as if these constituted evidence as to the authentic motives of practising capitalists.

By ways of remedying this weakness it is relatively easy to imagine the kind of independent evidence as to the meaning of economic activities by which the validity of Weber's argument might be ascertained. If ascetic Protestant businessmen and businesswomen could, in fact, be shown to have justified their activities in terms of performing the duties of a calling then there would be reasonable grounds for maintaining the correctness of his thesis. If pre-Reformation capitalists employed similar motives, however, his case would seem to be suspect. This would also appear to be the conclusion to be drawn from data which demonstrated that ascetic Protestants conducted their business activities according to principles which were wholly unrelated to the idea of diligently pursuing a vocation. In principle, then, there is no reason why we cannot look for evidence of the economic motives of pre- and post-Reformation capitalists independent of the sphere of religious doctrine and of that which is suggested by religious texts themselves. Whether or not, in practical terms, the data exist to yield such information for the periods in question is, of course, another matter.[48]

One other tradition among Weber's critics warrants a mention at this point. As we have observed, Weber's argument is in principle falsifiable, and is *not* merely an impenetrable circle in which the two major variables are defined in terms of each other behind the screen of a methodology of 'ideal-types'. Nevertheless, the provisional and extremely particularized nature of his thesis makes it difficult to gauge the potency of certain criticisms relating to the concept of 'the spirit of modern capitalism' itself. Weber identifies a motivation towards diligence in business as a duty or calling which is *the* distinguishing feature of the modern capitalist mentality but provides little or no admissible evidence by way of substantiating this argument. What then are we to make of the frequently repeated criticism that Weber ignores other aspects of, and other sources of, the modern capitalist world-view? Does not the new attitude also involve a particular orientation towards, for example, technology, science, and the application of these? And, although the interpretation which was placed on Protestant doctrine may have been important, cannot the capitalistic attitudes of the Puritans also be attributed, in part, to a range of social and political circumstances, such as the facts that they were a persecuted minority and were concentrated in urban environments?[49] Moreover, what is to be made of those critical commentaries on Weber's thesis which start from a different conception of 'the spirit of modern capitalism' to that proposed by Weber himself?[50] This posture is generally adopted, of course, as the first step towards a claim that 'the spirit of (modern) capitalism' existed prior to and independently of the Protestant Reformation. Samuelsson, for example, defining the modern capitalist mentality as a 'new spirit of creativeness, of protest against the old order, of inquiry and widening horizons', maintains that this spirit was common in the Italian and Hanseatic League cities of the Middle Ages, and among the sea explorers of late medieval Spain and Portugal, long before it became personified in the economic make-up of the Protestant capitalist-industrialists.[51]

In reply it can only be said that these arguments may or may not be true but they fail to challenge directly Weber's own. To redefine 'the spirit of modern capitalism' at the outset, rather than attempt to discover by empirical investigation precisely what were and were not the motives genuinely involved in economic conduct in pre- and post-Reformation Europe, is not to falsify Weber's thesis but to avoid it. The redefinition of concepts, by way of challenging a testable thesis, is a poor substitute for empirical research.

Labourers and wages

The methodological and practical difficulties that are involved in subjecting the conventional interpretation of Weber's thesis to empirical scrutiny re-emerge if we consider an additional dimension of his argument which is often neglected and has certainly been overshadowed by arguments about the motives and activities of capitalist entrepreneurs. I refer here to the application of Weber's argument to the history and study of the economic orientations, not of capitalists, but of labourers.

Weber's discussion of the effects of ascetic Protestantism on those of the labouring classes who subscribed to its teachings is frequently overlooked because of its fragmented nature. It comprises a number of incidental paragraphs and asides scattered throughout his discussion of the economic mentalities of diverse business communities and classes. A certain amount of reading between the lines is required if we are to arrive at a coherent statement of his position. Summing up his remarks, however, the gist of Weber's argument seems to be that there are directly parallel effects among labouring people to those he alleges to have occurred among the capitalist classes themselves. The norms of economic traditionalism among workers were undermined by the Protestant ethic. Hitherto, labour had expressed a consistent preference for increased leisure over increased income on the one hand (witness Weber's example, cited in Chapter 3, of the backward-sloping supply curve of labour among Silesian mowers); and, on the other, labour had grasped ruthlessly and unhesitatingly at any opportunity for windfall gains which happened to present itself. Calvinist and neo-Calvinist teaching undermined this orientation towards the world of work in two directions. First, the emphases on diligence in a calling and on one's life in this world as a period of 'stewardship' (the parable of the steward who increased his 'talents' to his master's glory being frequently told in Calvinist sermons) gave workers an interest in systematically increasing the returns which they gained for their labour, and for this reason they became willing (unlike the Silesian mower) to increase their exertions in exchange for higher wages. Second, these same doctrines – especially when reinforced by others which emphasized the importance of accounting systematically for the use of time and of hard and continuous bodily labour for those without capital to invest – created a tractable workforce that was willing to adapt to new time- and work-disciplines and rhythms. Gone were the spontaneous taking of holidays (reflected in the institution of 'Saint Monday') and the erratic work patterns of the labourer who moved freely in and out of work and from one task to another according to personal inclination. In their place inner-worldly asceticism created a docile, pliable, hard-working, consistent, reliable, and willing labour-force, fodder for the factories of the industrial revolutions, whose members were motivated by a desire to execute diligently the obligations imposed on them by their calling or vocation in life – however humble.[52]

The case for the defence

Can this account be substantiated? Once again, as in the case of the diverse orientations towards profit and the accumulation of capital, Weber's interpretation seems *prima facie* to fit such data as are available. The *schadenfreudlich* avarice of, for example, the medieval European peasant seems to be widely acknowledged.[53] At the same time, acquisitive opportunism was combined with an easy-going and casual attitude towards work and time neatly caught by the colloquial usage of the Spanish term *mañana* – 'worry about it tomorrow'. 'The peasant', Hill reminds us,

regulates his life by the sun and the seasons; but when Melanchthon made an appointment he fixed not only the hour but the minute as well. . . . A Soviet cartoon of the nineteen-thirties showed a man running to catch a train, who breathlessly asked a peasant by the side of the road what the time was. 'In the tenth hour', was the reply. The cartoon was labouring the same point as many a seventeenth-century sermon.[54]

Voluntary under-employment in medieval and late medieval Europe manifested itself in such phenomena as the spontaneous taking of holidays, long hours spent socializing in the home and tavern, the unhurried pace of life, the discontinuous pattern of work caused by frequent stoppages for recreation, the late arrivals for work and the early departures from it, and so forth.[55]

Similarly, the lengths to which the early factory masters had to go to foster a time- and work-discipline among traditionalistic non-Calvinist labour-forces are well documented, and records show that they imposed financial and corporal punishments for lack of punctuality and effort, implemented 'clocking-in' procedures, erected hierarchies of supervisors, and issued detailed work-schedules, rules, and regulations, in order to achieve this end.[56] The telling point in Weber's favour here would seem to be that many factory owners, acting almost as if they were themselves entirely conversant with Weber's thesis, launched 'moral crusades' and attempted to convert whole sections of their labour-force to Nonconformism (and especially Methodism) in the belief that an 'ascetic Protestant' workforce was an efficient, diligent, and reliable one.[57]

But the problems with this type of data, as it stands, will by now be familiar to the reader. We have shown how much of the evidence that has been presented in support of Weber's thesis as it applies to the business classes is, on detailed inspection, less than wholly convincing since the interpretation which is placed upon it is only one among several equally plausible accounts, and, indeed, rests on a fairly mechanical (and certainly unsubstantiated) imputing of meaning to conduct which systematically ignores a whole range of conditions of action whose influence on the activities in question may be crucial to our understanding of them. The data concerning the labour-discipline and economic orientations of the working class are subject to the same qualifications.

The prosecution: the meaning of labour

We know, for example, that in addition to any 'internalized' ideological predispositions brought by individuals to their work a large number of objective factors will be relevant in determining how hard and for how long they are prepared to labour. Among potential influences on one's 'motivation to work' the following might be included: the extent to which the task itself is intrinsically satisfying or 'alienating'; the availability of attractive alternatives to labour (for example, the comradeship of shared recreational pastimes in a close-knit mining community); the availability of desirable goods and services on which increased remunerations might be spent; and the number and nature of the dependents relying on the income of the individual worker. The list of conditions of action which may well be relevant to any worker's calculation of how much effort and time to invest in a given task is potentially enormous.[58] The main weakness of Weber's and his supporters' case with respect to the effects of ascetic Protestantism on labour is, therefore, that in considering the empirical data that are available as to the patterns of workers' conduct, they again ask us to accept that the meaning of an individual's behaviour is somehow self-evident from a record of economic activity itself.

It is not difficult to think of situations in which workers' conduct, by itself, tells us little or nothing about their abstract 'motivation to work' and, indeed, may be positively misleading in this regard. We have already noted the restrictions placed on productivity by medieval guilds and corporations. Whether or not local markets were limited and static is beside the point: the authorities and the craftworkers themselves believed them to be so. Since self-aggrandisement and expansion could only be carried out at the expense of a fellow worker, the individual was constrained in his or her labour – whatever the motivation to work may or may not have been. Guild regulations as to daily output and selling prices, the complicated statutes governing apprenticeship and the division and mobility of labour, and the laws pertaining to forestalling, regrating, and the preservation of monopoly can all be seen in this light as, at bottom, functions of the medieval view of the market.[59] Thrupp has suggested, for example, that craft guilds deliberately restricted output more or less in inverse ratio to the influence of merchants over their trade. Where goods were to be sold locally, output was restricted; where they were produced for export abroad by merchants, amounts could be manufactured that were beyond what it was felt the local market could absorb.[60]

Similarly, the backward-sloping supply curve of labour does not necessarily indicate that workers are 'traditionalistic' in their orientation to economic behaviour; that is, that they are 'lazy' or that, in principle, they prefer increased leisure to increased remuneration. Recent studies of the supposedly changing attitudes towards work among African tribesmen in a 'modernizing' economy offer an alternative conclusion. Conventional wisdom has it that indigenous labourers in the Zambian copper belt, for example, changed their orientation towards work during the colonial period; a change evident in the shift from an 'unorthodox' to an 'orthodox' response to economic incentives. The supposed preference for leisure which produced a backward-sloping supply curve of labour disappeared, it is alleged, as workers became increasingly familiar with, and desirous of, Western consumer durables that could be bought only with money earned by working in the European-owned mines. For the Weberian 'carrot' of 'proof of salvation' the mine owners had substituted twentieth-century 'beads and trinkets'.

Further examination reveals, however, that the availability of consumer goods procurable by earning wages from non-African employers stayed more or less constant in the hinterland of the copper belt throughout the colonial period. In any case, many of these items could be and had been obtained by barter before colonial rule. The argument for the inherent 'traditionalism' of African labour rests, therefore, on a 'fallacy of limited wants'. A more plausible explanation of the increased willingness of African tribesmen to move to the towns, work in the mines, and adopt new time- and work-disciplines can be gained from observing the changed living conditions of mine labourers during the period. At the outset, employers excluded women from the mining towns – despite the high costs of transportation to and fro between work and tribal areas – and many among the early labourers returned home to find their wives taken by another man. In addition, employers offered no medical protection against European diseases (death rates in the towns were consequently extremely high), forced unfamiliar urban staple foods and appalling punishments for breaches of labour-discipline on their workers, and allowed cartels of shopkeepers to defraud them of their wages. As these and other disincentives were gradually removed so labourers became more responsive to the opportunities to earn money wages and to intensify their efforts in exchange for wage increases. Summing up the argument against the thesis that labourers were 'traditionalistic' in orientation at the outset, and only gradually became 'modern' in their attitudes and behaviour when enticed to do so by the attractions of owning Western consumer durables, Miracle and Fetter conclude that

a better explanation is that it was a change in economic conditions within which African laborers acted which produced the reported changes in labor response. . . . An examination of the nature of the process of molding tribal economies into larger and structurally different regional and colonial economies strongly suggests that in the early years of colonial rule a sharply backward-bending labor-supply curve would have been just as consistent with maximization of individual worker welfare as a more gently backward-bending or positively sloped curve was at later periods.[61]

By itself, then, the existence of a backward-bending supply curve of labour – which may or may not indicate an attitude of 'economic traditionalism' among workers – actually proves nothing. The economic behaviour which generates it is entangled in a web of political and social institutions and in an economic context which is itself not constant. The curve has therefore to be interpreted. Under-employment may be involuntary as well as voluntary. The labourer's location in the socio-political structure, his or her definition of the situation, intentions and motives are all potentially important here. Perceived opportunities for saving, investing, and for social mobility; the nature of familial obligations and institutional arrangements regarding the distribution of possible rewards; resentment against new patterns of authority; and the social, political, and medical dangers of increased effort in certain directions, may all make the economic behaviour which produces the curve perfectly consistent with rational, maximizing (or more precisely cost-minimizing) behaviour. This is a matter, again, for empirical investigation in each instance.[62]

The simple fact is that, as in the case of the business classes and their attitudes towards profits, the *meaning* of economic activity, the motives that lie at the back of the individual's participation in it, cannot be determined by straightforward deduction from observed conduct itself. The methodological principle to be upheld in both cases is expressed succinctly in the dictum that 'Two men, performing the same *motions* side by side, might be said to be performing different *acts*, in proportion as they differed in their attitudes towards their work'.[63] The problem is, of course, that detailed information about people's attitudes towards work is extremely rare for the periods in question.[64] Would that it were possible to interview a fifteenth-century peasant or craftworker and observe his or her daily conduct in depth. Such records as have been passed down to us are largely accounts of general routine – not of meanings, motives, or attitudes – and so the scope for interpretation of these is immense. There is little doubt that his or her work habits would be as strenuous and intense as those of the factory worker of the industrial revolution – possibly more so. And given that it is quite possible to explain away the discontinuities in pre-industrial patterns of work in terms of such things as the erratic and nature-dependent characteristics of the technology of the day, seasonal changes in working conditions, and cycles of disease and illness,[65] perhaps the most appropriate judgement to pass on Weber's interpretation of the economic conduct of the 'traditionalistic' labourer of pre-Reformation Europe would be one of 'not proven'.

In the face of the acknowledged difficulty of obtaining data concerning what people *actually* thought about work and of their motives or reasons for participating in it in a particular fashion, commentators have adopted Weber's procedure of reading the programmatic ethical teachings of the Church as to the ideal in this matter as if these constituted evidence of the substantive motivations and work orientations of the different groups within the working classes.[66] This, of course, is a poor substitute for appropriate empirical data and investigation – and there's the rub. We cannot, as Edward Thompson has put it, interview tombstones. Yet if we were to try and state the most serious practical difficulty with Weber's thesis in a single sentence it would be that, in order to test it, we are required to do precisely that. Why? Because Weber makes it clear that his argument applies only to the ascetic Protestantism of the late sixteenth and seventeenth century.[67] By the eighteenth century, he maintains, the new capitalist mentality has so established itself that it has taken on self-sustaining characteristics and (witness the case of Franklin) has become wholly independent of its religious origins. The last thing that Weber is suggesting is that twentieth-century entrepreneurs or labourers universally view their economic activities as a calling or duty – far less one which has its roots in religious precepts. 'The capitalistic economy of the present day', he writes, is an immense cosmos into which the individual is born, and which presents itself to him, at least as an individual, as an unalterable order of things in which he must live. It forces the individual, in so far as he is involved in the system of market relationships, to conform to capitalistic rules of action. The manufacturer who in the long run acts counter to these norms, will just as inevitably be eliminated from the economic scene as the worker who cannot or will not adapt himself to them will be thrown into the streets without a job.[68]

True, Weber confuses the chronological issue slightly by introducing into his essays a discussion of eighteenth-century Methodism, but it is clear from a close reading of his text that this inclusion is intended only to strengthen his argument about the connection between religion and the modern capitalist mentality, since Weber interprets the Methodist revival – at least at its outset – to be a specific response to the Mammonism of the secular, bourgeois ethic which had by this time established itself. Nevertheless, it is plain from his essays that it is those European states which experienced widely the ascetic Protestantism of the seventeenth century that provide the testing-ground for his argument.[69]

How, then, are we to get at the meaning of economic activities for seventeenth-century capitalists and labourers? Clearly, the particular data required in order to make empirically substantial statements as to the motives of these men and women is going to be very sparse for the period in question.[70] Neither of the two principal means by which commentators have attempted to surmount this difficulty seems satisfactory. The problems involved in the first of these, the attempt to read motives mechanically into certain types of economic action, have been noted extensively. Even more dubious are the innumerable 'tests' of Weber's thesis that have been carried out using data from other times and places. The religious inclinations of twentieth-century American industrialists – the fact that, for example, Carnegie invoked Darwin and Spencer rather than Calvin – may be fascinating for many other reasons, but their relevance from the point of view of testing Weber's Protestant ethic thesis entirely escapes this author at least.[71] The study of the economic attitudes of different Muslim communities in contemporary South-East Asia is, similarly, interesting from several points of view, but it is simply preposterous to claim, as one critic has, that 'There is no reason why conclusions from such a study cannot be used to decide the central issue in the controversy around the Weber thesis.'[72] The fact seems to have escaped some commentators that, had Weber intended his thesis to be valid universally and up to the twentieth century, he himself could have conducted a survey of

Protestant, Catholic, and Jewish attitudes to wealth and economic activities, drawing samples from all corners of the globe, thus sparing his critics the trouble.[73]

At the end of the day, then, we find ourselves making a plea for additional and (most important of all) more *appropriate* research. The conclusion to which we have been moving steadily throughout this chapter, namely, that Weber's thesis is testable in principle though as yet inadequately tested in practice, is intended as a direct challenge to the many commentators who have attempted to proclaim the debate about the thesis closed. On the contrary, when we remove from the arena the clutter of inadmissible evidence which has been proffered by many of the combatants, we can see that serious discussion has barely begun.

6   Continuities in a controversy

The argument of this essay has been straightforward. It was to challenge directly the many commentators who have proclaimed the debate about Max Weber's Protestant ethic thesis to be closed, either on the grounds that the thesis has been conclusively falsified or corroborated, or that subsequent discussion has adequately explored every aspect of Weber's case. To the contrary, I have argued that few among Weber's critics (and almost none of his followers) have taken his argument at its face value, and set about systematic empirical investigation of the relationship which Weber claims to have identified between the Protestant ethic and a changing orientation towards economic activities in parts of sixteenth- and seventeenth-century Europe. I have attempted, in previous chapters, to illustrate some of the shortcomings both in Weber's own presentation of this argument, and in those of certain of his detractors, from the point of view of such a study. As the exposition proceeded it became clear that the types of data which would be required in order to arbitrate between Weber and his critics on empirical grounds are both temporally and geographically specific and, since they relate to the precise motives of historical actors, likely to be difficult to uncover for the period in question. Far from being exhausted, then, really serious discussion of the thesis – by which is meant here the investigation of Weber's argument, as it *actually* appears in his essays, and against *appropriate* empirical data – is conspicuous in the literature only by its relative absence. His thesis about the consequences for everday conduct of certain Protestant doctrines, though testable in principle, remains inadequately tested in practice – despite the voluminous literature which it has occasioned. Many contributors to the lengthy debate have simply talked around the central issues and past both each other and Weber himself. A few examples will perhaps serve to illustrate this point and encourage students who wish to pursue the matter to map out the terrain for themselves.

An exchange – of sorts

The historical critique

In Chapters 2 and 3 of this essay I attempted to show how, and explain why, Weber's thesis is unambiguously concerned with 'the spirit of modern capitalism'. His explanandum is an orientation towards everyday life as a whole and economic conduct in particular. He most certainly does not argue that ascetic Protestantism is a sufficient cause of economic, or even capitalist development; indeed, as was observed, he reserves the most impassioned and sarcastic of his replies for those among the early German commentators who accuse him of such 'idealism'.

He may as well have spared himself the trouble. Critics have continued to 'Hegelianize' his thesis. The principal culprits here have been historians, who have commonly objected to Weber's thesis on the grounds, first, that 'capitalism' existed prior to, and has occurred independently of, ascetic Protestantism; and, second, that Weber ignores the many factors other than religion which were important for its development. The first of these objections is put succinctly by Hartwell, who maintains that 'a basic dilemma is posed by the facts that capitalism has risen and flourished with and without Protestantism, and that Protestantism has risen and flourished with and without capitalism'.[1] To take but a few frequently cited examples, capitalism existed in Italy, France, Spain, and Portugal long before the Reformation era; whereas, conversely, ascetic Protestantism seems to have given no impetus to capitalist development in Switzerland, Scotland, Hungary, and parts of the Netherlands. (Indeed, so the argument goes, by the conservatism of its explicit teachings on wealth it may well have hindered it.)[2] Moreover, critics continue, even if it were true that certain types of Protestantism did encourage the growth of capitalism, it is still the case that Weber ignores the many other factors that played a much larger part in such a development: the Renaissance, the Crusades, and the discovery and exploitation of the Americas and of sea routes to the Far East; the influences of Roman Law, of improvements in techniques of production and exchange, and of the rise of the modern centralized state; the transformation of agriculture; the relative movements of wages and prices; and a host of additional elements too numerous to mention in the present context.[3]

It is clear that, among historical commentators generally, these charges arise out of a quite considerable confusion as to Weber's explanandum. His thesis is commonly interpreted as an argument that ascetic Protestantism was wholly or in part responsible for 'capitalism', 'economic progress', 'economic development', 'industrialization', 'entrepreneurs', 'economic growth', and even 'commerce and industry' *per se*.[4] Whether because of (perhaps understandable) confusion generated by the inclusion of Weber's 1920 'Author's introduction' as the opening part of his essays in translation, or (dare we suggest it) through not having familiarized themselves with the argument first-hand, historians have gradually come to conflate Weber's two arguments that the Protestant ethic fostered the modern capitalist mentality, and that this mentality was, under specific economic circumstances, important for the direction of economic development in the West, such that his thesis is reduced, as we have observed, to the proposition that 'ascetic Protestantism caused modern capitalism'.[5] Historical instances in which either may be said to have existed without the other are therefore erroneously taken as providing conclusive falsification of 'Weber's thesis' and as sufficient grounds upon which to declare discussion of the matter closed.

A sociological response

Sociologists have been quick to suggest that claims such as these could be made only in ignorance of Weber's other writings. They maintain, for example, that we have merely to read Weber's essays on China or India, *Economy and Society*, or his *General Economic History*, to see that his conception of causation is pluralistic. 'Protestantism', for Weber, 'is not *the* cause, but *one* of the causes of capitalism, or rather, it is *one* of the causes of *certain aspects* of capitalism.'[6] Weber is not laying capitalism *tout court* at the feet of John Calvin or even of Richard Baxter. He claims only that ascetic Protestantism changed the attitudes of the faithful towards their everyday and economic activities; not that it created the money economy, the banking system, factories, or any other aspects of modern occidental economic life. In short,

At the level of causality, the 'thesis' is extremely cautious and limited. Limited in the first place because it does not apply to capitalism in its entirety as an historical phenomenon, but only to certain specific characteristics of occidental capitalism; and the protestant ethic has been but one of the causes, amongst others, of these particular characteristics. Limited also to the period of nascent capitalism. . . . Limited finally because, far from suggesting the direct action of theological doctrines on the economic sphere, it postulates the existence of indispensable mediations, in particular psychological motivations deriving from religious beliefs.[7]

Historians have therefore been berated for their failure to put Weber's original essays into their proper context of his writings on the sociology of religion as a whole and of his later studies of the rise of capitalism in the West.[8]

This sociological counter-attack would seem to be entirely justified.[9] It is hard to see how the charge that Weber is a latter-day Hegelian can be sustained except by a studious refusal to acknowledge the fact that his essays on 'the Protestant ethic' were not the only pieces which he ever published.[10] Consider, for example, the account that is offered of the transition from feudalism to capitalism in Europe in Weber's lectures on *General Economic History*. Here he documents, among other things, the factors which, during (largely) the sixteenth century, led European societies in general and England in particular to develop economically in a fundamentally different direction from those followed by other great agrarian civilizations such as China and India. First among these is the differentiation of the European peasant household functions of ownership, production, and consumption, such that only the last is retained by the household itself. The business and the household, both as physical entities and functional concentrations of capital, became separated. This differentiation was at least partly due to the dissolution of the manorial system which led to the creation of both free land and labour markets and hence to the establishment of these commodities as the private properties of individuals. The manorial system had been 'undermined from within' by 'the mere fact of the development of a market', since this had introduced profit, money, and production for exchange rather than use, and thus eroded the household and subsistence economy of the manors. The early establishment in England of the market itself was at least in part due to the centralized state and rational legal system imposed by the Norman Conquest – and so Weber's exposition and causal regress proceeds. Need we continue with the details?

The fact is that, whatever the accuracy of Weber's account of the nature of the economic development of the Occident,[11] it most certainly cannot be depicted as idealist or, indeed, monocausal with respect to any factor whatsoever. At times the direction of causality proceeds from economic to political while at other times it is reversed; elsewhere it is legal developments that are accorded primacy; then on another occasion it may be ideological. Weber invokes, in short, pluralistic explanations for the occurrence and direction of economic change in the West. Entirely typical, for example, is the following short extract from his account:

All earlier forms of capitalism relate to spoils, taxes, the pickings of office or official usury, and finally to tribute and actual need. . . . All this, however, relates to occasional economic activity of an irrational character, while no rational system of labor organization developed out of these arrangements.

Rational capitalism, on the contrary, is organized with a view to market opportunities, hence to economic objectives in the real sense of the word, and the more rational it is the more closely it relates to mass demand and the provision for mass needs. It was reserved to the modern western development after the close of the middle ages to elevate this capitalism into a system, while in all of antiquity there was but one capitalist class whose rationalism might be compared with that of modern capitalism, namely, the Roman knighthood. . . .

The capitalism of the late middle ages began to be directed toward market opportunities, and the contrast between it and the capitalism of antiquity appears in the development after the cities have lost their freedom. Here again we find a fundamental distinction in the lines of development as between antiquity and medieval and modern times. In antiquity the freedom of the cities was swept away by a bureaucratically organized world empire within which there was no longer a place for political capitalism. . . .
. . . the modern city . . . came under the power of competing national states in a condition of perpetual struggle for power in peace or war. This competitive struggle created the largest opportunities for modern western capitalism. The separate states had to compete for mobile capital, which dictated to them the conditions under which it would assist them in power. Out of this alliance of the State with capital, dictated by necessity, arose the national citizen class, the bourgeoisie in the modern sense of the word. Hence it is the closed national state which afforded to capitalism its chance for development. . . .[12]

Weber's historical narrative, in this particular text at least, is far from being crudely monocausal. Indeed, it is the near contrary which is the case. Such is the magnitude of the task which Weber sets himself – identifying the diverse origins of modern Western civilization in all its economic aspects – that it is often unclear whether the innumerable 'conditions' that are cited are causes, attributes, or consequences of what he intends by 'capitalism', so complex is the web of inter-relationships that he identifies.

Nor is it legitimate for historians to point to a bustling 'capitalism' in the pre-Reformation commercial centres of Europe, or its slow progress in certain Protestant countries during the centuries after the

Reformation, as if these concurrences *self-evidently* refuted Weber's case. The fallacy underlying criticism which deems the existence of 'pre-Reformation capitalism' to be problematic for Weber's argument has already been exposed. His essays are an attempt to describe the origins of a unique and specifically 'modern' attitude towards profits and work; capitalistic acquisition related to all sorts of other attitudes, and capitalist enterprises imbued with such attitudes, are acknowledged as long having predated Luther and Calvin. But what about objections deriving from the demonstrable persistence of economic backwardness in certain Protestant lands during the seventeenth century? Here again it appears not to be Weber, but his critics, who are guilty of historical naïveté.

In his replies to Fischer and Rachfahl, for example, Weber again emphasizes the fact that his primary concern is with the origins of the modern capitalist mentality. To this end he has investigated the congruence between this world-view (as illustrated in the writings of Franklin) and the doctrines of ascetic Protestantism. His argument is about (and legitimate criticism should contest) the psychological consequences of these doctrines and the possible direction which such consequences gave to everyday conduct. Weber concedes freely that this approach takes as given the prior relationship between the rational, methodical approach to economic life characteristic of modern capitalists, and the direction of economic development in the West.[13] However, he continues, just as it was assumed at the outset that the existence of such a world-view was important in this development, so also is it axiomatic that numerous other objective factors were equally so. His quip about Siberian Baptist wholesalers and Arabian Calvinist manufacturers, for example, occurs in the context of an emphatic denial that he is offering the 'spiritualistic' thesis that, irrespective of the social, political, and economic conditions under which it appears, the 'capitalist mentality' (arising out of ascetic Protestantism) will inevitably create certain economic forms and developments.[14] As Weber is well aware, a huge number of diverse factors are responsible for the precise nature of the modern economic order; it cannot be derived entirely from ascetic Protestantism.[15] In other words, the world-view engendered by the Protestant Churches and sects in question can only have the influence on the direction of economic development and change that Weber claims, where the various other preconditions for such change are also present. 'The spirit of capitalism' will be associated with modern, rational, capitalistic forms of enterprise, only where the objective possibility for the development of such enterprises exists.[16]

The fact that certain Protestant lands long remained 'economically backward' therefore fails to negate either of Weber's arguments. Assuming that the 'Protestant' theologies of the areas in question were of the 'inner-worldly ascetic' type discussed by Weber, there remains the possibility that one or more economic, political, or social factors were operative in blocking capitalist developments and economic growth. This possibility can only be explored by, and discounted through, extensive empirical analysis. To date, however, critics have been content merely to cite the cases of Scotland, Belgium, and so forth, as if these were somehow transparently problematic for Weber's case. My own study of the experience of the first of these so-called 'counter instances' suggests that it, at least, raises no such problems. Scots Calvinist-capitalists were amply imbued with an appropriate capitalist mentality (deriving, it seems, from their Protestantism), but their efforts had few discernible consequences for economic development because of the unfavourable circumstances in which they were made and which they proved unable to transcend. The 'conditions of action' circumscribing their activities included a number of severely detrimental economic and political relationships between Scotland and certain neighbouring states, inadequate supplies of suitably skilled labour and of liquid capital for investment, and the inappropriate fiscal and industrial policies pursued by the state. Thus, as Eldridge has correctly observed, 'the fact that Calvinism in Scotland was not associated with marked capitalistic development of the economy is no refutation of Weber's position', since it was never Weber's claim that ascetic Protestantism was sufficient to generate spontaneous economic growth in the absence of what Marxists might call a suitable 'base' for such a transformation.[17] Here again, the inappropriate data offered by many who are critical of Weber's thesis – growth rates in the economy, the size of the manufacturing sector as a proportion of the economy as a whole, the quality and quantity of goods produced, and so forth – point to the widespread confusion that exists in the historical camp concerning both the claims made in Weber's essays and the explananda of his causal propositions.

We can readily concur, therefore, with the sociological dismissal of the charge of idealism against Weber:

Weberian thought is not an inversion of historical materialism. Nothing would be more untrue than to imagine that Weber maintained a thesis exactly opposite to Marx's and explained the economy in terms of religion instead of religion in terms of the economy. . . . . Weber did not propose an exclusive causality of religion. What he did show is that men's economic activities may be governed by their systems of belief, just as at a given moment systems of belief may be governed by the economic system. He has therefore encouraged us to recognise that there is no determination of beliefs by economic-social reality, or at any rate that it is unjustifiable to assume a determination of this kind *a priori*.[18]

The problem with Weber's sociological apologists, however, is that they have tended to rest their case at this point. To the historical accusation of *simplicité* and downright inaccuracy, as far as the essays on the Protestant ethic are concerned, they reply only that Weber's critics have 'failed to appreciate the wider context of his work'. Precisely what sociologists have not attempted, on any serious scale, is an empirical verification of the central proposition of Weber's essays themselves.

Robert Moore's defence of Weber is entirely typical in this respect. Observing that 'the charge of historical naïveté is often levelled at Weber by British historians', and that he is therefore accused of 'adopting a *simpliste* approach to the question of the relations between religion and social change', Moore declares unequivocally that 'This charge cannot be substantiated.' 'It seems', in his opinion, 'to be founded on a reading of the essays *The Protestant Ethic and the Spirit of Capitalism* only and takes no account of this work's place in Weber's *Religionssoziologie* and his historical and comparative studies.' No one reading these works could possibly mistake Weber for a doctrinaire idealist or as historically unsophisticated. This, as we have just observed, is a fair commentary on the literature in question. We might, however, have expected the next step in Moore's argument to be the provision of such data as would confirm Weber's thesis to be historically accurate, or at least a discussion of the types of data that might facilitate such a demonstration; but we would be wrong. The idea that Weber's argument might be lacking somewhat in empirical documentation is not entertained. We are invited, instead, to accept his thesis on the grounds that his essays can be related to his 'wider sociological concerns' and his other works, a relationship which critics such as Samuelsson have failed to appreciate. Especially significant among these wider concerns is Weber's attempt to construct an ideal-typical and *verstehende* methodology for the social sciences. All this may be true, of course, but it begs entirely the original question concerning the historical accuracy of Weber's argument itself.[19]

Moore's treatment is singled out here, not because it is especially unsatisfactory, but simply because it fairly represents and illustrates particularly well the way in which generations of sociologists have avoided coming to terms with the empirical nuts and bolts of Weber's argument through appealing to his wider, and in particular his methodological, objectives. The point is that, in fact, it does not follow from the failure of the historical *critique* to engage Weber's thesis at points where it is genuinely weak that the thesis itself is therefore vindicated. To relate Weber's original essays to the arguments of his comparative studies, *General Economic History*, or *Economy and Society*, and to show how they illustrate aspects of his methodology such as the ideal-types, is not self-evidently sufficient proof of the accuracy of the substantive argument of the essays themselves. This is not to say that such continuities in Weber's work cannot be identified; indeed, it was suggested in Chapter 3 that Weber's concept of 'the spirit of modern capitalism' can be better understood through an appreciation of his ideas about 'value-relevant' concept formation in the social sciences. But the intellectual continuities that can be pointed to between Weber's methodological and substantive concerns elsewhere, and his argument about the effects of ascetic Protestant doctrine on the everyday life of the average believer, have not resolved the issue of whether or not the latter argument is tenable one whit; they have, instead, merely avoided it. Sociologists simply cannot escape the problems of historical counter-evidence, or more accurately (as I have argued) of the lack of substantiating evidence, by pleading for 'the big picture'.

Weber and Marx

Might it not be the case, however, that there are aspects of Weber's theses which must of necessity be settled on grounds other than the strictly empirical? Almost certainly there are. It may well become apparent, from investigation, that appropriate data simply do not exist, for the periods in question, in quantities sufficient to facilitate rigorous empirical scrutiny of every component of Weber's argument. If this is the case, however, we ought to be entirely clear about what, if anything, has been settled in subsequent discussion, and on what grounds. Where Weber's thesis about the consequences of ascetic Protestantism for economic conduct is rejected or accepted on the basis of, for example, a prior commitment to his overall approach to the study of social action, this should be clearly recognized, and the issue in question acknowledged to be one which commentators have been unable to resolve empirically. The relationship between Marx's and Weber's respective accounts of the connection between religion and the capitalist mentality would seem to be a case in point.

The Marxist critique

Marxists have, in fact, tended to be among the most lenient of Weber's critics. Marx's own picture of the mentality of the modern capitalist is almost identical to that painted by Weber, combining as it does the dual tendencies towards the pursuit of profit in production and of frugality in consumption, a conjunction which leads irresistibly to 'primitive modern capitalistic accumulation'. Again, like Weber, Marx concedes that capitalists, having once made their fortunes in such a manner, rapidly abandon their initial asceticism and acquire tastes and appetites for material comforts appropriate to their new stations in life.[20] What motivated the early capitalists was, however, class rather than religious interest. For Marx it is a specific relationship to the means of production, rather than to one's deity, that generates the material interest of the capitalist classes in the accumulation of capital. Religion, as part of the ideological 'super-structure' in any social formation, is simply an ideal and distorted expression of the true relationships of subordination and domination between classes. Since, in rendering these relationships opaque, it legitimates and makes harmonious the social relations from which it arises, religion therefore serves the interests of the dominant class in society. Engels explains how the general Marxian theory of ideology applies to the specific case of the Protestant Reformation in these terms:

When Europe emerged from the Middle Ages, the rising middle class of the towns constituted its revolutionary element. It had conquered a recognised position within mediaeval feudal organisation, but this position, also, had become too narrow for its expansive power. The development of the middle class, the *bourgeoisie*, became incompatible with the maintenance of the feudal system; the feudal system, therefore, had to fall.

But the great international centre of feudalism was the Roman Catholic Church. It united the whole of feudalised Western Europe, in spite of internal wars, into one grand political system. . . . It surrounded feudal institutions with the halo of divine consecration. . . . Before profane feudalism could be successfully attacked in each country and in detail, this, its sacred central organisation, had to be destroyed. . . .

. . . [Therefore] the class most directly interested in the struggle against the pretensions of the Roman Church was the bourgeoisie; and . . . every struggle against feudalism, at that time, had to take on a religious disguise, had to be directed against the Church in the first instance. . . .

The long fight of the bourgeoisie against feudalism culminated in three great, decisive battles.

The first was what is called the Protestant Reformation in Germany. The war cry raised against the Church was responded to by two insurrections of a political nature. . . . Both were defeated, chiefly in consequence of the indecision of the parties most concerned, the burghers of the towns – an indecision into the causes of which we cannot here enter. . . .

But where Luther failed, Calvin won the day. Calvin's creed was one fit for the boldest of the bourgeoisie of his time. His predestination doctrine was the religious expression of the fact that in the commercial world of competition success or failure does not depend upon a man's activity or cleverness, but upon circumstances uncontrollable by him. It is not of him that willeth or of him that runneth, but of the mercy of unknown superior economic powers; and this was especially true at a period of economic revolution, when all old commercial routes and centres were replaced by new ones, when India and America were opened to the world, and when even the most sacred articles of economic faith – the value of gold and silver – began to totter and break down. Calvin's church constitution was thoroughly democratic and republican; and where the kingdom of God was republicanised, could kingdoms of this world remain subject to monarchs, bishops and lords? . . .

In Calvinism, the second great bourgeois upheaval found its doctrine ready cut and dried. This upheaval took place in England. . . .

The Great French Revolution was the third uprising of the bourgeoisie, but the first that had entirely cast off the religious cloak, and was fought out on undisguised political lines. . . .[21]

Calvinism and the rise of capitalism are indeed, as Weber suggests, closely related; but the relationship between the 'ethos' of modern capitalism (the attitudes and conduct of the early capitalists) and Calvinist doctrine is precisely the opposite of that which the Weberian account proposes. According to Weber, Calvinist theology, developing autonomously out of Lutheranism by systematizing the doctrines of the latter, had the entirely unintended consequence of generating in believers an interest in methodical conduct of a type which was almost certain, *ceteris paribus*, to lead to the accumulation of capital. For Marx and Engels, however, the doctrines of the Reformed Churches are simply an ideological representation of social class relationships which had arisen out of, and were determined by, specific developments in the sphere of production. The ascendant capitalist class therefore held a prior class interest in accumulating capital ruthlessly and systematically and was attracted to Calvinist and neo-Calvinist beliefs only because these offered convenient justification for its economic practices. As a result, Reformed doctrine came more and more to reflect the interests of this class by prescribing for apparently religious reasons behaviour which increasingly was suited to its economic objectives. In short, it is the capitalist 'ethic' that explains the origins and development of Calvinist beliefs, rather than vice versa.

There is no need here to go into the extremely complex question of the precise nature of the Marxian account of the rise of capitalism or of the relationship between ideological and infrastructural elements in specific social formations. In any case, Marxism currently embraces a wide range of positions on these issues, and it is by no means easy to see how the contrasting and often contradictory interpretations might be reconciled. The divergent accounts of the transition from feudalism to capitalism offered by, for example, Dobb, Sweezy, Anderson, and Wallerstein are perhaps symptomatic of the fact that Marx himself offered at least three separate and perhaps not easily reconcilable accounts of the origins of capitalism during the course of his lifetime.[22] More serious, however, are the contemporary schisms within Marxism regarding the interpretation of Marx's central metaphor of 'base and superstructure'. The issue here boils down to one of establishing precisely what determines what, how, and why. Marxist theory, as Raymond Williams has pointed out, offers at least two fundamentally different interpretations of the key term 'determine'. 'There is, on the one hand', he writes, 'the notion of an external cause which totally predicts or prefigures, indeed totally controls subsequent activity. But there is also . . . a notion of determination as setting limits, exerting pressures.'[23] Whereas earlier, more mechanistic Marxists tended to adhere to the former viewpoint, more recently it is the latter which has become fashionable. Nevertheless, the parameters of disagreement within even the 'limiting conditions' interpretation are still large, and currently include versions of idealism, structuralism, functionalism, culturalism, and a number of loosely related attempts to reconcile these and apply a sophisticated 'non-deterministic' Marxist analysis which accords due weight to 'consciousness' and 'agency', in addition to 'structure', to the study of empirical problems of both historical and contemporary relevance.[24] There are, it seems, fundamental issues yet to be resolved. How 'autonomous' is 'relatively autonomous'?

When is 'the last instance'? And, if we concede some measure of genuine interaction between the spheres of production and other spheres of social life, what then is distinctively 'Marxist' about the methodologies of the approaches in question?[25]

It would be imprudent for an outsider implicitly to impose an hegemony in the Marxist camp by selecting only one of these positions to represent 'the Marxist theory of ideology'. This would only be to invite scorn from those excluded from the chosen orthodoxy since, as Paul Hirst rightly comments in his contribution to a recent exchange between 'culturalist' and 'structuralist' Marxists,

There is no such thing as 'orthodox Marxism'. All 'orthodoxies' – Kautsky's, Lukács', Stalin's – are particular theoretical constructions culled out of the possibilities within the complex whole of Marx and Engels' discourse. [Edward] Thompson has every right to call himself and to be a Marxist – he is as heterodox as I am and no less.

Moreover,

There is no more unity to 'Althusserianism' than there was to a previous *bête noire* 'structuralism'. Many different theories and styles of work are grouped under this catchphrase. . . .[26]

Fortunately, it is not necessary, for our purposes, to intervene in these debates, since however divergent the ways in which Marxists conceive of ideology in its relationships to modes of production and class structures, at the end of the day a majority of those who would call themselves by that name make common use of empirical data which relate Calvinist religious beliefs to capitalist activities in post-Reformation Europe. Where capitalists profess Calvinist beliefs, and especially where they may be shown to be appealing to these in order to explain their economic behaviour, such appeals are commonly interpreted to be simply a convenient 'justification' for conduct which in reality arises out of objective class interests. These 'justifications' may be offered in good faith, because the capitalist class does not yet perceive its own objective interests, or they may be employed in a more Machiavellian manner, as when capitalists seek consciously to employ religion as a means of socially legitimating their enterprise or of controlling their labour-force. In both cases, however, the 'real' reasons for the capitalists' behaviour are economic rather than religious. They are pursuing class interests arising out of a specific relationship to the means of production, interests which exist independently of the religious sphere, and developed autonomously of it. The origins of the 'capitalist mentality' and capitalist conduct are, ultimately, economic.

The other side of the causal chain

A variety of Marxists and, in fact, a significant number of non-Marxists have interpreted the history of Calvinism and capitalism in the aforementioned terms. A number of the former have followed Engels's analysis and suggested that, 'in the last instance', it is the class interests of the capitalists which account for the development of Calvinist beliefs although, at the level of individual actors, a 'dialectical' relationship between class interest and ideological representation can be observed. The nascent capitalist was attracted to Calvinism because it appeared to offer some justification for his or her economic practices and this, in turn, reinforced the commitment to the activities themselves.

Christopher Hill, for example, claims to have demonstrated 'how perfectly the theology of the Puritan preachers fitted the needs of a revolutionary class',[27] on the grounds that

The protestant revolt melted down the iron ideological framework which held society in its ancient mould. Where capitalism already existed, it had henceforth freer scope. But men did not become capitalists because they were protestants, nor protestants because they were capitalists. In a society already becoming capitalist, protestantism facilitated the triumph of new values. There was no inherent theological reason for the protestant emphasis on frugality, hard work, accumulation; but that emphasis was a natural consequence of the religion of the heart in a society where capitalist industry was developing. It was, if we like, a rationalization; but it flowed naturally from protestant theology, whose main significance, for our present purposes, is that in any given society it enabled religion to be moulded by those who dominated in that society.[28]

The connection between Protestantism and capitalist activity therefore arises out of the appeal which the former had from the point of view of the material interests of the latter. Protestant theology justified the pursuit of profits as an expression of diligence in a calling, and encouraged the poor to labour ceaselessly at their master's bequest, both by the threat of divine retribution for laziness and by emphasizing the dignity of labour. The stress on the role of the individual conscience as the guiding light in conducting one's life (as compared to Roman Catholic casuistry, which tended to emphasize the formal and external) justified the challenges of the rising bourgeoisie to established political and social authority by granting legitimacy to its economic and related practices. Parochial discipline promised to solve the problem of the 'idle poor' by punishing sturdy beggars.[29]

Not surprisingly, then,

Calvinism everywhere pervades the classes which are most directly in contact with the constituent elements of capitalism. It recruits among the 'industrial population', that is to say among employers and employees in businesses using new techniques; among maritime insurers and organisers of lotteries and wagers; among the large merchants and money-changers who frequent the stock exchanges and who resent the absolute power of the great bankers of the Curie, and their factors; among projectors, inventors of new processes.... Thus, following Marx, we can define protestantism as the bourgeois religion *par excellence*, a definition reaffirmed by his son-in-law Lafargue: protestantism is the authentic religious expression of the capitalist form of production and exchange.[30]

It is for precisely this reason that, for example, English Puritanism was strongest among small employers in the economically advanced areas of London, the Home Counties, East Anglia, and in towns, small-manufacturing and clothing areas generally.[31] It 'appealed especially to those smaller employers and self-employed men, whether in town or country, for whom frugality and hard work might make all the difference between prosperity and failure to survive in the world of growing competition'.[32] In short, Calvinism did not create the interest of the capitalist class in the systematic accumulation of capital; it merely provided a helpful justification for an interest which was already struggling to assert itself and, Calvinism or not, would eventually have been triumphant. The history of Calvinism and capitalism vindicates Marx and Engels rather than Weber.[33]

A variety of non-Marxists have proposed a similar interpretation of the relationship between Calvinist ethic and capitalist spirit. Reviewing the controversy about Weber's thesis in 1944 Fischoff observed that

while there is readiness enough to accept the congruity between Calvinism and capitalism, it has been suggested that a consideration of the crucial question of timing will show that Calvinism emerged later than capitalism where the latter became decisively powerful. Hence the conclusion that Calvinism could not have causally influenced capitalism, and that its subsequent favourable disposition to capitalist practice and ethics is rather to be construed as an adaptation.[34]

The argument to which Fischoff was referring has its roots in the charge that Weber has studied only 'one side of the causal chain' and has ignored the economic origins of the Reformation. Had he studied the latter, critics claim, he would have observed that the Reformation was accomplished largely by the middle classes precisely because, with the rise of the towns and commercial life, the new bourgeoisie had interests in personal liberty, economic freedom, and a measure of political self-determination which it expressed in a widespread challenge to the established order. The middle classes therefore sought to abolish formalistic and ecclesiastic restrictions on trade and business, and their support for the Reformation reflects the fact that they were already imbued with that spirit of 'capitalistic individualism' which Weber mistakenly interprets as a consequence of their religious commitment, rather than its principal cause.[35] The relationship between Puritanism and the clothing industry in England is, in fact, the very opposite of that suggested by Weber's argument. 'Puritanism did not create the economic attitudes of the industry; Protestantism was accepted, for strategic reasons, by part of English commerce as a support to already existing economic values.'[36]

This is not to say, however, that the Reformation, once secured, did not react back upon the world-views and conduct of the classes and strata which had carried it through. A great many commentators have proposed what Forcese calls a 'feedback effect' between Protestantism and capitalistic individualism.[37] Yinger, for example, has argued that Weber's consciously one-sided approach to the relationship in question

runs the risk . . . of seeming to disregard the ways in which Calvinism was shaped and interpreted in ways that were harmonious with the inclinations of its adherents. . . . Calvinism did not create the spirit of capitalism, but the needs and tendencies of capitalists were involved in the process which selected from the various possibilities of interpretation of Calvinism.

The important place Calvin gave to the doctrine of predestination, similarly, need not have had the consequences which Weber describes, had it been developed by persons in a different social situation. With Calvin, it demonstrated that pure, unmerited grace comes from God, because man, by his 'fall' has lost the ability to achieve grace. Calvin had no trust either in works or in sacramental forms and rites. This might easily lead to mysticism and quietism. If it encouraged 'worldly asceticism' among the commercial groups that embraced Calvinism, it is because such an interpretation had some meaning to those who were winning positions of influence in a dynamic society. Having accepted such an interpretation, however, they were bound to some degree by its implications – thrift, hard work, self-denial.[38]

Similarly, in Henri Sée's opinion, Calvinism 'stimulated the energies and individualism of its adherents', as Weber maintains, but only because 'the individualism characterising the Calvinistic Reform fitted well with the individualism which characterised the economic life of the centers of capitalistic enterprise during the sixteenth century'. It spread chiefly throughout the urban centres of France, England, and the Low Countries, 'among the bourgeois and merchant classes who were naturally apt to become imbued with the capitalist spirit even without submitting to the influence of the reformers' doctrines'. The relationship between the capitalistic and Calvinist world-views is therefore one of 'action and reaction' or of 'convergence'.[39]

Many of these critics turn against Weber his own distinction between the early Calvinism of the sixteenth century and that of the seventeenth-century neo-Calvinists. Precisely what this 'internal evolution' towards the ideal-typical 'Protestant ethic' signals, it is claimed, and precisely what Weber ignores, is the way in which the Calvinistic middle classes sought to steer Calvin's original teachings in the direction of their own economic and class interests. The Calvinist ethic is sympathetic to the capitalist spirit, not because it created it, but because of 'a process of churchly adaptation to its environment' (although, in the manner of a feedback mechanism, the religious doctrines once established may have acted back upon the motivations and economic conduct of adherents). Puritan ministers were, in short, increasingly inclined to preach exactly what their middle and lower middle class audiences wanted to hear. For example, early Calvinists only rarely mention the duty of diligence in a worldly calling, whereas by the time of Richard Baxter this doctrine has become a pronounced feature of Calvinist teaching. The relationship between 'capitalist individualism' and the 'Calvinist ethic' proposed by Weber can therefore more appropriately be reversed:

The doctrine of the 'calling' did not breed a spirit of capitalism. The spirit of capitalism was responsible for a gradual modification and attrition of the Puritan doctrine; and this attrition had barely begun in England before the Restoration.[40]

The gradual Calvinist accommodation to the notion of 'legitimate interest' and the progressive relaxation of the economic casuistry of the Roman Catholic Church can also be viewed in this light. Both testify to the fact that 'the Churches, one and all, have had to accommodate themselves to an extraneous development of a busy commercial spirit; that capitalism has created, or found already existent, its own spirit, and set the Churches the task of assimilating it'.[41]

A claim

How are we to resolve this issue? Was the Calvinist ethic an important source of the spirit of modern capitalism, as Weber maintains, or is it the independent influence of the latter which explains the nature and development of Calvinist teaching, as is suggested above?

It is difficult to see how these questions may be answered empirically. In the words of one researcher,

Lutheranism quickly established itself in the cities of Germany, and the merchants had much to do with carrying it to the Low Countries. Twenty years later, in these same Low Countries, as in Great Britain, Calvinism would find an excellent breeding ground. Historians have been tempted to seek in the Reformation the religious expression of a social movement, but the temptation has rarely produced any serious attempts at research along these lines. Can we speak of a revolt aiming at both the traditional religious order and the traditional social order? A cursory survey of the period might well lead to this conclusion, but once the researcher begins to probe for specific data, he encounters so many difficulties that most historians of the Reformation prefer not to bother with the question at all.[42]

Of course, illustrations can be brought forward of capitalists who appear to be appealing to Calvinist theology simply as a convenient way of legitimating their attitude towards profit; an attitude which can more obviously be related to their interests elsewhere, particularly economic ones. Conversely, certain data appear to confirm the sincerity of the religious beliefs held by Calvinist businessmen and businesswomen, and hence of their religious motives for practising certain types of economic conduct. But data such as these are rare and, in any case, apply only to the isolated individuals for whom they can be unearthed. It seems unlikely that we will be able to find, for the sixteenth and seventeenth centuries, empirical materials of sufficient quality and quantity as would permit an empirical resolution of the issue as to whether the Protestant ethic decisively shaped the capitalist mentality of entire social strata, or vice versa.

If the chicken and egg problem of the relationship between capitalist spirit and Calvinist ethic seems unlikely to be decided on empirical grounds, how then are we to arbitrate between Weber and his critics in this matter? The answer would seem to be that one may choose to align oneself with one party or another only on grounds deriving from considerations of general sociological theory. One is, for example, inclined either to accept or reject the possibilities that ideas can exert an independent influence on social conduct, or that changing attitudes are inevitably, sometimes, or never the result of a change in objective circumstances (of whatever kind), simply on the grounds of a prior commitment to a particular model of social action. In other words, discussion of which changed first – the world (Marx) or people's understanding of it (Weber) – is likely to be interminable because what is at issue is not the status of this or that body of empirical material, but is, rather, the validity of competing frameworks for the interpretation of social reality. One follows Marx or Weber on the issue of the relationship between the Calvinist ethic and the capitalist mentality, not by adducing empirical materials (since these are almost always open to alternative interpretations from another direction), but by a declaration of theoretical commitment.

At this point, of course, the issues become extremely complicated because the relationship between the theoretical frameworks of Weberian sociology and Marxism is clearly a matter of some controversy. Thus, for example, depending upon the particular interpretation of Weberian and Marxian theory that one adopts, one may conclude alternatively that Weber's 'Protestant ethic thesis' is wholly antagonistic to the Marxian account of the relationship between Calvinism and capitalism, indeed achieves 'the positive overcoming of the "materialistic" view of history'; that there are close similarities between the two approaches such that each complements the other; or even that Weber's entire argument 'fits without difficulty into the Marxian scheme'.[43]

My own opinions on this matter are as much a statement of personal theoretical preference as are those of anyone else. I have argued that Weber did not compose his essays on the Protestant ethic specifically in order to challenge the framework of historical materialism. The origins of his essays are, as was suggested in Chapter 2, complex and diverse, but a desire on Weber's part to engage directly the 'ghost of Marx' does not seem to have figured prominently in these.[44] Nevertheless, irrespective of the genealogy of Weber's argument, one of its inescapable results is, I believe, to challenge directly the Marxist account of the relationships between ideology (as part of the 'superstructure' of a social formation) and the infrastructural productive base, and between ideas, interests, and actions in general. The two approaches simply cannot be reconciled on these issues.[45] Marx declares that

The ideas of the ruling class are in every epoch the ruling ideas, i.e. the class which is the ruling *material* force of society, is at the same time its ruling *intellectual* force. The class which has the means of material production at its disposal, has control at the same time over the means of mental production, so that thereby, generally speaking, the ideas of those who lack the means of mental production are subject to it. The ruling ideas are nothing more than the ideal expression of the dominant material relationships, the dominant material relationships grasped as ideas; hence of the relationships which make the one class the ruling one, therefore, the ideas of its dominance.[46]

Weber's denial of this particular conception of the relationship between ideas, interests, and action, between the economic and non-economic aspects of social existence, could hardly be more emphatic:

I would like to protest the statement . . . that some one factor, be it technology or economy, can be the 'ultimate' or 'true' cause of another. If we look at the causal lines, we see them run, at one time, from technical to economic and political matters, at another from political to religious and economic ones, etc. There is no resting point. In my opinion, the view of historical materialism, frequently espoused, that the economic is in some sense the ultimate point in the chain of causes is completely finished as a scientific proposition.[47]

It can be argued, of course, that the matter is considerably more complex than this; and in many ways this is a fair comment. A number of observers have pointed out, for example, that Weber held separate opinions of Marx's personal contribution (and, according to his wife at least, he expressed 'great admiration' for the latter's 'brilliant constructions'[48]); of Marxism as a political philosophy and movement; and of the value of contemporary Marxist analyses of historical and social problems.[49] Thus, while it is clear that he saw the 'one-sided' approach of 'the great thinker' himself to be useful only for heuristic purposes as an 'ideal-type',[50] his repeated and emphatic denials of the 'scientific validity' of the Marxian schema *per se* may have been, in part, a reaction to the vulgar materialism of the theorists associated with the Second International and the German Social Democratic Party. Perhaps, as many have claimed, the Marxism which Weber rejects is an overly deterministic and simplistic version of the original theory.[51]

Similarities can also be documented between aspects of the two men's substantive analyses of modern capitalist society. Marx felt that the influence of capitalism as a unique social form was so all-embracing that it placed people in 'definite relations that are indispensable and independent of their will'. This accords well with Weber's remarks on the role of Protestant asceticism in the modern world:

The Puritan wanted to work in a calling; we are forced to do so. For when asceticism was carried out of monastic cells into everyday life, and began to dominate worldly morality, it did its part in building the tremendous cosmos of the modern economic order. This order is now bound to the technical and economic conditions of machine production which to-day determine the lives of all the individuals who are born into this mechanism, not only those directly concerned with economic acquisition, with irresistible force. Perhaps it will so determine them until the last ton of fossilized fuel is burnt. In Baxter's view the care for external goods should only lie on the shoulders of the 'saint like a light cloak, which can be thrown aside at any moment'. But fate has decreed that the cloak should become an iron cage.[52]

Marx's and Weber's descriptions of capitalist society are, indeed, remarkably similar in this and many other respects.[53]

It is also true that, in outlining the relationship between their respective methodologies, we not only have to specify which Marx we are addressing, but also which Weber. Thus, while the Weber of *The Protestant Ethic and the Spirit of Capitalism* may well be difficult to reconcile with a Marxian framework, his later works do not appear to be as antagonistic to the latter point of view.

Consider, as an example, Weber's account of the relationships between ideas, interests, and social action. The argument of the original essays on the Protestant ethic specifically claims that religious ideas exerted an independent influence on the direction of social action by giving the faithful a unique interest in methodical conduct in their everyday lives. Weber's thesis is, quite simply, that certain Protestant doctrines *caused* the rise of the modern capitalist mentality; they are the source of this mentality rather than a rationalization of it. 'Above all', he insists, 'this sort of religious ethic cannot be regarded as a reflex of economic conditions.'[54] Of course, Weber concedes, to argue this proposition is to focus only upon a single moment in the chain of causation. One aspect of the unfulfilled research scenario which he outlined at the end of the original essays was, in fact, 'to investigate how Protestant Asceticism was in turn influenced in its development and its character by the totality of social conditions, especially economic'.[55] That he did not doubt such an influence is really a matter beyond dispute:

For those to whom no causal explanation is adequate without an economic (or materialistic as it is unfortunately still called) interpretation, it may be remarked that I consider the influence of economic development on the fate of religious ideas to be very important and shall later attempt to show how in our case the process of mutual adaptation of the two took place. On the other hand, those religious ideas themselves simply cannot be deduced from economic circumstances. They are in themselves, that is beyond doubt, the most powerful plastic elements of national character, and contain a law of development and a compelling force entirely their own.[56]

Thus, while Weber is not seeking 'to substitute for a one-sided materialistic an equally one-sided spiritualistic causal interpretation of culture and history',[57] nevertheless it is his claim that, without ascetic Protestantism, the capitalist mentality of the modern era would not have developed the methodical, systematic, and originally ascetic characteristics that it displayed in parts of Western Europe during the seventeenth century; and, as the comparison with China and India suggests, the absence of such an ethic would, in all probability, have exerted a profound influence on the direction of subsequent economic development. The argument of the original essays seems, in short, to challenge directly at least one accepted version of the Marxian framework.

The challenge is not so readily apparent, however, in Weber's later study of 'The sociology of religion'. A complete exposition of Weber's argument is clearly beyond the scope of the present essay since his objective here is no less than a systematic exploration of the distinctive theological characteristics of Christianity as compared to the other 'great religions' of the world, a brief which leads him to consider, among other things, the religious objectives of diverse theologies, the prescribed means by which believers may attain these, the structure and organization of religious communities, and the possible political, sexual, artistic, and economic consequences of certain religious ethics. What should be noted, however, is that Weber explicitly investigates 'the other side of the causal chain' – the influence of social and material life on religious phenomena – by emphasizing the ways in which different theologies are suited to the respective existential needs and everyday situations of various social strata. Theodicies of dominance, mobility, and escape are appropriate to the needs and positions of elites, the middle classes (or 'civic strata'), and disprivileged strata (peasantry, urban lower classes, and pariah groups) respectively. He claims, as an example, that 'Other things being equal, strata with high social and economic privilege will scarcely be prone to evolve the idea of salvation. Rather, they assign to religion the primary function of *legitimising* their own life pattern and situation in the world.'[58] Thus the caste system and Hinduism generally are interpreted by Weber to be, in large part, the creation of a Brahman elite which sought principally to justify and perpetuate its privileged position – an interpretation which leads certain commentators to the conclusion that Weber's view of the relationship between 'material interests' and 'religious ideas' is, in fact, somewhat closer to that of Marx than might be suspected from the original thesis about the consequences of the Protestant ethic.[59]

Weber's concept of 'elective affinity', according to some, carries him further in the same direction. While the precise meaning of his argument is rendered obscure by his inconsistent usage of this concept,[60] Weber seems, by suggesting an 'elective affinity' between Protestant teachings and the capitalist mentality, to be claiming only that there is a 'convergence' or 'resonance' between the ideas expressed in the former and the interests implicit in the latter, and not that the Protestant ethic actually created and explains the nature of the modern capitalist world-view. The demonstration of such an 'elective affinity', critics maintain, 'is not in itself sufficient for the isolation of causes'.[61] Rather, it merely suggests that

as soon as a group of adherents is attracted to a particular idea or ethical system, which in origin is purely concerned with problems of salvation and ultimate meaning, they will begin to 'elect' those features of the original idea with which they have an 'affinity' or 'point of coincidence'. . . . Ideas that have been selected and reinterpreted from the original doctrinal formulation eventually tend to establish an affinity with the material interests of particular social strata. Furthermore, ideas that do not establish such an affinity are likely to be discarded.[62]

The argument of *The Protestant Ethic and the Spirit of Capitalism* can then be interpreted in a manner which renders it strikingly similar to the Marxist account of the Calvinist ethic–spirit of capitalism relationship:

Weber's thesis is that the fundamental *existential problem* facing the entrepreneur in the early stages of capitalism was to justify or explain why he regarded success in business as a calling worthy of his great devotion and virtually total commitment. Thus, according to Weber, the entrepreneur would welcome any belief system, and a means to express it, that would provide a rationale for his own deepest commitments. Indeed, such a belief system would be one for which he could hold a deep and abiding elective affinity. The Protestant ethic, according to Weber, was just such a belief system, one which could give expression to the essence and strivings of the entrepreneurial capitalist.[63]

Behaviour which had previously only been tolerated was now ideologically justified. 'The Protestant ethic did not serve so much to confer rationality upon enonomic activity as to give the bourgeois the feeling that their way of life was legitimate.'[64]

While it must be conceded that these and similar related issues make the relationship between Marx's and Weber's account of the connection between the Protestant and capitalist minds a matter of considerable complexity, and one which cannot be fully explored here, nevertheless they are not sufficient to undermine the claim made earlier that the respective positions adopted by these theorists are, ultimately, irreconcilable. It is true, as Runciman points out, that

Weber never attempts to formalize his implicit theory of the relation between substructure and superstructure; it tends either to be stated baldly as a fact ('*es konnte nicht ausbleiben dass...*') or expounded in terms of metaphors, such as ideas being 'stamped' (*geprägt*) by the substructure or in turn functioning as 'signalmen' (*Weichensteller*) who decide along which ideological tracks material interests will be shunted.[65]

But this is precisely because, as an *a priori* proposition, Weber denies all forms of necessary determinism in the social sphere. Empirical research alone can establish, in each instance, whether ideas exert a direct and independent influence on social action (as in the case of ascetic Protestantism and economic conduct); function in the legitimation of social institutions or structures and hierarchies of dominance (as they appear to have done at various times in Chinese and Indian history); or, as in the case indicated by Runciman, serve to refract interests in the manner of 'switchmen'. All three situations are empirical possibilities. (And neither the categories nor the situations are mutually exclusive.)

Moreover, even if it is conceded that Protestant doctrines granted the bourgeoisie a 'vocabulary' or 'rhetoric' in terms of which they might justify the systematic accumulation of capital, this does not disprove the thesis that the latter is the consequence of the former and, therefore, may be said to have been caused by it (if only in part). The 'rhetorics (or vocabularies) of motive' which are implied in any ideology can have a causal as well as a legitimating significance. Social actors are aware that they might be required to justify their actions to various groups of significant others. Precisely because social actions are social and involve or affect others, and because actors are generally held to be responsible for these, they may be called to account for them. But the 'legitimations' that are offered in such accounts are not exclusively ex post facto 'rationalizations'. Actors may, or course, retrospectively excuse their activities in terms other than those which, in reality, provided the motivational impetus behind them. But social action and social dialogue do not generally take this form and it seems implausible that the nascent bourgeoisie of the seventeenth century collectively lied on the scale required by the Marxist interpretation of the Calvinist ethic–spirit of capitalism relationship. In the absence of ascetic Protestantism, as Weber claims, capitalists could not reasonably have accounted for their economic practices, and since the religious ideas in question cannot be reduced to or deduced from the class interest and position of these individuals, it can fairly be claimed that Protestant teaching caused the rise of the modern capitalist mentality. In the absence of the former, the latter would not have developed in the direction in which both Weberians and Marxists agree that it did.[66]

Marxists would, of course, contest this whole argument on the grounds that it rests on the mistaken premise that Marxist theory denies any significance to actors' accounts of their own practices except as retrospective legitimations for conduct which in reality arises out of entirely different factors. But at this point we are back where we started, namely, with our claim that Marxist and Weberian frameworks are ultimately irreconcilable. In the particular example in question, suggestions of 'false consciousness' or 'objective interests' by the former clash with the Weberian principle most concisely expressed in the famous aphorism of W. I. Thomas, 'if men define situations as real, they are real in their consequences'. While both Weber and Marx would accept that social actors do treat complexes of subjective meaning as adequate grounds for social conduct, and do act in accordance with these, Marx's claim that such conduct can be the result of an 'ideological' reading of an underlying objective situation and is therefore irreducibly of a material or class nature in origin would certainly be contested by Weber. Without abandoning fundamental postulates on one side or the other – that is, surrendering either the independent causal role of ideas, or the priority of the economic sphere – the two perspectives cannot be reconciled. Weber, after an early flirtation with evolutionary perspectives in studies such as his *Roman Agrarian History*, developed and sustained a sophist-icated critique of evolutionism and determinism, including those versions of these doctrines which, in my understanding, must be central to any Marxist framework.[67]

Ultimately, then, whatever the substantive similarities that may be identified in their respective empirical and historical analyses, there remains an unbridgeable epistemological gap between the Marxian and Weberian frameworks. Weber's insistence on the logical and methodological separation of fact and value cannot be reconciled with Marx's epistemology of *praxis*. The latter's philosophy of history, whatever the precise nature of the 'determinism' that operates between the productive and other spheres of social life, makes a claim to answer scientifically questions about the meaning and objectives of the course of history. Weber, on the other hand, can have no truck with an epistemology which does not concede the irreducibility of competing values. 'Science today', he insists,

is a 'vocation' organised in special disciplines in the service of self-clarification and knowledge of interrelated facts. It is not the gift of grace of seers and prophets dispensing sacred values and revelations, nor does it partake of the contemplation of sages and philosophers about the meaning of the universe. This, to be sure, is the inescapable condition of our historical situation. We cannot evade it so long as we remain true to ourselves. And if Tolstoi's question recurs to you: as science does not, who is to answer the question: 'What shall we do, and, how shall we arrange our lives?' or, in the words used here tonight: 'Which of the warring gods should we serve? Or should we serve perhaps an entirely different god, and who is he?' then one can say that only a prophet or a savior can give the answers.[68]

Perhaps it is the similarity between the promises held out by Calvin and Marx, and Weber's timely reminder that a belief-system may grow to have a direction and consequences of which the original prophet would wholly have disapproved, that makes generations of Marxists turn again and again to comment upon and contest Weber's Protestant ethic thesis and so help keep controversy alive. But speculations such as this should properly be reserved for another occasion.

Weberology and teleology

There remains, finally, the matter of what will here be called 'the Parsonsian legacy' to the debate about Weber's Protestant ethic thesis. Too much should not be read into this choice of terminology since the legacy in question is intellectual rather than substantive, and comprises only a certain continuity of perspective on Weber's sociology, such that Parsonsian designs upon it are perpetuated.

It is widely acknowledged that Talcott Parsons's claim to have identified in Weber's work an underlying trend towards developing a systematic theory of social action (and, incidentally, a convergence with Durkheim and Pareto at this point) cannot be substantiated. Parsons's 'convergence thesis', and in particular his 'completion' of Weber's 'fragmentary ideal-types' into a unified theoretical whole, rests upon his reading into Weber's methodology certain tendencies and an overall direction which simply are not there. Parsons's resultant 'General Theory of Action' represents a type of universalistic and organological approach to the study of social reality of which Weber was, in fact, explicitly critical in his methodological essays.[69]

One other acknowledged problem with Parsonsian theory is its ahistoricity. Parsons, especially in his later 'developmental' or 'evolutionary' works, writes as if societies as divergent as the hunting and gathering groups of the Kalahari, on the one hand, and the contemporary United States, on the other, can be analysed using exactly the same conceptual, theoretical, and explanatory framework. In his judgement, the social and general action processes at work in the latter are simply more developed versions of those comprising the former. By comparison, of course, Weber is historically senstive, denies the possibility of universalistic laws in historical explanation, and seeks instead only to identify the 'adequate causes' for historically specific configurations or events.[70]

To speak of a 'Parsonsian legacy' to the discussion about Weber's thesis, then, is to claim that, while almost all of the commentators to be mentioned below would deny the utility of Parsonsian theory *per se*, and in all probability would contest his interpretation of Weber, nevertheless they embody the spirit of the Parsonsian approach to Weberian sociology by perpetuating both of these tendencies. Weber's Protestant ethic thesis is, in other words, 'universalized' and made 'ahistorical' in ways which Weber never envisaged it should. A few examples of these approaches are given in the following paragraphs. They are offered more or less without comment, certainly without documented criticism, since the argument against such interpretations is nothing less than the substance of this essay itself. The present text returns to a fairly old-fashioned interpretation of Weber's thesis, pointing as it does to the temporal and geographical specificity of the argument, its precise intellectual origins in an internal controversy about 'economic ethics' or world-views, and the difficulties involved in subjecting Weber's extremely particularized proposition to empirical examination. The points of contention about which this and any of the following interpretations diverge will be obvious.

The march of rationalization

One of the major strands of the Parsonsian legacy to Weberian sociology generally is represented by an ongoing search to find a common theme underlying Weber's apparently fragmented contribution to the study of social existence. Discussion of his particular essays on 'The Protestant ethic and the spirit of capitalism' therefore proceeds on the assumption that these must be related systematically to Weber's wider sociology before they can properly be understood. A number of closely similar interpretations of Weber's 'Protestant ethic thesis' have been offered in this context and, for the sake of convenience, these will be treated generically here, as being commonly 'teleological'. This label, it will be remembered, was introduced in Chapter 2. Its use with respect to the following commentaries on Weber's essays implies nothing beyond a broad recognition that, in such interpretations, the initial argument about the economic conse-quence of the Protestant ethic is viewed as being the opening tactic in a more grandly conceived Weberian strategy of outlining a comparative history of cultures, in preference to its being read as a specific response to the writings of Weber's immediate predecessors. (It was suggested at the outset, of course, that the latter 'chronological' approach more accurately identified the origins of Weber's argument and, more importantly, offered a better and more fruitful understanding of its peculiar structure and characteristics.)

Currently one of the most fashionable of the 'teleological' readings of Weber's argument is that which finds one, or even *the*, underlying thread in Weber's thought to lie in the priority he supposedly accords to an autonomous process of 'rationalization' in the sphere of religion. In Tenbruck's[71] version of this thesis, for example, it is observed that Weber outlines the progressively rational solutions that are adopted by men and women seeking to solve the problem of theodicy. As the charismatic figures of primitive religions proved fallible in eliminating suffering and misfortune, so progressively more encompassing solutions were offered, each transcending its predecessor by attempting to unify more and more of the isolated events of reality into a systematic world-view capable of offering an explanation for all of the miseries of humanity. In this way religions develop an inner logic of their own. They unfold by following an autonomously developing course of rationalization, each stage being logically consistent with, but more comprehensive than, its predecessor, a process evident in the progressive rationalization of Christian teachings which accomplished the gradual 'de-magification' of the world and culminated in the ruthless logic of the Calvinist doctrine of predestination. Calvinism itself, by creating the ethos of worldly asceticism, and thence of modern capitalism, paved the way for the increasing rationalization of the modern world in non-religious directions and spheres. Weber's sociology therefore offers a strong counter-thrust to the Marxian view of history which sees reality as being progressively rationalized, wholly in the direction of economic interests. In Weber's view, by comparison, religious developments are held to be more than a simple reflection of material interests; indeed, they advance according to a logic of their own and have an independent influence on the direction of practical conduct. In accounting for the sequence of historical processes, attention is in this way focused on the 'transformative capacities' of religion; in short, on the independent role of ideology in determining the overall direction of historical change.

A number of commentators have interpreted Weber's essays on the Protestant ethic along more or less similar lines.[72] Despite the many important internal differences between their respective accounts, details of which cannot be investigated here, they may fairly be classified together since they share a broadly common perspective (based on a one-sided rendering of Weber's sociology of religion) with which this essay is clearly in disagreement.

First, by reading Weber's *Religionssoziologie* as if he had written all of his essays at the same time (commencing with the retrospective 'Introduction' of 1920) and for the solitary purpose of attributing the 'rationalization' of life in the West to developments in the religious sphere, they arrive at a 'spiritualistic' interpretation of his Protestant ethic thesis which Weber himself openly repudiated and which has been contested in the chapters above. From the reasonable suggestion that Weber was arguing to the effect that, in specific instances, ideas may develop under the thrust of their own logic to their point of rational internal consistency and, in so doing, affect the course of social action and historical events generally, the unreasonable conclusion is drawn that the rise of the West is mainly to be understood as a product of a rationalization process at the level of religious ideas. In the opinion of Kolko, for example, Weber's objective was to establish 'universally relevant historical laws'. Accordingly, having once identified the causal importance of the Protestant ethic, he 'made his position increasingly untenable by declaring that the Ethic was not merely a necessary condition of rationalized institutions but also a sufficient condition regardless of other factors'. His Protestant ethic thesis is offered as a 'causal law of history' which asserts that Calvinism is '*the* causal factor' in the history of the modern West. In short, according to Kolko,

> the Protestant Ethic serves as the equivalent of a historical prime mover, a Geist, similar in function to those deeply embedded in the German philosophical tradition. . . . Weber in reality proposes a comprehensive historical law which does not include all *relevant* historical events which the verification of any law must incorporate. There was, after all, a Renaissance in Europe, the development of stable currency, advanced bookkeeping, free labor, capital accumulation, basic technology, etc, before Calvin, and this too suggests at least the possibility of alternative theories which Weber did not discuss.[73]

What status now are we to accord to Weber's lengthy discussions, in *General Economic History, Economy and Society,* and indeed in his 'Replies' to the German critics of the essays of 1905, of the diverse economic, technological, political, administrative, and social-structural origins of modern capitalist society? Only by reading these texts in a very peculiar way can we arrive at the conclusion that Weber offers an idealistic or emanationist theory of history.

This is not to deny that Weber's sociology of religion does contain a discussion of autonomous processes of religious rationalization; his essays on 'The social psychology of the world religions' and 'Religious rejections of the world and their directions' are notable in this respect. But, and this is really the gist of his argument in *The Protestant Ethic and the Spirit of Capitalism* and *The Sociology of Religion*, Weber was insistent that ideas become significant in history and are causally effective in shaping social conduct because, at certain points, a class or status group with specific material or ideal interests takes up, sustains, and develops these ideas, and is influenced by them. He accepts, as we have seen, that ideas are both shaped by and, in turn, help shape interests and action. As a general principle, however, the 'inner logic' of their development does not proceed independently of all other spheres of social reality.

Secondly, and partly as a result of this common tendency towards an idealistic interpretation of his sociology, these authors are inclined to conflate Weber's separate arguments about the origins of the spirit of capitalism, and of modern capitalistic economic development *per se*, into a unitary thesis about the origins and consequences of the rationalization of life in the West. Particular emphasis is placed on Weber's 'Author's introduction' to the *Religionssoziologie* series, and on the aforementioned essays on 'The social psychology of the world religions' and 'Religious rejections of the world'. These pieces are approached as if they were declarations of intent by Weber to the effect that he was bent on investigating the totality of the ramifications of rationalization processes in the West – in architecture, music, art, science, government, economic life – and his essays on the Protestant ethic were simply a preliminary attempt to show how rational capitalism in its economic aspects is essentially a product of the Reformation. Luethy, for example, maintains that

only in the whole context of his monumental, labyrinthine, and tormented work does Max Weber's thesis achieve its complete and subtle meaning ... in this context the words 'capitalism' or 'spirit of capitalism' are used in a very particular sense: they mean no less than the entire inner structure governing Western society's attitudes, not only its economy but also its legal system, its political structure, its institutionalised sciences and technology, its mathematically-based music and architecture. Its economic modes of operation, works discipline, and accountancy methods are all regarded by him as the mere *pars per toto* of a whole civilization-type for which Weber's final word is rationality – a rationality which permeates all fields of social behaviour, the organisation of labour and management as well as the creative sciences, law and order, philosophy and the arts, the state and politics, and the dominant forms of private life. This rationality, driven by its own internal dynamic, has overthrown (or tamed) every form of resistance offered by pre-rational human nature, magic and tradition, instinct and spontaneity. Finally with the Reformation, it has forced its way into the innermost temple wherein the motives behind human behaviour are generated, into the very heart of religious belief, there to destroy all the dark, magical, mysterious tabernacles – image, cult, and tradition – for which it substitutes the Bible as the authentic truth, supposedly unshakeable, accessible to critical examination, and susceptible of proof.

This is what the Reformation means for Weber. . . .[74]

Such an interpretation rests upon our reading the chronological sequence of Weber's writings on religion and the rise of capitalism backwards and, more importantly, it obscures the fact that the explanandum of his initial essays is neither modern capitalism itself, nor the rationality of Occidental life in all its aspects, but is, quite specifically, the particular 'spirit of modern capitalist economic practice'.[75] Weber readily concedes that, given the importance of the economic sphere in contemporary capitalist societies, the 'process of rationalisation in the field of technique and economic organisation undoubtedly determines an important part of the ideals of life of modern bourgeois society'. But the development of the spirit of modern capitalism cannot be understood as being merely one aspect of a march towards rationalism as a whole, in all spheres of social existence. It is evident, to Weber,

that such a simple way of putting the question will not work, simply because of the fact that the history of rationalism shows a development which by no means follows parallel lines in the various departments of life. The raionalization of private law, for instance . . . was achieved in the highest hitherto known degree in the Roman law of late antiquity. But it remained most backward in some of the countries with the highest degree of economic rationalization, notably in England. . . . In fact, one may – this simple proposition, which is often forgotten, should be placed at the beginning of every study which essays to deal with rationalism – rationalize life from fundamentally different basic points of view and in very different directions. Rationalism is an historical concept which covers a whole world of different things.[76]

He is not, therefore, seeking to describe or explain the dimensions and development of rationalism as a whole. Rather, his limited and specific objective is 'to find out whose intellectual child the particular concrete form of rational thought was, from which the ideas of a calling and the devotion to labour in the calling has grown'.[77] It was, according to Weber, the child of ascetic Protestantism.

It is true, of course, that Weber suggests the Protestant Reformation had consequences other than those pertaining to people's attitudes towards economic activity. In the second part of the programme for future research that is spelled out at the end of the essays on the Protestant ethic, he makes it clear that, having related the Protestant world-view to bourgeois capitalistic practices,

The next task would be . . . to show the significance of ascetic rationalism, which has only been touched in the foregoing sketch, for the content of practical social ethics, thus for the types of organization and the functions of social groups from the conventicle to the State. Then its relations to humanistic rationalism, its ideals of life and cultural influence; further to the development of philosophical and scientific empiricism, to technical development and to spiritual ideals would have to be analysed. Then its historical development from the mediaeval beginnings of worldly asceticism to its dissolution into pure utilitarianism would have to be traced out through all the areas of ascetic religion. Only then could the quantitative cultural significance of ascetic Protestantism in its relation to the other plastic elements of modern culture be estimated.[78]

Weber's scattered attendant remarks, in the original essays, concerning the possible political, sexual, and artistic implications of Protestant 'worldly asceticism' and its relationship to the development of the exact sciences, are pursued at marginally greater length in his 'Sociology of religion' essay and 'Introduction' of 1920, and incidentally throughout the comparative studies of the world religions, but nowhere in his subsequent studies does he attempt seriously to pursue the task outlined in 1905.

It is, therefore, difficult to see how we might justify the claim that Weber saw the 'Protestant ethic' in particular, or even 'inner-spiritual and cultural' factors in general, as all-embracing historical 'prime-movers'. Yet Luethy, like Kolko, claims that Weber describes the Protestant world-view

as though the essential thread had suddenly been discovered which would lead dialectically from the nailing of Luther's ninety-five theses on the Wittenberg church door to the assembly lines of Detroit and the ramifications of Standard Oil.[79]

Contrast Weber's declaration in his original essays (a statement which seems to have escaped Luethy's attention), that

the above sketch has deliberately taken up only the relations in which an influence of religious ideas on the material culture is really beyond doubt. It would have been easy to proceed beyond that to a regular construction which logically deduced everthing characteristic of modern culture from Protestant asceticism. But that sort of thing may be left to the dilettante who believes in the unity of the group mind and its reducibility to a single group formula.[80]

Clearly, to suggest that Weber attributes the development of, for example, 'positive science' and 'modern democracy' to rational Calvinist religiosity, is to extend his thesis even beyond the claims made in 1920, far less those put forward by the author of *The Protestant Ethic and the Spirit of Capitalism*.

New directions

Of course, some of the most exciting texts in what has come conventionally to be regarded as the 'Protestant ethic literature' have sought explicitly to go beyond Weber's initial insights. For example, Robert Merton's argument, well-known in sociological circles, regarding the relationship between Puritanism and the development of the sciences, is an intervention in a debate which, as Merton rightly observes, is in no way concerned to confirm or refute Weber's 'Protestant ethic thesis' (although Merton and many other participants acknowledge Weber's incidental contribution to discussion of the relationship in question). Most of the contributors to this particular literature are aware that attempts to connect Protestantism and the rise of science long precede Weber; that the latter's central concern is to explore the consequences of ascetic Protestantism in the realm of economic activity; and that the observed relationship of the Reformation to the development of 'positive science' need have no necessary implications for the correctness or otherwise of 'Weber's thesis'. Only a very few commentators have laboured under the misapprehension that, by investigating the relationship between Protestantism and 'scientific endeavour' either at the time of the Reformation or even in the world of today, they were somehow 'testing the Weber thesis'.[81]

Somewhat less discerning are the studies related to Gerhard Lenski's influential work on the 'the religious factor' in the modern United States. Lenski himself makes it clear that the temporal parameters of Weber's argument about the Protestant ethic specifically exclude the possibility of its being tested in twentieth-century America. His target is not Weber, but rather those 'positivists' and 'determinists' (Comte and Marx are mentioned) who would deny the significance of religion in the modern world, and who viewed it as a rapidly declining social force.[82] Against this alleged thrust of progressive secularization, Lenski presents survey data, which in his view uphold what he takes to be the general Weberian and Durkheimian principle that religion will continue, even in the economically advanced areas of the world, to exert an independent influence on such things as political, economic, familial, and educational orientations and practices.

Lenski's reading of the classical theorists is not at issue here. What is important, from our point of view, is that his findings generated a whole industry in North American 'Protestant ethic studies'. Endless replications and extensions of his arguments confirmed or contested relationships between self-professed religiosity or Church affiliation, on the one hand, and, on the other, a range of dependent variables which included intergenerational and intragenerational mobility, educational achievement and aspirations, personal income, occupational classification, and 'achievement motivation'. The operationalization procedures utilized in many of these studies are questionable. For example, researchers identified 'the Protestant ethic' with a declared nominal affiliation to any Protestant denomination, and equated Weber's explanandum with 'entrepreneurial success' as measured by intergenerational mobility, or with 'rational control orientation' as measured by 'the Personal Powerlessness Subscale of Seeman's Index of Dimensions of Alienation'. Quite apart from this and other shortcomings, however, it is evident that some of the contributors to the debate were unfamiliar with the possibility that, since time passes, causal and other relational propositions may have an historical specificity. It is difficult otherwise to explain the fact that, although the majority of commentators seem to follow Lenski and are aware that it is *his* propositions to which their remarks are addressed, a substantial minority appear to believe that, by investigating the relationship between Church affiliation and socio-economic achievement in North America in the late twentieth century, they are executing a direct test of 'Weber's Protestant ethic thesis'.[83]

'Weber's thesis' has also been widely discussed in the general context of the possibility that 'ideologies' may have implications for the propensity of adherents to engage in practices which are conducive to 'modernization' or 'economic development' in the so-called 'Third World' countries of today. Here again his argument about the consequences of Protestant asceticism has been used in ways which range from the entirely legitimate to the wholly outrageous. Economists of development have long cited Weber in support of propositions dear to the German historical economists of the nineteenth century: namely, that a range of social, legal, cultural, political, symbolic, familial, and other 'non-economic' factors play an important and often fundamental role in stimulating or hindering economic growth; and that, among such factors, 'ideology' ranks high, since people's propensity to save, work, reinvest, and consume – in short the whole spectrum of their economic orientations and conduct – depends in part upon the meaning that they attribute to economic activities. Political, nationalistic, and religious ideologies can therefore play a significant part in shaping certain processes related to economic development since they may alter significantly people's orientations towards the world of work and wealth.[84] André Gunder Frank is, of course, correct in his assertion that some of these commentators pursue this argument to a position of untenable idealism, since they appear to claim that economic development in contemporary less-developed countries can be wholly internally generated by the simple devices of creating an 'achievement-oriented' elite or business community, and a disciplined labour-force with a positive motivation to work. As Frank points out, neither 'The Protestant ethic' nor any latter-day functional equivalent is capable of generating autonomously a process of self-sustained economic growth, simply through creating a mass 'need for achievement'. The role of foreign trade and aid, the structure of market and power relationships, and the long histories of colonial exploitation cannot be overlooked in explaining 'underdevelopment'. Moreover, where economic theorists of development have in fact acknowledged the structural context of underdevelopment, they have tended to assume *a priori* that foreign trade, aid, and imports of Western technology and capital are necessarily beneficial to the recipients, an assumption upon which Frank and his followers have rightly cast doubts.[85] Less palatable is Frank's dismissal of Weber's thesis on the grounds that it cannot explain the current underdevelopment of large parts of Latin America, Africa, and the Far East. Weber's essays on the Protestant ethic do not offer 'a coherent theory of underdevelopment' for the simple reason that this was not Weber's purpose in writing them.[86]

Fascinating though these literatures are on the diverse relationships between the Reformation and the development of the sciences, between denominational affiliations and socio-economic achievement in the United States, and ideology and economic processes in lessdeveloped countries, they have nothing whatsoever to do with testing Weber's thesis about the relationship between the Protestant ethic and the spirit of capitalism. Participants in these debates may, of course, choose to generalize Weber's argument about the possible relationships between religious ideas, material interests, and economic conduct, and so explore the contemporary roles of nationalism, religion, and political philosophies in transforming everyday conduct. 'Functional equivalents' to the Protestant ethic may be identified and their roles investigated. Perhaps, as has been suggested, this is the direction which the whole controversy should now take.[87] The purpose of this essay is not to contest such a promising turn in the discussion; it is simply to suggest that, before extending the search for 'the spirit of capitalism' in new and undoubtedly worthwhile directions, we ought to be clear about the grounds on which such a quest is proceeding. Apologists and critics alike will, in future, have to be somewhat more discerning in their use of, and claims for, 'Weber's Protestant ethic thesis'.

7 Conclusion

The conclusions to which I have been moving steadily throughout this essay will by now be apparent. My broad appraisal of the controversy about Max Weber's Protestant ethic thesis is that the masterly argument of *The Protestant Ethic and the Spirit of Capitalism* has but sporadically been matched in quality during the course of the debate occasioned by this text. Despite certain quite significant weaknesses in Weber's essays, he presents a thesis that is sociologically sophisticated, historically specific, and – within the practical limitations imposed by extant data – open to empirical discussion. He attempts to deal theoretically, historically, and empirically with the complex relationships between social structures and processes, on the one hand, and, on the other, the actors who confront, interpret, and may transform specific social and historical realities. Few who have taken up Weber's argument have displayed his resourcefulness and skills. Working often with a crude and bastardized version of his thesis, most critics have pursued inadmissible data in the wrong times and places. Alternatively, many of Weber's supporters have eschewed the realm of the empirical altogether in favour of an 'internally generated' defence of his case, and have argued simply by assertion that, such is Weber's methodological achievement and so impressive is the scope of his comparative sociology, that his Protestant ethic thesis 'must' stand. Sociologists in particular have proceeded on the assumption that, if the specific criticisms raised by historians could be systematically eliminated as 'irrelevant' since they were found to be wanting in relation to Weber's 'wider methodological aims', then his thesis about the consequences of ascetic Protestantism would be vindicated on the grounds that all objections to it had been undermined. Rarely have sociologists themselves squared up to the empirical shortcomings of Weber's argument.

I hope that I have shown both aggressive and uninformed empiricism and a wholesale retreat into epistemological disputation – two methodological strategies which have characterized the debate thus far – to be equally unproductive from the point of view of resolving the major substantive issues raised by Weber's theses. As has been observed, parts of his argument seem to be empirically corroborated, other portions remain plausible but as yet unverified, while certain aspects would seem, in the absence of appropriate data, to be matters of methodological dispute and theoretical preference. From a non-partisan standpoint, therefore, we might see the whole 'Protestant ethic controversy' to have been dogged from the outset by the grinding of particular religious, political, or theoretical axes; by a widespread tendency to oversimplify Weber's argument through increasing reliance on inaccurate secondary expositions of it; and by the routine employment of certain rhetorical devices (mere assertion, unsub-stantiated generalization, setting up and demolishing of 'straw-men' alternatives to dogmatically held positions, and the polemical use of violent and powerful language itself) in order to disguise intellectual and empirical weaknesses in some of the arguments being proposed and defended.

In sum, after nearly three-quarters of a century of sustained research, commentary, and debate, we are scarcely better placed now than were combatants at the outset to offer informed arbitration between those who view Weber's account of the economic conse-quences of ascetic Protestantism as an immensely important and durable insight into the history of Western capitalist society, and those for whom it remains an imaginative but wholly unsubstantiated flight of speculation.

This is not to say that we have learned nothing from the controversy itself. Among the more obvious practical lessons, for example, attention might be drawn to the evident necessity of familiarizing oneself directly with the arguments of those whom one is intent upon criticizing. Other virtues clearly underwritten would seem to be those of intellectual honesty and modesty: honesty regarding the limitations of one's own research, for example, and modesty concerning the scope of the claims and generalizations that are based upon it. Moreover, whatever the epistemological difficulties of distinguishing 'fact' and 'value', the Protestant ethic debate provides a clear warning against introducing personal theological or socio-political aspirations and values into discussions in the fields of historical and sociological analysis. Inevitably such intrusions serve merely to obscure the issues and mystify the events themselves. A dialogue between conflicting articles of faith expands the horizons of historical and sociological inquiry little if at all.

Above all else, however, there is an important methodological lesson to be drawn from the controversy and it is one which future generations of historians and sociologists would be ill advised to ignore. The debate may not have taught us a great deal about the economic motivation of late medieval and early modern businessmen and businesswomen, or the everyday lives of seventeenth-century Protestants, but it most certainly sounds an important warning with respect to the practice of sociology and history themselves. The clear message is that sociology and history must move forward together – or not at all.

This idea is, of course, scarcely original. Weber's own methodological writings affirm the inseparability of the two disciplines.[1] Moreover, while it would be erroneous to suggest that history and sociology were completely estranged during the heyday of institutional historiography and structural-functional sociology, nevertheless the extent to which they were developing as more or less self-contained spheres of intellectual activity can be gauged from the strength of the call for their 'reunion' that was to be heard when the positivistic orthodoxies of both disciplines were explicitly challenged from the late 1950s onwards. The timely plea of E. H. Carr fell on sympathetic ears in both camps: 'the more sociological history becomes, and the more historical sociology becomes, the better for both. Let the frontier between them be kept wide open for two-way traffic'.[2]

The controversy about Weber's Protestant ethic thesis can therefore be seen as a singularly apposite illustration of the need to take Carr's appeal to heart. Too many historians, bent on challenging Weber's argument, simply mined the economic and religious source materials of the sixteenth and seventeenth centuries for information that was in any way germane to the field of 'religion and capitalism', without first pausing to consider the precise nature of Weber's arguments and the sorts of data that might be relevant in respect of them. The significance of their findings therefore remained, in many cases, entirely obscure – at least from the point of view of Weber's theses. Most historians participating in the controversy forgot that aspects of reality become significant and worth knowing only in terms of a specific problem, issue, or framework of meaning. In short, they neglected the role of self-conscious and articulate theorizing in history. The crudely empiricist and unreflective nature of the principal historical interventions in the Protestant ethic controversy are a pertinent reminder of the weaknesses of an atheoretical or covertly theoretical history of the kind which is still prevalent in many quarters of the discipline today.[3]

Sociologists emerge from the debate with scarcely more credit. As has been observed, many retreated from the realm of the empirical entirely and defended Weber exclusively on methodological and epistemological grounds and in terms of his larger theoretical framework. Of course, a number of sociologists do refer to the specific historical processes at issue, but throughout they appear to have been operating with an epistemological and methodological double standard, whereby positivistic assumptions and procedures were to be scorned in the study and explanation of contemporary social reality but, when it came to utilizing historical materials, the most crude forms of positivism were unequivocally respectable. Thus, on the one hand, the problems of how sociologists might know the meaning of contemporary social actions for the agents involved became a matter of intense epistemological debate (witness the 'phenomenological revolution' and rise of epistemological 'anomie' or pluralism in the 1960s); while, on the other hand, the motivation of those involved in various mercantile and religious activities in past centuries was entirely unambiguous and readily transparent from the most meagre accounts of the forms taken by the activities themselves. The sociological contribution to the debate about Weber's text therefore serves to highlight the dangers of crudely positivistic historical sociology of the kind which is all too common elsewhere in the discipline. Goldthorpe, for example, contrasts Weber's theoretically informed interest in the 'specific historicity' of events past and present (part of what Goldthorpe takes to be the 'classic tradition' in sociology) with the uncritical deployment of historical 'facts' by practitioners of both the political right and left in defence of certain *a priori* and historicist theoretical frameworks claiming universal applicability:

not a few present-day sociologists seeking to work in the classic tradition would be well served by rather more 'inhibition', particularly in their use of history as derived from *secondary* sources. Most ironically one may observe writers (for example on the New Left) who would be among the first to decry survey-based research as 'positivistic', themselves displaying at least as crude a positivism in treating the 'facts' contained in historical works as if they were something like stamps or butterflies to be diligently collected, arranged in attractive patterns and then displayed for admiration. But such facts must always be understood as simply *inferences* – the most interesting being usually the most complex and debatable – drawn from the 'relics' at the historian's disposal. The methodological basis of any kind of historical sociology wholly or largely reliant upon secondary sources should, I believe, be regarded as no less problematical and as requiring no less critical scrutiny than that, say, of the most ambitious mathematical or quantitative sociology.[4]

In short, therefore, the discussions in history and sociology about Max Weber's Protestant ethic thesis should be studied by all who seek to illuminate the nature of the relationships between the two disciplines, and to lay bare the foundations of a truly 'historical sociology' or 'social history'. Indeed, it is at precisely this point that participants in the controversy have made their most positive and original contribution, since their sterile exchanges point to the conclusion that even Carr's prescriptions for cross-disciplinary co-operation are too conservative. The implication of Carr's analysis is that history and sociology are to be viewed as distinct practices with an identifiable boundary between them – across which, of course, Carr wishes to see a great deal more traffic. Certainly, as Carr and countless others have pointed out, the past cannot be viewed as 'just one damn thing after another'. Historians who see their task to be the accumulation and reporting, in strict chronological sequence, of the 'facts' of the past 'as it really happened', simply theorize implicitly and informally and, therefore, obscurely and naïvely. But in recognizing that histories are interpretations of the world couched in terms of particular frames of reference, we ought not to be misled into suggesting that historians can turn to sociology for their theoretical salvation, as if the latter discipline were an 'already constituted' and 'theoretically mature' science. Sociological theories, models, or concepts cannot be collected and pasted – like stamps – on to complex historical realities, since these theories and concepts are themselves problematic, as is only too obvious from the discussions that bear testimony to the recent 'crisis in Western sociology'. Historians, in other words, must do their own theorizing.[5]

Similarly, too many sociologists simply pay lip-service to the past by prefacing their – otherwise ahistorical – accounts of contemporary social structures and actions with an entirely separate and unrelated section entitled 'Historical background'. It is not simply the case, as Carr implies, that these recalcitrants must take more account of the interpretations of the past that are offered by their historical colleagues. Rather than accept the secondary accounts proffered by historians as non-problematic 'data', sociologists must investigate the historical sources themselves, and with the same scepticism and articulation of theory as they might normally be expected to apply to the study of contemporary social processes and phenomena.

What can be learned from the controversy about Weber's Protestant ethic, therefore, is that both sociology and history share common objectives: to uncover the meaning of social actions and relationships as agents participate in these and, via comparative analysis, to arrive at causal explanations of these actions, of social structures and processes, and of the course of social change in the development of civilizations. History and sociology cannot be treated as if they represent self-contained approaches for investigating entirely different and unrelated aspects of social reality. The differences between them are neither of kind nor even, I would suggest, of degree. Because they appreciated this, sociologists of the 'classic tradition' made a crucial observation, forgetfulness of which has led many into the wilderness of structural-functionalism and phenomenology: they recognized that sociology was an historical discipline. And, in the words of Fustel de Coulange: 'History is not the accumulation of events of all kinds which occurred in the past. It is the science of human societies.' It is, in short, sociology. The administrative error, because of which the two groups of practitioners currently pursue the same objectives in the separate contexts of discrete literatures and departments, ought to be rectified as a matter of urgency.

Appendix

Chronology of Weber's principal writings in translation

German original		English translation	
1894	'Entwickelungstendenzen in der Lage der ostelbischen Landarbeiter', *Preussische Jahrbücher*, 77, pp. 437–73	1979	'Developmental tendencies in the situation of East Elbian rural labourers', *Economy and Society*, 8, pp. 172–205
1896	'Die sozialen Gründe des Untergangs der antiken Kultur', *Die Wahrheit*, 6, pp. 57–77	1950	'The social causes of the decay of ancient civilization', *Journal of General Education*, 5, pp. 75–88
1903–6	'Roscher und Knies und die logischen Probleme der historischen Nationalökonomie, *Jahrbuch für Gesetzgebung, Verwaltung und Volkswirtschaft im Deutschen Reich*, 27, pp. 1181–221; 29, pp. 1323–84; 30, pp. 81–120	1975	*Roscher and Knies: The Logical Problems of Historical Economics* (New York: Free Press)
1904	'Die "Objektivität" sozialwissenschaftlicher und sozialpolitischer Erkenntnis', *Archiv für*	1949	' "Objectivity" in social science and social policy', in Max Weber, *The Methodology of*

Year			English translation
			the Social Sciences, ed. E. A. Shils and H. A. Finch (New York: Free Press), pp. 49–112
1905	*Sozialwissenschaft und Sozialpolitik*, 19, pp. 22–87		See below (p. 178)
	'Die protestantische Ethik und der "Geist" des Kapitalismus', *Archiv für Sozialwissenschaft und Sozialpolitik*, 20, pp. 1–54; 21, pp. 1–110		
1906	' "Kirchen" und "Sekten" ', *Frankfurter Zeitung*, 13 April 1906; 15 April 1906		See below (p. 178)
	'Kritische Studien auf dem Gebiet der kulturwissenschaftlichen Logik', *Archiv für Sozialwissenschaft und Sozialpolitik*, 22, pp. 143–207	1949	'Critical studies in the logic of the cultural sciences', in Shils and Finch, op. cit., pp. 113–88
1907	'Kritische Bemerkungen zu den vorstehenden "Kritischen Beiträgen" ', *Archiv für Sozialwissenschaft und Sozialpolitik*, 25, pp. 243–9 [Reply to Fischer]		None available
	'R. Stammlers "Überwindung" der materialistischen Geschichtsauffassung', *Archiv für Sozialwissenschaft und Sozialpolitik*, 24, pp. 94–151	1977	*Critique of Stammler* (New York: Free Press)
1908	'Bemerkungen zu der vorstehenden "Replik" ', *Archiv für Sozialwissenschaft und Sozialpolitik*, 26, pp. 275–83 [Reply to Fischer]		None available

German original		English translation	
	'Die Grenznutzlehre und das "psychophysische Grundgesetz"', *Archiv für Sozialwissenschaft und Sozialpolitik*, 27, pp. 546–58	1975	'Marginal utility theory and "the fundamental law of psychophysics"', *Social Science Quarterly*, 56, pp. 21–36
	'Erhebungen über Auslese und Anpassung (Berufswahl und Berufsschicksal) der Arbeiterschaft der geschlossenen Grossindustrie' (Manuscript)	1971	'A research strategy for the study of occupational careers and mobility patterns: methodological introduction for the survey of the society for social policy concerning selection and adaptation (choice and course of occupation) for the workers of major industrial enterprises', in J. E. T. Eldridge (ed.) *Max Weber* (London: Nelson), pp. 103–55
	Unpublished fragment	1972	'Georg Simmel as sociologist', *Social Research*, 39, 155–63
1909	'Agrarverhältnisse im Altertum', *Handwörterbuch der Staatswissenschaften*, 3rd edn, 1, pp. 52–188	1976	*The Agrarian Sociology of Ancient Civilizations* (London: New Left Books)
1910	'Antikritisches zum "Geist" des Kapitalismus', *Archiv für Sozialwissenschaft und Sozialpolitik*, 30, pp. 176–202 [Reply to Rachfahl]		None available
	'Antikritisches Schlusswort zum "Geist des Kapitalismus"', *Archiv für Sozialwissen-*	1978	'Anticritical last word on "The spirit of capitalism", by Max Weber, *American*

Journal of Sociology, 83, pp. 1105–31
(translation incomplete)

1948 'The social psychology of the world religions', in H. H. Gerth and C. W. Mills (eds.), *From Max Weber: Essays in Sociology* (London: Routledge and Kegan Paul), pp. 267–301

1951 *The Religion of China: Confucianism and Taoism* (Glencoe, Ill.: Free Press)

1948 'Religious rejections of the world and their directions', in Gerth and Mills, op. cit., pp. 323–59

1958 *The Religion of India: The Sociology of Hinduism and Buddhism* (Glencoe, Ill.: Free Press)

1952 *Ancient Judaism* (Glencoe, Ill.: Free Press)

1949 'The meaning of "ethical neutrality" in Sociology and Economics', in Shils and Finch, op. cit., pp. 1–47

schaft und Sozialpolitik, 31, pp. 554–99 [Reply to Rachfahl]

1916–19 'Die Wirtschaftsethik der Weltreligionen: Religionssoziologische Skizzen'
– 'Einleitung'

– 'Der Konfuzianismus', I-IV

– 'Zwischenbetrachtung: Stufen und Richtungen der Religiösen Weltablehnung', *Archiv für Sozialwissenschaft und Sozialpolitik*, 41, pp. 1–87, 335–421

– 'Hinduismus und Buddhismus', I-III, *Archiv für Sozialwissenschaft und Sozialpolitik*, 41, pp. 613–744; 42, pp. 345–461, 687–814

– 'Das antike Judentum', I-II, *Archiv für Sozialwissenschaft und Sozialpolitik*, 44, pp. 52–138, 349–443, 601–26; 46, pp. 40–113, 311–66, 541–604

1917–18 'Der Sinn der "Wertfreiheit" der soziologischen und ökonomischen Wissenschaften', *Logos*, 8, pp. 40–88

German original	English translation
1919 'Wissenschaft als Beruf', 'Politik als Beruf', both in *Geistige Arbeit als Beruf: Vier Vorträge vor dem Freistudentischen Bund*, (München: Duncker und Humblot)	1948 'Science as a vocation', 'Politics as a vocation', in Gerth and Mills, op. cit., pp. 129–56, 77–128
1920 *Gesammelte Aufsätze zur Religionssoziologie – 1* (Tübingen: J. C. B. Mohr (Paul Siebeck). This is a collection of essays that were originally published in the *Archiv für Sozialwissenschaft und Sozialpolitik*, with a new introduction specially written for the compilation. It comprises:	
– 'Vorbemerkung' (1920)	1930 'Author's introduction', in Max Weber, *The Protestant Ethic and the Spirit of Capitalism*. London: Unwin
– 'Die protestantische Ethik und der "Geist" des Kapitalismus' (a slightly extended version of the essays of 1905, with additional footnotes, see above, p. 175)	1930 Weber, *The Protestant Ethic and the Spirit of Capitalism*, pp. 35–284
– 'Die protestantische Sekten und der Geist des Kapitalismus' (an extended version of the *Frankfurter Zeitung* articles of 1906, see above, p. 175)	1948 'The Protestant sects and the spirit of capitalism', in Gerth and Mills, op. cit., pp. 302–22
– 'Einleitung'; 'Der Konfuzianismus';	See above (p. 177)

'Zwischenbetrachtung' (the 'Introduction', study of Confucianism and Taoism, and 'Intermediate reflections', that form the first two articles in the 'Economic ethic of world religions' series, see above, p. 177)

1922	*Wirtschaft und Gesselschaft* (Tübingen: J. C. B. Mohr (Paul Siebeck), edited by Marianne Weber from Weber's papers after his death. Part 1 written 1918–20; Part 2 written 1910–14	1968	*Economy and Society*, 3 vols. (New York: Bedminster Press), incorporating segments earlier translated as *The Theory of Social and Economic Organization* (New York: Oxford University Press 1947); *Max Weber on Law in Economy and Society* (Cambridge, Mass.: Harvard University Press 1954); *The Sociology of Religion* (Boston: Beacon Press 1963); Gerth and Mills, op. cit., chs. 6, 7, 8 and 10; and other smaller fragments
1923	*Wirtschaftsgeschichte: Abriss der universalen Sozial- und Wirtschaftsgeschichte,* ed. S. Hellmann and M. Palyi, (München: Duncker und Humblot) compiled from lecture notes by Weber's students after his death	1923	*General Economic History* (London: Allen and Unwin)

Notes

1 Introduction

1 For example Hyma (1937, pp. 203, 226ff., 246), Samuelsson (1961, pp. 26, 151–4), and Dickens (1971, pp. 178–80).

2 A number of texts offering selected readings from the debate have appeared over the years, including Green (1965), Kitch (1967), Eisenstadt (1968a), Besnard (1970), and Seyfarth and Sprondel (1973). Among countless retrospective essays, Fischoff's (1944) and Nelson's (1973) reviews of the literature are exemplary, although the former is now slightly dated.

3 Good examples from the early literature are O'Brien (1923, pp. 170–80), Brodrick (1934), and Fanfani (1935), but more recently see Biéler (1961, pp. 477–514).

4 For example see Robertson (1933, p. xi) and Mandrou (1966, p. 106).

5 Parsons, for example, has consistently maintained this stance.

6 See, by way of illustration, the exchanges between Robertson (1933) and Parsons (1935), or Luethy (1964, 1965) and Nelson (1964). Means (1965) has also made this point forcefully, and suggests that sociologists are unaware of historical evidence which may present problems for Weber's argument because his thesis has attained the status, in sociological circles, of 'received doctrine' or 'an unanalyzed article of faith'.

7 George and George (1961, p. 74).

8 This is the origin of my own attempt (1980b), as a sociologist, to defend Weber against his historical critics, not on methodological grounds, but on the basis of empirical evidence pertaining to the frequently cited so-called 'refuting instance' of Scotland.

9 Masur (1963, pp. 192f.); see also Moore (1971).

10 See Roth (1975, p. 367).

11 White (1969, p. 197).

12 Of late, for example, Weber's thesis has spawned some fairly esoteric research, including a computerized semiotic analysis of the French translation of the original text itself, and an implausible attempt to identify the premises and practice of modern psychotherapy as the

legacy of Protestant dualism (Ankerl, 1972; Rotenberg, 1978). Any attempt to follow up literature such as this would clearly lead the present text to assume unacceptable proportions.

13   cf. Marshall (1979, 1980a).

14   The idiosyncratic and piecemeal manner in which Weber's texts have been translated into English has often served to obscure both their chronological and intellectual relationships to each other. See the Appendix on pages 174–9, which, it is hoped, will help the student locate the various translations in their original context.

15   Bruun (1972, p. 3).

16   For example, see Little (1970, pp. 1–22), Luethy (1965, p. 92), and Gilchrist (1969, pp. 122–39).

17   On the difficulties created by Weber's style of writing in general, see Marianne Weber (1975, pp. 309, 368) and Weyembergh (1971, p. xi). Ritualistic complaints about the difficulties of the text of the essays on the Protestant ethic pale somewhat when one considers the extent to which Weber's argument has been misrepresented over the years. On this point, compare Fischoff (1944, p. 70), Nelson (1973, p. 81), and Weber (1907, pp. 243, 245). Weber's critics themselves have often been guilty of holding several conflicting positions simultaneously. In the space of two pages, for example, Heaton (1963, pp. 220–21) succeeds in arguing first, that Weber's Protestant ethic thesis is correct, then that it is entirely wrong, and finally that it is correct in parts.

2   The spirit of modern capitalism – 1

1   Weber (1971, pp. 47f.).

2   ibid., pp. 48–50.

3   In fact the French and German editions of *The Protestant Ethic and the Spirit of Capitalism* also follow this format.

4   Marianne Weber (1975, pp. 57, 67ff.).

5   See Giddens (1972, pp. 28–30).

6   Moore (1977).

7   Weber (1971, pp. 191, 280).

8   ibid., p. 35.

9   ibid., p. 191. See also Weber (1910a, pp. 191f.; 1910b, p. 581). For additional discussions of the precursors of Weber who also postulated a relationship between Protestantism and capitalism, see Besnard (1970, pp. 7f.), Bendix and Roth (1971, pp. 299–310), M. Hill (1973, pp. 103f.), and Trevor-Roper (1963, p. 19), and for an assessment of Offenbacher's statistics and Weber's interpretation of them, see Turksma (1962, pp. 461–9). C. Hill (1966, pp. 131ff.), like Weber, concludes that 'It was a seventeenth-century commonplace that

Protestantism was peculiarly suited to a commercial and industrial community, and that popish religion created an unaptness for trade, hard work and accumulation.'

10   Goodman (1975), Cahnman (1964), Therborn (1976, pp. 272–95), and Burger (1976, pp. 140–53), among others, have previously explored Weber's contribution in the context of the *Methodenstreit*, but only from the point of view of locating the origins of his methodology for the social sciences, specifically the notion of ideal-types.

11   Oberschall (1965, p. 12). Some idea of how the various issues were and became intertwined can be gained from Sheehan's (1966) biography of a scholar who was involved in most of them, Lujo Brentano.

12   Principal among the other controversies of the day were those which arose out of discussions concerning the intellectual and institutional relationships between the various social sciences and humanities; the structure and methods of teaching in German universities; the role of values in the social sciences; the merits of economic liberalism and tariff protectionism as alternative economic strategies for German states; and the 'Working Class Question', where debate centred on the issues of support for various political parties, one's attitude towards socialism, trades unionism, government bureaucracy, and Prussian dominance in Germany.

13   Samuelsson (1961, pp. 50ff., 81ff., 151f.).

14   Weber (1971, pp. 152, 197). The nature of mercantilist theory is itself contentious. Useful overviews of the relevant issues can be found in Wilson (1958, 1967) and Coleman (1969). Mercantilists may well have started from the assumption of the rational self-maximizing economic actor, and with the avowed object of diverting this self-interest into the channels most appropriate to the 'national' or 'public' good (Clark 1972, pp. 28–9; Cunningham 1912–15, vol. 1, p. 562), but the extent to which their writings are descriptive rather than prescriptive is debatable. The writings of Thomas Mun, like those of many of his peers, both advocate and can be taken as symbols of the moral respectability of profits, but it was he too who wrote:

It is true indeed that many merchants here in England, finding less encouragement given to their profession than in other countries, and seeing themselves not so well esteemed as their noble vocation requires, and according to the great consequence of the same, do not therefore labour to attain unto the excellency of their profession; neither is it practised by the Nobility of this kingdom as it is in other states from the father to the son throughout their generations, to the great increase of their wealth and maintenance of their names and families. Whereas the memory of our richest merchants is suddenly extinguished; the son, being left rich, scorns the profession of his father, conceiving more honour to be a gentleman (although but in name), to consume his estate in dark ignorance and excess, than to follow the steps of his father as an industrious merchant to maintain and advance his fortunes. [Quoted in Stone 1965, pp. 128–9]

His was a complaint that is common in mercantilist texts. It is, therefore, at least as plausible to argue that economic theorizing or ideology is ahead of everyday economic practices, at this point, as it is vice versa (see Marshall 1980a).

15 Quoted in Appleby (1978, p. 7).

16 For an introduction to Smith's thought see Deane (1979) and the references given there.

17 See Deane (1979, pp. 84, 88, 92), and Gide and Rist (1915, pp. 393–5).

18 Gide and Rist (1915, p. 379).

19 Good introductions to the German Historical Schools of Economics can be found in Bell (1953, pp. 328–59) and Haney (1964, pp. 537–51).

20 Quoted in Therborn (1976, p. 306).

21 On List see Hoselitz (1965, pp. 195–205).

22 Quoted in Gide and Rist (1915, p. 382).

23 See Hoselitz (1965, pp. 205–10), Gide and Rist (1915, pp. 383f.).

24 See Bell (1953, pp. 336f.), Gide and Rist (1915, pp. 384f.).

25 Quoted in Gide and Rist (1915, pp. 400f.).

26 On the differences between the younger and older schools of German historical economics see Gide and Rist (1915, pp. 385ff.), Haney (1964, pp. 544ff.), and Hutchison (1953, pp. 180–5).

27 Gide and Rist (1915, pp. 389–98), Burger (1976, pp. 143–50), Hoselitz (1965, pp. 210–24).

28 Burger (1976, pp. 140–3).

29 See Bell (1953, pp. 426–9), Lachmann (1970, pp. 23–6).

30 For a discussion of these early studies see Roth's 'Introduction' to Weber (1968). (A *Habilitationsschrift* is a second dissertation required of those seeking permanent teaching posts in German universities.) Weber confirmed his non-determinist stance in subsequent studies of 'capitalism' in antiquity, addressing himself to the factors accounting for the decline of the large empires, and which distinguish the forms of economic organization typical of these societies from those that are peculiar to the rational capitalism of the West (see Weber, 1950, 1976).

31 A number of commentators have observed the intellectual continuity between Weber's East Elbian studies and his essays on the Protestant ethic. See, for example, Mommsen (1959, pp. 29ff.), Bendix (1969, ch. 2), Antoni (1962, pp. 128f., 148f.), and Giddens (1971, pp. 121ff.).

32 Weber, *Die Verhältnisse der Landarbeiter im ostelbischen Deutschland* (1892), cited in Lazarsfeld and Oberschall (1965, p. 186). For a complete bibliography of Weber's writings on agrarian labourers, see Käsler (1975), and for a concise summary of his argument, Weber (1970f).

33 See, for example, Weber (1972a) in Eldridge (1972, pp. 149ff.), Oberschall (1965, pp. 121f.), Schmidt (1976), and Eldridge (1971).

34 For references see Käsler (1975) and for a discussion Bendix (1969, ch. 2).

35 Weber (1971, pp. 51f., 193).

36 See Marianne Weber (1975, pp. 252f., 260).

37 Simmel (1978, pp. 204–80).

38 ibid., p. 232. This argument has been restated more recently by Kenneth Burke (1962, pp. 91–6).

39 Simmel (1978, p. 236).

40 ibid., p. 237.

41 ibid., p. 227.

42 ibid., p. 256.

43 Weber (1971, p. 51).

44 Weber (1972b, p. 161).

45 Unfortunately, Sombart's *Der Moderne Kapitalismus* remains untranslated, except in fragments. The English title *The Quintessence of Capitalism* is, confusingly, a translation of *Der Bourgeois* (1913).

46 Parsons (1928, p. 646) has rightly commented on the incomprehensibility of Sombart's insistence on distinguishing between these two systems, since the dominant characteristic of any system appears to be its spirit, and in this case both are possessed of practically the same spirit.

47 For additional material and commentary see Mitzman (1973, pp. 133–264), Knight (1928), and Hoselitz (1965, pp. 224–30).

48 These are mentioned briefly and in somewhat different fashion by Sutton (1965, pp. 326ff.) and Ashton (1954, pp. 57–62).

3 The spirit of modern capitalism – 2

1 Weber (1971, pp. 58f.).

2 Weber (1923, pp. 354f.); see also Weber (1970b, p. 296).

3 Weber (1971, pp. 60ff.).

4 ibid., pp. 66f.

5 ibid., p. 55.

6 Weber (1923, pp. 355f.); see also Weber (1907, p. 247; 1910b, p. 575; 1971, pp. 63f., 75f., 276).

7 Weber (1971, pp. 56f.).

8 ibid., p. 58; see also Weber (1910a, pp. 189f.).

9 Weber (1971, pp. 51, 56–8, 69, 73; 1968, p. 1118).

10 'I have finished Rickert. He is *very* good; in large part I find in him the thoughts that I have had myself, though not in logically finished form. I have reservations about his terminology.' (Letter from Weber to his wife, 1902, quoted in Marianne Weber, 1975, p. 260.)

11 For example see Jordan (1938), Bruun (1972), and Butts (1973).

12 Weber's concept of 'value-relevance' has been widely misrepresented. The best and most accurate exposition of his argument is offered by von Schelting (1934), whose interpretation is closely adhered to by Burger (1976).

13 Rickert (1902, 1962).

14 Rickert (1962, pp. 99f.).

15 Goldenweiser (1938, p. 627).

16 Weber (1969, pp. 76f., and in general pp. 68–85, 156–60).

17 Weber (1969, pp. 24f., 57, 81f., 84, 111, 135, 159; 1970e, pp. 147f., 152).

18 Weber (1969, pp. 72ff., 82ff.).

19 Weber (1968, pp. 4–22; 1969, pp. 164–88).

20 Compare the different evaluations of, for example, Sahay (1971, 1972) and Runciman (1972).

21 Compare, for example, the account that is offered here and in Marshall (1975, pp. 39–44), with the interpretations put forward by Blum (1944), Dawe (1971), Gouldner (1975), and Parsons (1971a).

22 On the former issue compare the radically systematizing approaches of von Schelting (1934), Weyembergh (1971), and Parsons (1968), with the different fractionizing stances adopted by Rex (1971), Antoni (1962), and Torrance (1974). On the possible relationships between Weber's methodological writings and his empirical studies in general compare the conclusions reached by Sahay (1972, pp. 38f.) and Parsons (1968, p. 503) with those of Turner (1974, p. 3) and Bendix (1946, p. 521).

23 Weber (1910a, pp. 181, 199; 1910b, pp. 566, 580f.; 1971, pp. 47f., 71, 200).

24 Weber (1907, pp. 247f.; 1910a, pp. 188–90, 201f.; 1910b, pp. 565f., 575, 596; 1923, pp. 334, 356; 1968, pp. 99, 164–6, 479f., 611–15, 629f., 1118; 1970a, p. 309; 1971, pp. 17, 19f., 53, 55f., 71f., 198f., 260, 276.

25 Weber (1910b, p. 569; 1971, p. 58).

26 Weber (1923, p. 357; 1971, pp. 73f.).

27 Weber (1971, pp. 74f., 55).

28 ibid., pp. 53f.

29 ibid., pp. 181f; see also ibid., pp. 54ff., 72f., 90f., 282, 283f., and Weber (1970a, pp. 312, 322).

30 Weber (1923, pp. 312–14).

31 ibid., pp. 275–8, 286, 341–3, and Weber (1971, pp. 17–27).

32 This point has also been made by Smelser (1976, pp. 119f.) and Baechler (1968, pp. 224–5).

33 Weber actually concedes this structure to his essays by posing both questions explicitly in a later article (1908, p. 280).

34 See Fischer (1968a, 1968b), Rachfahl (1968a, 1968b), and Brentano (1923).

35 Weber (1907, p. 243, 245; 1908, pp. 275; 1910a, pp. 192, 202; 1910b, pp. 554–9).

36 Weber (1907, p. 244; 1908, p. 277; 1910a, p. 200; 1910b, pp. 556f., 572, 579).

37 Weber (1907, p. 244; 1908, p. 277; 1910a, pp. 192, 197; 1910b, pp. 572, 597); see also Weber (1970a, p. 322; 1971, pp. 72f., 91f., 273f.).

38 Weber (1907, p. 246).

39 Weber (1971, pp. 55f., 90f., 186, 282, 283).

40 Weber (1910a, p. 201; 1910b, pp. 579ff., 597ff.).

41 Weber (1907, p. 246; 1910a, pp. 200f.; 1910b, pp. 579f., 597f.).

42 See, for example, the criticisms of Robertson (1933), Fanfani (1935), Hyma (1937), and Samuelsson (1961), and the discussion in Chapter 6 below.

43 See Weber (1964, 1962).

44 Weber (1923, pp. 275–8, 352–4).

45 ibid., pp. 354–68.

46 Weber (1971, pp. 35–7).

47 ibid., pp. 17f.

48 ibid., pp. 19f.

49 ibid., pp. 20–2.

50 ibid., p. 51.

51 See, for example, the way in which Weber oscillates between these differing usages in his key chapter on 'The spirit of capitalism' (1971, pp. 51–64).

52 For example, see Cancian (1975) and LaPiere (1934).

53 This is essentially the principal objection which 'substantivist' economic anthropologists (Polanyi 1977; Arensberg 1957; Fusfield 1957) raise against 'formalists' who seek to apply neo-classical economic theory to the study of primitive economies (as in, for example, Herskovitz 1952). For a good review of this debate see LeClair and Schneider (1968), in particular the 'Introduction' by the editors and the contribution by Salisbury.

54 MacIntyre (1962, p. 54).

55 This is, for example, the procedure followed by LaPiere (1934).

56 For example see Swanson (1967, pp. 251f.) and Supple (1963, pp. 59ff.).

57 For an excellent discussion of the problems associated with different theoretical approaches to the relationships between 'ideas' and 'social

life', see Stark (1977, pp. 245–73).

58   Weber (1971, pp. 64f.); on this point, see also Eldridge (1972, pp. 40–1).

59   Weber (1910a, pp. 201f.; 1970b, pp. 267f.).

60   Weber (1910a, p. 200).

61   Weber (1971, pp. 64f.).

4 The Protestant Ethic

1   Weber (1971, pp. 95–6); see also Hyma (1937, pp. 190ff.) and Hill (1966, pp. 13–29).

2   Weber (1971, pp. 96–7).

3   ibid., pp. 155ff.

4   Compare, on this point, Brentano (1923, pp. 393–6), Robertson (1933, pp. 1–4), and Weber (1910b, p. 577; 1971, pp. 204–10).

5   Weber (1971, p. 80); for a similar account see Mehl (1970, p. 207).

6   Weber (1971, p. 83).

7   ibid., pp. 112–14.

8   ibid., p. 85. Weber's interpretation of the Lutheran conception of the 'calling', and of Lutheran doctrines generally in so far as these are relevant to his argument, has been confirmed in essentials by Daniel (1972).

9   Weber (1971, pp. 86–7).

10   ibid., p. 102.

11   ibid., pp. 99–101.

12   ibid., pp. 103–4.

13   ibid., pp. 104–5.

14   ibid., pp. 110–12.

15   ibid., pp. 114–15.

16   ibid., pp. 232–3, 225. Less plausible sources for the 'psychological sanction' in Calvinism have been suggested by Kingdon (1972, pp. 4, 12), Antoni (1962, pp. 156–60), and Stark (1966), who offer respectively the institution of the Calvinist consistory, the Calvinist acceptance of the legitimacy of lending money on interest, and the positive side of the Calvinist doctrine of the Fall (we have lost the Garden of Eden but gained the wide acres of the Earth and have been commanded to make wheat and barley where before there was nothing but wasteland), as possible alternatives to Weber's account.

17   Weber (1971, pp. 155–69).

18   ibid., pp. 131–2, 143, 148–52.

19   ibid., pp. 121–8, 170.

20   ibid., p. 197; see also Weber (1910b, pp. 582–4). This is also the significant difference between ascetic Protestant prescriptions for methodical economic conduct, underwritten by threats of eternal

damnation, and the intellectual defence of profits as 'morally respectable under given circumstances' offered by secular theoreticians on grounds relating to mercantilist social and economic policies. (Compare Johnson 1960, chs. 12, 13, 15; Letwin 1963, ch. 3; Appleby 1978.) Hirschman (1977, pp. 129–30), in his excellent study of 'political arguments for capitalism before its triumph', concedes the importance of Weber's point by leaving a space for the latter's thesis in his own account:

Weber and his followers as well as most of his critics were primarily interested in the psychological processes through which some groups of men became single-minded in the rational pursuit of capitalist accumulation. My story takes it for granted that some men became so impelled and focuses instead on the reaction to the new phenomenon by what is called today the intellectual, managerial, and administrative elite. That reaction was favourable, not because the money-making activities were approved in themselves, but because they were thought to have a beneficial side effect: they kept the men who were engaged in them 'out of mischief', as it were, and had, more specifically, the virtue of imposing restraints on princely caprice, arbitrary government, and adventurous foreign policies. Weber claims that capitalistic behaviour and activities were the indirect (and originally unintended) result of a desperate *search for individual salvation.* My claim is that the diffusion of capitalist forms owed much to an equally desperate search for a way of *avoiding society's ruin*, permanently threatening at the time because of precarious arrangements for internal and external order. Clearly both claims could be valid at the same time: one relates to the motivations of the aspiring new elites, the other to those of various gatekeepers.

21 Weber (1971, pp. 128–39).
22 ibid., pp. 121–2.
23 ibid., p. 145.
24 ibid., pp. 151–2.
25 Weber (1970a, p. 321; also 1971, p. 126). Weber's interpretation of the consequences for everyday life of sectarian organizational principles has been vindicated by Johnson (1971, pp. 473–6). For a detailed discussion of his essay on the Protestant sects see Berger (1971).
26 Weber (1971, p. 117).
27 ibid., pp. 117–18.
28 Weber (1910a, pp. 178–82; 1910b, p. 569; 1971, pp. 118–21). By itself, therefore, the mere existence of ascetic monasticism during the Middle Ages does not, as Hallam (1975) seems to believe, provide evidence against Weber's thesis about the unique 'worldly' asceticism of certain branches of Protestantism.
29 Weber (1971, p. 172).
30 ibid., pp. 172, 180.
31 ibid., p. 174.
32 Compare Weber (1971, pp. 187–8, 218, 284) and Troeltsch (1931).

Troeltsch's masterpiece is so engaging that its length is scarcely noticed by the reader, but the faint-hearted may wish to settle for the abbreviated version of his observations on the Protestant Churches in his *Protestantism and Progress* (1912). Assessing his colleague's thesis, Troeltsch concludes: 'Weber has, in my opinion, completely proved his case . . .' (1912, p. 138).

33   See, for example, Hauser, (1927, pp. 70–3), Hyma (1937, pp. 68–81), Lecerf (1949, pp. 100–3), Means (1965, p. 3), and Samuelsson (1961, pp. 36–7), but compare Freund (1968, pp. 5–6).

34   Reid (1962, p. 9).

35   Weber (1971, p. 220). See also ibid., pp. 215, 274; 1907, p. 246; 1910a, p. 181; and for an excellent overview of the diverse strands of the Calvinist movement McNeill (1967).

36   Biéler (1961, pp. 493–4, 496).

37   Hudson (1949, pp. 9ff.). See also Brentano (1923, pp. 402ff.).

38   See Samuelsson (1961, pp. 30–2), Lecerf (1949, p. 104), George and George (1961, pp. 150–1, 166), Jaccard (1960, pp. 166–7), Gilchrist (1969, pp. 129–30), Hauser (1927, pp. 70–9), Dickens (1971, pp. 178–9), George (1957), Moehlman (1934), Green (1964, p. 175), Holl (1959, pp. 83–7), Hyma (1937, pp. 68–90), Hamilton (1929, pp. 342–3), and Luethy (1964, pp. 36–8).

39   Weber (1971, p. 157).

40   This interpretation of Weber's account has nevertheless been proposed by, among others, Lecerf (1949, p. 104), Jaccard (1960, p. 167), and Argyle (1974, pp. 22–3).

41   Compare Hamilton (1929, pp. 342f.), Gilchrist (1969, pp. 134–5, 138), and George and George (1961, pp. 152–4).

42   Weber (1971, p. 259).

43   Weber (1910b, pp. 581–2; 1970a, p. 321; 1971, pp. 89f., 97f., 192, 203, 217, 229).

44   Weber (1971, p. 157).

45   ibid., p. 171.

46   Rachfahl (1968a, pp. 82–93), Sombart (1967, pp. 236–50), Brentano (1923, pp. 376–7).

47   Robertson (1933, p. 28).

48   ibid., p. 164; see also Sombart (1967, pp. 251–62).

49   Tawney (1972, p. xi), Parsons (1935).

50   Brodrick (1934).

51   See Kitch (1967, p. 148), Hudson (1949, p. 9), Fischoff (1944, p. 73), Hyma (1938, pp. 322ff.), Holl (1959, pp. 68–9), George and George (1961, pp. 126–43).

52   See, for example, Scoville (1960, pp. 131–55), See (1927, pp. 61–2), Luethy (1964, pp. 29–30), and Holl (1959, p. 90). Compare Weber (1971, pp. 39f., 165f., 189f., 191, 270; 1968, pp. 468–71, 492–9,

611–23, 1200–4), and Halbwachs (1925, pp. 134–5).
53   Trevor-Roper (1963), Luethy (1965, p. 94). Swanson (1967, pp. 248–
      50) has also argued the near opposite; namely, that where Protestant
      merchants and artisans participated directly in the political processes
      of 'hierarchic, balanced, or limited centralist regimes' their special
      economic interests and activities gradually became legitimized, and so
      were less effectively restricted than in regimes from which they were
      excluded political participation.
54   Thus, for example, the 'traditionalistic' business practices of any
      'Protestant' merchant become, for Ball (1977, pp. 124ff.), evidence
      against Weber's thesis. Similarly, C. H. George and K. George (1961,
      pp. 6–10) are not prepared to accept an ideal-typification of so complex
      and diverse a belief-system as Puritanism (especially according to
      criteria deriving from the Calvinist doctrine of predestination), yet they
      have no hesitation in simplifying Roman Catholicism to the point
      where they rely almost exclusively on selected writings by St Thomas
      Aquinas as being wholly representative of 'the Roman Catholic
      position'. See also Weber's complaints about Rachfahl's tendency to
      regard all Protestantism as being 'ascetic' in Weber's sense (Weber
      1910a, pp. 180–1).
55   Besnard (1970, p. 40).
56   Compare Moore (1971) and Freund (1968).
57   Hyma (1937, pp. 141–66; 1938); see also George and George (1961,
      pp. 65–8).
58   George and George (1958, p. 369).
59   ibid., and 1961, pp. 3–19.
60   Little (1966, pp. 425–6); see also Little (1970).
61   Walzer (1966, pp. 12–13); see also Walzer (1963).
62   See in particular my own extensive study of sixteenth- and seventeenth-
      century Scottish Calvinism (1980b, pp. 39–112), but also Troeltsch
      (1931), Jonassen (1947), Hertz (1962), and Eisen (1975, 1979).
63   This is not to say that all Calvinist or Calvinist-inspired theology is
      internally wholly consistent. Weber (1971, pp. 102ff.) quite mistakenly
      tends to view Calvinism as a belief-system which became progressively
      more logically consistent over the years. As Hill (1966, p. 249) and
      others have rightly pointed out, much of Calvinist thinking, even as late
      as the time of the Puritans, is in formal terms inherently contradictory.
      But the Calvinist pastors were about the business of changing the
      conduct and lives of their charges; not for them the subtleties of
      academic dispute and rhetoric. Instead, where any possible 'escape
      clause' existed by which the believer might be permitted the luxury of
      an assurance of his or her election in the *absence* of appropriate
      'saintly' everyday conduct, this was closed off by the simple expedient
      of 'secondary elaboration'. Expository texts and sermons are full of

examples of this phenomenon. Calvinism, as Kenneth Burke (1961, pp. 220–4) observes, may not be logically rigorous, but as a belief-system it is extraordinarily powerful since it is full of 'amplifying devices' which prevent the believer from drawing the 'wrong' (fatalistic) conclusions, and from questioning or rejecting any single part of the theology as an independent proposition. One has to accept (or reject) the theology wholesale. The parallels with Azande witchcraft and Popperian-style 'closed societies' are obvious. (Compare Evans-Pritchard, 1937, Popper 1966, Marwick 1973, and the papers collected in Wilson 1977.)

64 Bendix and Roth (1971, p. 191); see also Robertson (1972, p. 181), Walzer (1963, pp. 71–3), and Weinryb (1975, p. 47). This criticism also applies, *mutatis mutandis*, to Weber's remarks about the religions of China, India, Judea, and Islam. His speculations as to the likely consequences for everyday conduct of the theologies of the other great world religions may be well argued and intellectually reasonable. However, in the absence of any empirical evidence as to the substantive effect of the belief-systems in question on the consciousness and conduct of the average believer, it can only be said that Weber's arguments are more or less *plausible* than those offered by critics who choose to hypothesize along different lines. For assessments of the strengths and weaknesses of Weber's comparative studies of world religions (his interpretation of texts, the quality of his sources, weaknesses in his methodology, and the like), see van der Sprenkel (1963), Raphaël (1970) Petersen (1979), Sahay (1969), Madan (1979), and Turner (1974).

5 The heart of the matter

1 Weber (1970b, p. 267).
2 Compare Sombart (1967, pp. 103–24) and Weber (1971, pp. 194–8). See also, among Weber's critics, Brentano (1916, pp. 117–57), Robertson (1933, pp. 57–87), and Strauss (1953, pp. 60–1). In his defence, see Besnard (1970, pp. 67–8) and, ironically, de Roover (1958), who is here, as elsewhere, a vociferous proponent of the idea that 'capitalism' and 'rational bourgeois conduct' antecede the Reformation, although he agrees with Weber's interpretation of Alberti's *Weltanschauung* and maintains that Alberti can only be presented as a forerunner of Franklin by means of a 'gross misrepresentation of the facts', of which Sombart therefore stands accused.
3 Weber (1971, p. 197). Texts similar to those of Alberti can be found outside Protestantism in most European languages but, of course, Weber would apply the same criticism to all. (See, for example, the writings of Cotrugli, Savary, and others, reproduced in Kitch 1967, pp.

80–5, and Molho 1969, pp. 53–8). Mercantilist condemnations of 'luxury' and 'idleness' fall into the same category (compare Johnson 1960, ch. 14).

4   Weber (1971, pp. 200–2). Weber's general interpretation of the teachings of the medieval Church regarding profit and trade, and of the relationship between these and the economic consciousness and activities of the merchant classes, is confirmed in Bloch (1961, pp. 352–5), Cunningham (1912–15, vol. 1, pp. 252–9, 556–9), Evans (1921), Heaton (1963, pp. 190–3), Kedar (1976, pp. 59–60), Ehrenburg (1928, pp. 42–3), Tigar and Levy (1977, pp. 36–8, 106–7), and Sée (1928, pp. 37–9). Good reviews of canonist teachings on these subjects are Jarrett (1926, ch. 7), Kitch (1967, pp. 89–95, 117–25), Tilgher (1931, pp. 38–62), Nelson (1969), and Tawney (1925). Numerous commentators have observed the difference between the hostile teachings of the Church on the subjects of profits, usury, and trade during the early Middle Ages, and those of certain fifteenth-century schoolmen which are demonstrably more sympathetic to capital, as if this – self-evidently – falsified Weber's thesis through confirming Roman Catholicism to be as 'receptive' to the capitalist mentality as was ascetic Protestantism. (See, for example, de Roover 1963a; Gilchrist 1969, pp. 124ff.; Gough 1969, pp. 23–4; and Hyma 1937, pp. 6–15. Nelson 1947 leaves open the question of their significance for Weber's thesis.) The point is, of course, that the concessions of the medieval scholastics were reluctantly given and, at best, only made certain types of profit and economic transactions 'acceptable as a social necessity'. The merchant's activities were no longer inherently sinful and many of them could be performed with a relatively free conscience. But self-interest – pursuing economic transactions with the straightforward objective of making money – remained morally disreputable (see Origo 1963b, pp. 93–4, and de Roover 1955, p. 179; 1967, pp. 9–16). Ascetic Protestantism, on the other hand, made diligence in economic activities (and this included the accumulation and reinvestment of capital) the only means of proving one's salvation. It made it, in fact, a duty. The former was scarcely likely to change the economic consciousness and conduct of a capitalist class; the latter might well have.

5   Weber (1970b, p.280).

6   Jeannin (1972, pp. 8–9).

7   Ball (1977, p. 124).

8   Weber was, of course, fully aware that 'rational' book-keeping and accounting long preceded the Reformation, and accepted the importance of these for the development, of capitalist forms of enterprise (Weber 1923, pp. 275–8, 353–4; 1968, pp. 92–3; 1971, pp. 21–2, 67, 186), but his thesis about the origins of the modern capitalist attitude towards

profit is in no way weakened by this admission (compare Pollard 1965, pp.215–16; Kitch 1967, pp. 74–85). Double-entry book-keeping, for example, though not entirely unambiguous in its origins (in all probability these lie in Italy during the second half of the thirteenth century or the first decades of the fourteenth), was certainly in everyday use throughout commercial Europe for up to two centuries before the Reformation, depending upon the particular location in question (see de Roover 1978, and Goldthwaite 1968, ch. 1). The importance of the double-entry system for the development of capitalism is, in fact, a matter of some debate (see Yamey 1949, 1975).

9 Salzman (1926, p. 75).

10 Renouard (1968, pp. 223–31); see also Jeannin (1972, pp. 33, 105–13), Ramsay (1943, pp. 31–64), Salzman (1926, pp. 241–2), Jaccard (1960, pp. 159–61), and Abram (1909, p. 207).

11 Jeannin (1972, p. 128).

12 Carus-Wilson (1967, pp. 73–84).

13 See Ehrenburg (1928, p. 84), Renouard (1968, pp. 317–18), Goldthwaite (1968, pp. 33–4, 49, 52–107, 173–4), de Roover (1963b, pp. 6–7, 72, 340ff., 362ff.), Kitch (1967, p. 164), Origo (1963a), Ramsay (1943, pp. 31–64), Boissonade (1927, pp. 299–301), Thrupp (1948, pp. 130–54), and Thompson (1960, pp. 492–3).

14 Ferguson (1966, pp. 92–3).

15 Helleiner (1951, p. 106); see also Bendix (1956, pp. 22–116), Sombart (1967, pp. 13–20), Thrupp (1948, pp. 143, 166ff.), Burke (1961, pp. 142–58), and, for a case-study, Goldthwaite (1968, pp. 38–52). Braudel's (1977a, 1977b) categories of 'material life' and 'economic life' are also strongly reminiscent of Weber's ideas about economic traditionalism.

16 Ferguson (1966, p. 125).

17 See, for example, Gilchrist (1969, p. 130), Ehrenburg (1928, pp. 42–3), de Roover (1958, pp. 47–8), Pirenne (1956, pp. 82–91), Jeannin (1972, pp. 141–2), Kedar (1976, pp. 59–60), Renouard (1968, pp. 232–6), Webb (1962, pp. 149–51), and Le Bras (1963, p. 574).

18 See Grubb (1930), Mathias (1975, pp. 151–65).

19 Hill (1961, p. 39).

20 Detailed biographies of Cranfield and Banks include those by Prestwich (1966) and Coleman (1963). For a review of the business ventures of similar late medieval, early capitalist Protestant entrepreneurs, see Supple (1963), who offers the activities of such men as evidence against Weber's argument without first considering whether or not the individuals concerned were anything other than nominal Protestants. It must be noted, however, that the danger in this line of reasoning is that any group or stratum of 'bourgeois capitalists' who channel their profits from the sphere of business into the purchase of landed estates, and

thus become part of the 'notorious scramble for membership in the nobility', are summarily dismissed as being 'not strictly Calvinist' simply on the evidence provided by their aristocratic tendencies. Weber himself is not above this kind of 'secondary elaboration' in order to explain away data which are problematic for his thesis (see Weber 1971, pp. 278–9).

21 ibid., pp. 91–2.
22 ibid., pp. 54–7.
23 ibid., pp. 179–80.
24 ibid., pp. 65, 173–4, 278–80, 282.
25 See Mundy and Riesenberg (1958, pp. 37–9, 76–7), Wilson (1967, pp. 490–2), Barbour (1966, pp. 11–12), George and George (1961, pp. 146–7), Clark (1972, pp. 32–8), Samuelsson (1961, pp. 83–7), and Reynolds (1945).
26 Hill (1969, pp. 196–8), Grassby (1970, pp. 90, 107), Ball (1977, p. 127), Jeannin (1972, pp. 141–2), Supple (1963).
27 Compare Hill (1969, pp. 197–8).
28 Supple (1963, p. 60), Mundy and Riesenberg (1958, pp. 76–7).
29 Weber (1910a, p. 188; 1968, pp. 164–6, 612–15, 1156, 1203f.; 1971, pp. 58, 278).
30 O'Brien (1923, p. 91).
31 Power (1941, pp. 104–6).
32 Thrupp (1941). For similar accounts, see Mundy and Riesenberg (1958, pp. 76–7) and Carus-Wilson (1967, pp. xxix–xxx).
33 Kitch (1967, p. 176).
34 Ludloff (1957). For a further example of the complex 'conditions of action' within which economic activities are negotiated and undertaken, see the discussion of the 'entrepreneurial decisions and profit' of Andrea Barbarigo (1399–1449), merchant of Venice, in Lane (1944, pp. 131–6).
35 See, for example, Marshall (1980b, pp. 127–217), Hill (1969, pp. 184–5), Supple (1963), and Barbour (1966, pp. 74–129).
36 For example, see the accounts given of the activities of the partnerships of Raffaello di Francesco de' Medici and Company (1531–4) and Francesco di Giuliano di Raffaello de' Medici and Company (1556–8), in de Roover (1941), and of the partnership of Andrea di Francesco Banchi (1372–1462), in de Roover (1966).
37 Carus-Wilson (1967, p. xvi); see also Jeannin (1972, p. 103).
38 See Jarrett (1926, pp. 155–68), Evans (1921, p. 615).
39 Weber is not the only commentator to have adopted this methodological device in the hope of uncovering the world-view of historical actors who are known to us only by a record of their economic conduct in certain directions (investments, savings, expenditures, and the like). See also, for example, Gimpel's (1975, pp. 6, 99ff.) attempt to locate

the origins of the modern capitalist mentality in European 'industrial revolutions' of the eleventh to thirteenth centuries, by reading a certain economic *mentalité* into the spread of new agricultural, mining, building, commercial, administrative, and industrial techniques, of the mechanical clock, and the increasing division of labour and scale of business. Describing the same development Gras (1926, pp. 454–60) too maintains that 'parallel with the new forms went a new spirit' but, like Gimpel, his 'evidence' as to this new spirit consists largely of an imaginative but wholly speculative and unsubstantiated reading of a new 'ethos' into the observed changes in techniques and the scale of operations. Kedar (1976, pp. 133–6) is more honest. He acknowledges the near dearth of direct references by medieval merchants as to their motivation and attempts instead to infer different merchant 'moods' from a number of 'indicators' of questionable validity: the formulae of commercial contracts (supposedly indicative of the degree of 'risk' which traders were willing to take); lists of first names and names of ships (where saints names are common this is supposed to indicate a high degree of piety); proverbs; and literary sources or chronicles (written, it must be noted, not by the merchants themselves but by moralists who passed judgement on *their* interpretation of the traders' motives).

40   Schumpeter (1974, p. 109ff.), Kedar (1976, pp. 117–32).

41   Gough (1969, pp. 289–90). For a concise summary of, and commentary on, 'the Gentry debate', see Stone (1965).

42   Barbour (1966, pp. 140–2).

43   Weber (1971, p. 198).

44   See George and George (1961, p. 146), Robertson (1972, pp. 172–3), and Dixon (1973, p. 61).

45   Weber (1971, pp. 196, 53–4).

46   ibid., p. 276. Perhaps Weber's lapses in this direction explain the (otherwise bizarre) arguments offered by certain critics, that Franklin's texts are atypical of the mood of ascetic Protestant writings as a whole (Luethy 1964, pp. 26–7; Samuelsson 1961, pp. 55–67), and that Weber fails, in *The Protestant Ethic and the Spirit of Capitalism* (and elsewhere in his sociology of religion), to document satisfactorily the origins of his explanandum – the Protestant ethic (Razzell 1977)!

47   Compare Weber's (1971, pp. 73–4, 115ff., 159–60, 174–5) assumptions with the more sophisticated treatments of the relationship between canonist teaching and economic practice to be found in, for example, Evans (1921) and Thrupp (1941).

48   Cohen (1968, p. 198) has also challenged the argument that Weber's thesis is tautological, but from another direction:

A significant point concerning Weber's explanation is that the secular conduct of capitalism is *not* logically entailed by Calvinism – the religious doctrine does not urge men to accumulate capital and to invest it rationally – but results from a psychological change in motivation and values. It certainly cannot be argued that Weber's hypothesis is tautological, or purely logical, unless one insists that he attributed to Protestantism characteristics which are indistinguishable from those of the 'spirit of capitalism'.

49 See White (1969, p. 198), Sée (1927, pp. 61–2), Holl (1959, pp. 89–90), Scoville (1960, pp. 143–55), and Antoni (1962, p. 152).

50 Compare, for example, Brentano (1923, pp. 363–70), Knight (1928), George and George (1961, pp. 146–7). See also Gras (1926, pp. 457–60), Hobson (1954, pp. 21–3), Strieder (1929, pp. 3–4), Groethuysen (1968), and Bergier (1973, pp. 406–8) for independent discussions of 'the spirit of capitalism'.

51 Samuelsson (1961, pp. 48–50); see also Hallam (1975, p. 44), Luethy (1964), Wax and Wax (1955), Dobb (1951, p. 9), Fanfani (1935, pp. 138, 200–1), Heaton (1963, pp. 186–7), Jaccard (1960, pp. 166–7), Robertson (1933, pp. xi–xv, 168–206), Sée (1928, pp. 39–40), Means (1965, p. 4), and Macfarlane (1978).

52 Weber (1971, pp. 38–9, 62–3, 158–9, 177–8, 282).

53 See, for example, Unwin (1927, p. 295), Lane 1966, pp. 278–81), and Coulton (1926, pp. 242–7).

54 Hill (1966, p.130).

55 See Coleman (1956, pp. 290–2), Laslett (1975), Thomas (1964), Thompson (1967, pp. 56–79), and Langenfelt (1954).

56 See McKendrick (1961), Pollard (1963), Thompson (1967, pp. 79–97).

57 See, for example, Pollard (1963, pp. 267–70) and Moore (1974, pp. 78–92).

58 For an introductory discussion see Argyle (1974).

59 Heaton (1963, pp. 193–211), Thrupp (1941).

60 Thrupp (1942, p. 170).

61 Miracle and Fetter (1969, p. 242); see also Miracle (1976).

62 See Higgins (1955), Whyte and Williams (1968, pp. 51–8), Bauer and Yamey (1963, pp. 82–101), Moore (1964, pp. 381–5), Coleman (1956, pp. 282–90), and Hill (1969, pp. 214–20).

63 Burke (1962, p. 276).

64 Anthony (1977, pp. 36–8), Thomas (1964, pp. 54–6).

65 Thrupp (1972, pp. 252–5).

66 This device is widely employed by Tilgher (1931), Parias (n.d.), and Jaccard (1960).

67 Weber (1907, p. 245; 1971, pp. 75, 220, 273, 278).

68 Weber (1971, pp. 54–5); see also ibid., pp. 70, 72, 75, 181–2, Weber (1910a, p. 189; 190b, pp. 573–5, 593), and for a similar argument Baechler (1975, pp. 106–11).

69 Weber (1971, pp. 143, 174–6, 252). Among those who have correctly

recognized the spacial and temporal restrictions which Weber applies to his thesis are Freund (1968, pp. 8–9), and Demerath and Hammond (1969, pp. 102–3).

70   On the paucity of data of the kind in question see Grassby (1970, pp. 87–9), Fisher (1957), and the excellent paper by Rabb (1974), who also explores some of the problems this creates for those who wish to participate in discussions about the modern capitalist mentality and its possible origins.

71   Samuelsson (1961, pp. 67–79); see also Biéler (1961, p. 494), Gollin (1967), and Nafziger (1965).

72   Alatas (1963, pp. 33–4); see also Atkinson and Hoselitz (1958) and Morris (1967, pp. 594–602).

73   Compare Weber's temporal specificity with studies such as those by Barclay (1969) or Kosa and Rachiele (1963).

6 Continuities in a controversy

1   Hartwell (1971, p. 303).

2   See Rachfahl (1968a, pp. 93–125), Brentano (1923, pp. 363–425), See (1928, p. 96), Hamilton (1929, p. 342), Hyma (1937, pp. 141–66), Kolko (1960–1, pp. 247–55), Means (1965, pp. 3–4), Jaccard (1960, p. 166), Frank (1978, p. 29), Andreski (1964, pp. 9–14), Macfarlane (1978), and Marshall (1980b, pp. 27ff.).

3   See Rachfahl (1968a, 1968b), Brentano (1923, pp. 385, 421–5), Kolko (1959), Hyma (1937, pp. 168, 202), Hamilton (1929), Gough (1969, pp. 22–9), Sorokin (1966, p. 123), Swanson (1967), and Lukács (1972).

4   Numerous examples are cited in Marshall (1980b, p. 31), but see also Supple (1963, pp. 57–9), Kunkel (1970, pp. 219–20), and Israel (1966, pp. 589–90).

5   See Chapter 3, note 42 above, and Trevor-Roper (1963, pp. 21, 28–9), Hauser (1927, pp. 69–70), Luethy (1964). One eminent historian, writing in an authoritative student text, signals his fundamental misunderstanding of Weber's argument in this respect by referring critically to Weber's articles on (sic) 'The Protestant ethic and the rise of capitalism' (Marwick 1970, pp. 64–5). A reference in the same source to Weber as being the first author to suggest a connection between Protestantism and capitalism (p. 122) tends to confirm one's suspicion that the critic in question may not be entirely familiar with Weber's text. Weber has, of course, persistently been charged with 'idealism' by commentators writing from a Marxist standpoint (see, for example, Lukács 1972; Kolko 1959).

6   Aron (1957, p. 95); see also Jaspers (1965, pp. 234–5) and Raphaël (1970, p. 302).

7   Besnard (1970, p. 21).
8   See, for example, Freund (1968, pp. 4, 11–12), Hill (1973, pp. 99–
    100), Nelson (1973, pp. 80–2), Razzell (1977), Fischoff (1944),
    Besnard (1970, pp. 18–19), Bellah (1970, pp. 54–5), and Parsons
    (1935).
9   The experience of one eminent historian, at least, is enlightening in this
    respect. In the first edition of his *Religion and the Rise of Capitalism*,
    Tawney is unreservedly critical of the argument proposed in Weber's
    original essays, on the grounds that Weber's 'one-sided and over-
    strained' treatment leads him to ignore a host of additional factors
    which were clearly important for the development of capitalism in
    Holland and England in the sixteenth and seventeenth centuries,
    factors such as the Discoveries and the economic consequences of
    these. 'Of course', Tawney concedes, 'material and psychological
    changes went together, and of course the second reacted on the first.
    But it seems a little artificial to talk as though capitalist enterprise could
    not appear till religious changes had produced a capitalist spirit. It
    would be equally true, and equally one-sided, to say that the religious
    changes were purely the result of economic movements.' Weber is also
    charged with ignoring developments unconnected with religion (the
    political thought of the Renaissance, the 'speculations of business men
    and economists on money, prices, and the foreign exchanges') which
    were 'favourable to the growth of business enterprise and to an
    individualist attitude towards economic relations'. In the preface to the
    1937 edition of his study, however, Tawney having familiarized
    himself with the arguments of Weber's comparative studies of world
    religions and his *General Economic History* in the interim, he
    withdraws both of these criticisms conceding that it was clearly not
    Weber's intention to advance a 'comprehensive theory of the genesis
    and growth of Capitalism' in his original essays: 'If he did not in his
    articles refer to economic consequences of the discovery of America,
    or of the great depreciation, or of the rise to financial pre-eminence of
    the Catholic city of Antwerp, it was not that these bashful events had at
    last hit on an historian whose notice they could elude.' Tawney further
    concedes, graciously, that he simply 'overlooked' Weber's observations
    on Renaissance authors such as Alberti. His new appreciation of
    Weber's wider sociology has led him from outspoken criticism of
    Weber's thesis to a sympathetic defence of the latter against 'the
    epigoni who take in his washing' (Tawney 1972, pp. vii–xiii, 311–13).
10 As a sociologist my own assessment of the historians' charge of
    'idealism' would be even less charitable. Such a claim could only be
    pressed by wilful ignorance, not only of Weber's writings elsewhere,
    but of his original essays themselves (compare, for example, Weber,
    1971, p. 183).

11   For a critical review see Macfarlane (1978).

12   Weber (1923, pp. 334–5, 337). Compare also the following remarks, scarcely typical of an idealist interpretation of history, from the same source:

> An economic prerequisite for the appearance and existence of a factory . . . is mass demand, and also steady demand – that is, a certain organization of the market. An irregular market is fatal to the entrepreneur because the conjecture risk rests on his shoulders. . . . A further requisite is a relatively inexpensive production process. . . . In order to find a steady market, again, he must produce more cheaply than under the traditional technique of house industry and the putting-out system. Finally, the development of the factory is conditioned by a special social prerequisite in the presence of a sufficient supply of free labourers; it is impossible on the basis of slave labour. . . . This mass of labour was created in England, the classical land of the later factory capitalism, by the eviction of the peasants. [pp. 163–4]

> The labour contract . . . created the possibility of exact calculation, which again could only be carried out in connection with a combination of workshop and free worker. [p. 175]

> But for all this revolution in the means of work the development might have stopped and modern capitalism in its most characteristic form never appeared. Its victory was decided by coal and iron [which] . . . released technology and productive possibilities from the limitations of and the qualities inherent in organic materials. . . . Thus iron became the most important factor in the development of capitalism; what would have happened to this system or to Europe in the absence of this development we do not know. [pp. 304–5]

and finally,

> Without the stimulus of patent law the inventions crucial for the development of capitalism in the field of textile industry in the eighteenth century would not have been possible. [p. 312]

13   Weber (1908, pp. 277f.; 1910a, pp. 191f., 197; 1910b, pp. 579ff., 598). In fact, in the original essays themselves, Weber declares that the importance of the capitalist ethos for capitalist developments in the West 'is obvious', referring the reader to Sombart who, in his *Der Moderne Kapitalismus*, 'has already well pointed out this characteristic phenomenon' (Weber 1971, pp. 170, 276).

14   Weber (1907, pp. 244ff.).

15   Weber (1910b, p. 572; 1910a, p. 197).

16   Weber (1971, pp. 42–3, 190).

17   Marshall (1980b), Eldridge (1972, p. 40); see also Besnard (1970, pp. 26–32) and Bellah (1970, pp. 54–5), and compare Hyma's much cited studies of the Netherlands (1937, pp. 141–66; 1938). Among many weaknesses in the latter's interpretation of Weber's argument, most of which have been noted above, is a tendency to read almost any material whatsoever that pertains to economic activities as evidence against

'Weber's thesis': numbers of ships passing through the Sound; the growth of banking and the publishing trade; and the expansion of commerce and trade generally. Precisely how such data relate to the object of Weber's investigation – the attitude towards profit and business activities that he calls 'the spirit of modern capitalism' – is not discussed by Hyma. Unfortunately, from Hyma's point of view, its relevance is not entirely clear – to this reader at least.

18   Aron (1970, p. 224). See also Besnard (1970, pp. 17–18), Warner (1970, pp. 77–8), Eldridge (1972, pp. 35–40).

19   Moore (1971). Compare the approach of Tawney (1972, pp. xi–xii), who concedes his own errors in interpreting Weber's original articles as an exercise in idealism, but does not let this admission detract from the crucial question of attempting to discern 'what the facts were [concerning] . . . a connection between the religious movements of the sixteenth and seventeenth centuries and the outburst of economic energy which was remaking society in the Netherlands and England'.

20   Marx (1972, pp. 650ff).

21   Engels *Socialism: Utopian and Scientific* ('Special introduction to the English edition of 1892'), in Marx and Engels (1970a, pp. 383–7); see also his *Ludwig Feuerbach and the End of Classical German Philosophy*, ibid., pp. 618–20.

22   See Baechler (1975, pp. 5–26), and compare Dobb (1951), Sweezy (1954), Anderson (1974), and Wallerstein (1974).

23   Williams (1973, p. 4); see also Corrigan and Sayer (1978).

24   Good commentaries on the various Marxist theories of ideology have recently been offered by Larrain (1979) and Seliger (1979). Compare the divergent accounts of the relationship between 'base' and 'super-structure', and especially the contrasting theories of 'ideology', that are currently proposed by Hindess and Hirst 1975 (idealist); Althusser 1977, Althusser and Balibar 1970 (structuralist); Cohen 1978 (func-tionalist); Thompson 1978 (culturalist); and Culter *et al.* 1977–8 (variously all of the aforementioned). Recent attempts by certain Marxists to synthesize and develop two or more of these positions have left this reader, at least, puzzled as to what it might be (other than a specific rhetoric and style of discourse) that makes such attempts distinctively Marxist in a *methodological* sense. Certainly, the conception of 'determinism' that is employed in theorizing the relationships between the economic and non-economic aspects of social existence, and between social actors and the structures which comprise their milieu, is scarcely uniquely 'Marxist' and does not distinguish the enterprises in question from those of many mainstream Weberian sociologists. (See, for example, Johnson 1978, 1979a, 1979b, and Clarke 1979).

25   On the last of these questions see, for example, the discussion in

Schumpeter (1974, pp. 10–14).

26 Hirst (1979, pp. 420, 443).

27 Hill (1966, p. 249).

28 Hill (1961, p. 36); see also Hill (1969, pp. 26–7).

29 Hill (1963, 1966).

30 Dauphin-Meunier (1955, pp. 69–70).

31 Hill (1963, p. 84).

32 Hill (1966, p. 134).

33 See also, for similar accounts, Walker (1937), Dauphin-Meunier (1955, pp. 62–70), Marcuse (1971), Cox (1964, pp. 46–60), and Birnbaum (1959).

34 Fischoff (1944, p. 75).

35 See Pirenne (1956), Thompson (1960), Gras (1926), and McCormack (1969).

36 Means (1965, p. 5).

37 Forcese (1968, pp. 198–9).

38 Yinger (1967, pp. 215–16).

39 Sée (1927, pp. 61–2, 64; 1928, pp. 39–40, 185–6). For similar interpretations, see Hudson (1949) and Mauro (1970, pp. 323–9). Tawney's (1972) complex analysis and changing position with respect to Weber's original argument is reducible, in the final resort, to an almost identical stance. In his view it was the gradual abdication by religion of the spheres of economic and political activity – a secularization of the business world that is coincidental with, but not the consequence of, the Reformation – which permitted the rise of unrestrained capitalist individualism. At the same time, however, aspects of Calvinist teaching that were in harmony with the entrepreneurial and individual-istic mentality of the bourgeoisie were readily employed by post-Restoration businessmen and businesswomen as a convenient justifi-cation for economic enterprise, and in this way helped further their activities. Early Puritanism, following the teachings of Calvin, had displayed a dual ethic of individualism and social obligation. The ascendant middle classes selected from it only those elements which were suited to their purposes, namely those emphasizing the ethic of individualism. They conveniently ignored the ethic of social accounta-bility and, as can be seen from the teachings of the post-Restoration Puritans, in this way usurped the theology for their own ends. By the nineteenth century this process had reached the point where the business world was totally secularized and the individualistic elements of Protestant theology had given way entirely to the egoism of Samuel Smiles. The 'acquisitive society' had triumphed totally over the egalitarian one. The success of capitalism is, therefore, the failure of Protestantism.

40 Robertson (1933, p. 27); see also Alatas (1963, pp. 28–9), Green

(1964, p. 175), and Michaelsen (1953, pp. 325, 334–6).

41 Robertson (1933, pp. 164–5); see also Yinger (1970, pp. 380–95) and Zaret (1980a).

42 Jeannin (1972, p. 133).

43 Compare, for example, Marianne Weber (1975, p. 335), Warner (1970, p. 77), and Lichtheim (1971, p. 385).

44 Compare the many commentators who have taken Weber's essays to be primarily a direct response to Marx's account of the origins of capitalism. These include Salomon (1945, p. 596), Birnbaum (1953, pp. 125, 127, 140), Fischoff (1944, p. 60), Antoni (1962, pp. 149–50), and Prades (1969, pp. 87, 92).

45 This conclusion has also been reached by, among others, Freund (1979, p. 166) and Mommsen (1977, pp. 378–80).

46 Marx and Engels (1970b, pp. 64–5).

47 Weber (1924, p. 456).

48 Marianne Weber (1975, p. 335).

49 See Giddens (1970), Mommsen (1977), and Bendix and Roth (1971, pp. 239–45).

50 'Naturally', he writes,

all specifically Marxian 'laws' and developmental constructs – insofar as they are theoretically sound – are ideal-types. The eminent, indeed unique, *heuristic* significance of these ideal-types when they are used for the assessment of reality is known to everyone who has ever employed Marxian concepts and hypotheses. Similarly, their perniciousness, as soon as they are thought of as empirically valid or as real (*i.e.*, truly metaphysical) 'effective forces', 'tendencies', etc. is likewise known to those who have used them. [Weber 1969, p. 103]

See also ibid., p. 71.

51 See, for example, Giddens (1970), Gabel (1969), Besnard (1970, pp. 14–18), and Mommsen (1977, pp. 376–7).

52 Weber (1971, p. 181).

53 See Avineri (1972, pp. 105–16, 162–74), Birnbaum (1953, pp. 126–9).

54 Weber (1971, p. 266); see also Dixon (1973, pp. 60–1), Knight (1928, p. 131), Alatas (1963, pp. 24–6), Demerath and Hammond (1969, pp. 93–103), and Andreski (1964). The fact that Weber's methodology may also be an exercise in hermeneutics, as has been claimed most recently by Bauman (1978, ch. 3), does not alter the fact that an unambiguously causal relationship is proposed between Calvinist teachings and economic conduct in Weber's original essays. It should also be noted that, contrary to the beliefs held by certain Marxist writers, Weber was not naïve as to the hypocritical way in which eighteenth- and especially nineteenth-century capitalists employed religion as a means of controlling their workforce or legitimizing certain of their own harsh practices. The material benefits to be gained by

promoting religions which emphasized frugality and a work-ethic rapidly became apparent to later generations of Calvinist businessmen and businesswomen. By this time, of course, the genuinely religious basis to the capitalist mentality had entirely disappeared (Weber 1971, pp. 174–7).

55   Weber (1971, p. 183).

56   ibid., pp. 277–8; see also Weber (1970b, p. 268).

57   Weber (1971, p. 183); see also ibid., pp. 90–2.

58   Weber (1968, p. 491).

59   See, for example, Demerath and Hammond (1969, pp. 81ff.), Gerth and Mills (1970, pp. 63–4).

60   For a detailed analysis of the ways in which Weber employs the term, and a general history of the concept itself, see Howe (1978).

61   Giddens (1971, p. 131); see also Bendix (1969, pp. 63–4). I confess, however, that I fail to understand Bendix's claim that 'Weber's essay on Protestantism does not deal with the problem of causal imputation except incidentally', in view of the latter's clarification of his objectives in this study. Weber states explicitly that in dealing with the Calvinist faith he is interested in 'its influence on other historical processes as a causal factor'. He is concerned, therefore, with 'judgements of historical imputation' (Weber 1971, pp. 98–9; see also, for similarly unambiguous declarations, ibid., pp. 27, 90–2, 180). A limited causal imputation it may have been, and one which could only be assessed fully in the light of subsequent exploration of 'the other side of the causal chain', but causal it is nevertheless. It would have been strange had Weber tackled the problem otherwise, since he discerns the specific objective of sociology to be the 'interpretive understanding of social action', and thereby the provision of 'a causal explanation of its course and consequences' (Weber 1968, p. 4).

62   Hill (1973, pp. 108–9); see also Stark (1977, pp. 256–8), Bendix and Roth (1971, p. 268).

63   Winter (1974a, p. 1037); see also Giddens (1971, pp. 210–12), Jaccard (1960, p. 167), Forcese (1968, pp. 197–8), and Burke (1961, pp. 135–9).

64   Baechler (1975, p. 70); see also Mehl (1970, p. 207).

65   Runciman (1969, p. 183).

66   The discussion that has taken place over many years, within and between various schools of sociological thought, concerning the status of actors' accounts of their activities and the role of 'vocabularies of motive' in generating both the accounts and the activities themselves, stems in part at least from Weber's own definition of a motive as 'a complex of subjective meaning which seems to the actor himself or to the observer an adequate ground for the conduct in question' (Weber

1968, p. 11). For the parameters of the ensuing discussion and a review of the ways in which sociologists have dealt with, in particular, deviants' accounts of their alleged deviance, see Marshall (1981).

67 See, for example, Weber (1969, pp. 65–71; 1975, 1977).

68 Weber (1970e, pp. 152–3); see also Weber (1969, pp. 1–47, 57–8), and compare Marx, 'Theses on Feuerbach', in Marx and Engels (1970a, pp. 28, 30), and Marx and Engels (1970b, pp. 48, 56f., 62, 94f.).

69 Weber (1968, pp. 4–22; 1975). Critics of Parsons's (1968) 'convergence thesis' and his interpretation of Weber's sociology in general are legion, but see especially Sahay (1972, ch. 6), Butts (1975), Cohen *et al.*, (1975a, 1975b), and Zaret (1980b).

70 See Parsons (1964, 1966, 1971b), and for criticisms, Smith (1973) and Nisbet (1970); compare Weber (1969, pp. 164–88).

71 Tenbruck (1980).

72 See, for example, Luethy (1964, 1965), Mommsen (1965), Eisenstadt (1968b, 1971, 1973), Seyfarth (1973), Schluchter (1979), and Dux (1973). It must be conceded that I am here painting with fairly broad brush-strokes. Tenbruck, for example, is fully aware of the chronology of Weber's writings, and of the fact that he had not formulated the outline of his subsequent studies of 'The economic ethic of world religions' when he penned his essays on the Protestant ethic. Tenbruck's approach is not so much 'teleological' as 'retrospective'. The original essays are interpreted from the standpoint of Weber's comparative studies and read in such a manner as will make them consistent with his alleged concerns in these later texts. Nevertheless, recent 'retrospective' commentaries which are, in fact, sensitive to the chronology of Weber's *Religionssoziologie* arrive at the same end result as earlier, less sophisticated, and genuinely 'teleological' interpretations. Both effectively ignore the specific context of Weber's essays of 1905; disregard his concerns and writings prior to that date; and attempt to incorporate his essays into a much grander project, and more systematic theory of social action and social change, which are purportedly rooted in his comparative studies of world religions.

73 Kolko (1959, pp. 24–5).

74 Luethy (1964, p. 27).

75 Compare our approach with that of Giddens (1976, p. 5) and Schluchter (1979, pp. 19, 60). The latter writes: 'We take a unified approach that overcomes the isolated analysis of the Protestant ethic and sees it as part of a larger program for the analysis of rationalism and rationalization'; and 'The analytical end point of the [*Religionssoziologie*] studies was the religious ethics of ascetic Protestantism, about which Weber had written first.'

76   Weber (1971, pp. 77–8).
77   ibid., p. 78.
78   ibid., pp. 182–3.
79   Luethy (1964, pp. 28–9).
80   Weber (1971, pp. 283–4).
81   Compare the sophisticated approaches of Jones (1961), Merton (1968, pp. 628–60), Stimson (1948), Mason (1953a, 1953b, 1956, pp. 138–50), Kocher (1969), Hill (1964a, 1964b, 1965a, 1965b), Kearney (1964, 1965), Whitteridge (1965), and Rabb (1965, 1966), with the studies by Hooykaas (1956), Kennedy (1962), and Datta (1967). For an excellent review of the issues and much of the literature in this debate, see Rabb (1962).
82   Lenski (1963, pp. 2–3, 7–8, 357–9; 1965).
83   See, for example, Kim (1977) and Johnson (1962, 1966). More ambiguous on the questions of the historical referents of their conclusions and their relationship to Weber's argument are studies such as Ball (1965), Parenti (1967), Cameron (1969), Featherman (1971, 1972), and Welch (1978). Exempt from the charge of historical naïveté must be Lenski himself, of course, and also, among others, Greeley (1964), Babbie (1965), Winter (1974b), Wagner (1964), Schoenfeld (1964), and Summers *et al.* (1970). Overviews of this whole literature are provided by Bouma (1973), Means (1966), and McNamara (1974).
84   In this respect the mainstream of development economics has long been closer to the tradition of the German Historical Schools than has the more neo-classically inclined orthodoxy of the discipline as a whole. See, for example, Buchanan and Ellis (1955), Lewis (1955), Kindelberger (1958), Bonné (1960), Hoselitz (1962), Williamson and Buttrick (1962), Alexander (1962), Villard (1963), Pepelasis *et al.* (1964), Meier and Baldwin (1964), Okun and Richardson (1964), Bruton (1965), Bhagwati (1966), Hirschman (1966), Ward (1967), and Datta (1974).
85   Frank's (1971) principal targets are the 'Modernization School' including Parsons, Hoselitz, and Levy; Rostow and similar 'stages of growth' theorists; 'diffusionists' of various traditions who advocate the export of capital, technology, and institutions from the West to the developing world, as a remedy for economic stagnation; and the 'psychological' theories of development advocated by, for example, McClelland, Kunkel, and Hagen. (These categories are not mutually exclusive.) His criticism also holds good, however, for *some* of the authorities mentioned in the previous note.
86   Compare Frank (1978, p. 30).
87   See Bellah (1970, pt 2), Hansen (1963, 1964), Geertz (1955–6), and Nelson (1969, pp. 248–9; 1974).

7 Conclusion

1   See, for example, the discussions in Burger (1976, pp. 135–40), Therborn (1976, pp. 272–95), and Zaret (1980b).
2   Carr (1970, p. 66); see also Cahnman and Boskoff (1964).
3   For example, see Elton's (1978) prescriptions for historical practice. Note also Selbourne's (1980) recently expressed reservations concerning the *cinéma vérité* tendencies in the work of the History Workshop.
4   Goldthorpe (1977, pp. 189–90).
5   This conclusion has also been recently arrived at by social historians working within very different perspectives to that employed in the present study (see Judt 1979, and Stedman Jones 1976).

Bibliography

Abram, A. (1909), *Social England in the Fifteenth Century: A Study of the Effects of Economic Conditions*, London: Routledge

Alatas, Syed Hussein (1963), 'The Weber thesis and South East Asia', *Archives de Sociologie des Religions*, 15, pp. 21–34

Alexander, Robert, J. (1962), *A Primer of Economic Development*, New York: Macmillan

Althusser, Louis (1977), *For Marx*, London: New Left Books

Althusser, Louis and Balibar, Etienne (1970), *Reading Capital*, London: New Left Books

Anderson, Perry (1974), *Lineages of the Absolutist State*, London: New Left Books

Andreski, Stanislav (1964), 'Method and substantive theory in Max Weber', *British Journal of Sociology*, 15, pp. 1–18

Ankerl, Guy (1972), *Sociologues Allemands*, Neuchâtel: Éditions de la Baconnière

Anthony, P. D. (1977), *The Ideology of Work*, London: Tavistock

Antoni, Carlo (1962), *From History to Sociology*, London: Merlin Press

Appleby, Joyce Oldham (1978), *Economic Thought and Ideology in Seventeenth-Century England*, Princeton, NJ: Princeton University Press

Arensberg, Conrad M. (1957), 'Anthropology as history', in Karl Polanyi *et al.* (eds.), *Trade and Market in the Early Empires*, Glencoe, Ill.: Free Press, pp. 97–113

Argyle, Michael (1974), *The Social Psychology of Work*, Harmondsworth: Penguin

Aron, Raymond (1957), *German Sociology*, London: Heinemann
(1970), *Main Currents in Sociological Thought 2*, Harmondsworth: Penguin

Ashton, T. S. (1954), 'The treatment of capitalism by historians', in F. A. Hayek (ed.), *Capitalism and the Historians*, London: Routledge and Kegan Paul, pp. 33–63

Atkinson, John W., and Hoselitz, Bert F. (1958), 'Entrepreneurship and personality', *Explorations in Entrepreneurial History*, 10, pp. 107–12

Avineri, Schlomo (1972), *The Social and Political Thought of Karl Marx*, Cambridge: Cambridge University Press

Babbie, Earl R. (1965), 'The religious factor – looking forward', *Review of Religious Research*, 7, pp. 42–51

Baechler, Jean (1968), 'Essai sur les origines du système capitalist', *Archives Européennes de Sociologie*, 9, pp. 205–63

(1975), *The Origins of Capitalism*, Oxford: Blackwell

Ball, Donald W. (1965), 'Catholics, Calvinists, and rational control: further explorations in the Weberian thesis', *Sociological Analysis*, 26, pp. 181–8

Ball, J. N. (1977), *Merchants and Merchandise: The Expansion of Trade in Europe, 1500–1630*, London: Croom Helm

Barbour, Violet (1966), *Capitalism in Amsterdam in the Seventeenth Century*, Ann Arbor, Mich.: University of Michigan Press

Barclay, Harold B. (1969), 'The Protestant ethic versus the spirit of capitalism?', *Review of Religious Research*, 10, pp. 151–8

Bauman, Zygmunt (1978), *Hermeneutics and Social Science*, London: Hutchinson

Bauer, P. T., and Yamey, B. S. (1963), *The Economics of Under-Developed Countries*, Cambridge: Cambridge University Press

Bell, John Fred (1953), *A History of Economic Thought*, New York: The Ronald Press Company

Bellah, Robert N. (1970), *Beyond Belief: Essays on Religion in a Post-Traditional World*, New York: Harper and Row

Bendix, Reinhard (1946), 'Max Weber's interpretation of conduct and history', *American Journal of Sociology*, 51, pp. 518–26

(1956), *Work and Authority in Industry: Ideologies of Management in the Course of Industrialization*, New York: John Wiley

(1969), *Max Weber: An Intellectual Portrait*, London: Methuen

Bendix, Reinhard and Roth, Guenther (1971), *Scholarship and Partisanship: Essays on Max Weber*, Berkeley, Calif.: University of California Press

Berger, Stephen D. (1971), 'The sects and the breakthrough into the modern world: on the centrality of the sects in Weber's Protestant ethic thesis', *Sociological Quarterly*, 12, pp. 486–99

Bergier, J-F. (1973), 'The industrial bourgeoisie and the rise of the working class 1700–1914', in Carlo M. Cipolla (ed.), *The Industrial Revolution* (Fontana Economic History of Europe, vol. 3), London: Collins/Fontana, pp. 397–451

Besnard, Phillippe, ed. (1970), *Protestantisme et Capitalisme: la controverse post-Weberienne*, Paris: Librairie Armand Colin

Bhagwati, Jagdish (1966), *The Economics of Underdeveloped Countries*, London: Weidenfeld and Nicolson

Biéler, André (1961), *La Pensée Économique et Sociale de Calvin*, Genève: Georg

Birnbaum, Norman (1953), 'Conflicting interpretations of the rise of capital-

ism: Marx and Weber', *British Journal of Sociology*, 4, pp. 125–41
(1959), 'The Zwinglian reformation in Zurich', *Past and Present*, 15, pp. 27–47
Bloch, Marc (1961), *Feudal Society*, London: Routledge and Kegan Paul
Blum, Fred H. (1944), 'Max Weber's postulate of "freedom" from value judgements', *American Journal of Sociology*, 50, pp. 46–52
Boissonnade, P. (1927), *Life and Work in Medieval Europe*, London: Kegan Paul, Trench, Turner and Co.
Bonné, Alfred (1960), *Studies in Economic Development*, London: Routledge and Kegan Paul
Bouma, Gary D. (1973), 'Beyond Lenski: a critical review of recent "Protestant ethic" research', *Journal for the Scientific Study of Religion*, 12, pp. 141–55
Braudel, Fernand (1977a), *Capitalism and Material Life, 1400–1800*, London: Fontana/Collins
(1977b), *Afterthoughts on Material Civilization and Capitalism*, Baltimore, Md.: Johns Hopkins University Press
Brentano, Lujo (1916), *Die Anfänge des modernen Kapitalismus*, München: J. Roth
(1923), *Die wirtschaftende Mensch in der Geschichte: Gesammelte Reden und Aufsätze*, Leipzig: Felix Meiner
Brodrick, J. (1934), *The Economic Morals of the Jesuits: an answer to Dr. H. M. Robertson*, London: Oxford University Press
Bruton, Henry J. (1965), *Principles of Development Economics*, Englewood Cliffs, NJ: Prentice-Hall
Bruun, H. H. (1972), *Science, Values and Politics in Max Weber's Methodology*, Copenhagen: Munksgaard
Buchanan, Norman and Ellis, Howard S. (1955), *Approaches to Economic Development*, New York: Twentieth Century Fund
Burger, Thomas (1976), *Max Weber's Theory of Concept Formation: History, Laws, and Ideal Types*, Durham, NC: Duke University Press
Burke, Kenneth (1961), *Attitudes Toward History*, Boston: Beacon Press
(1962), *A Grammar of Motives and a Rhetoric of Motives*, Cleveland, Ohio: World Publishing Co.
Butts, Stewart (1973), 'Alternative epistemological frameworks for sociology', *Sociological Analysis and Theory*, 3, pp. 83–92
(1975), 'Parsons, Weber and the subjective point of view', *Sociological Analysis and Theory*, 5, pp. 185–217

Cahnman, Werner J. (1964), 'Max Weber and the methodological controversy in the social sciences', in Werner J. Cahnman and Alvin Boskoff (eds.), *Sociology and History: Theory and Research*, Glencoe, Ill.: Free Press, pp. 103–27

Cahnman, Werner J. and Boskoff, Alvin, eds. (1964), *Sociology and History: Theory and Research,* Glencoe, Ill.: Free Press

Cameron, Paul (1969), 'Attitude toward capitalism among Protestants and Catholics', *Journal for the Scientific Study of Religion,* 8, pp. 165–6

Cancian, Francesca, M. (1975), *What Are Norms? A Study of Beliefs and Action in a Maya Community,* London: Cambridge University Press

Carr, E. H. (1970), *What is History?,* Harmondsworth: Penguin

Carus-Wilson, E. M. (1967), *Medieval Merchant Venturers: Collected Studies,* London: Methuen

Clark, Sir George (1972), *The Seventeenth Century,* London: Oxford University Press

Clarke, Simon (1979), 'Socialist humanism and the critique of economism', *History Workshop,* 8, pp. 138–56

Cohen, G. A. (1978), *Karl Marx's Theory of History: A Defence,* Oxford: Clarendon Press

Cohen, Jere *et al.* (1975a), 'De-Parsonizing Weber: a critique of Parsons' interpretation of Weber's sociology', *American Sociological Review,* 40, pp. 229–41

   (1975b), 'On the divergence of Weber and Durkheim: a critique of Parsons' convergence thesis', *American Sociological Review,* 40, pp. 417–27

Cohen, P. S. (1968), *Modern Social Theory,* London: Heinemann

Coleman, D. C. (1956), 'Labour in the English economy of the seventeenth century', *Economic History Review,* Second Series, 8, pp. 280–95

   (1963), *Sir John Banks, Baronet and Businessman,* Oxford: Clarendon Press

Coleman, D. C. ed. (1969), *Revisions in Mercantilism,* London: Methuen

Corrigan, Philip, and Sayer, Derek (1978), 'Hindess and Hirst: a critical review', in Ralph Miliband and John Saville (eds.), *The Socialist Register, 1978,* London: Merlin Press, pp. 194–214

Coulton, G. G. (1926), *The Medieval Village,* Cambridge: Cambridge University Press

Cox, Oliver C. (1964), *Capitalism as a System,* New York: Monthly Review Press

Cunningham, W. (1912–15), *The Growth of English Industry and Commerce* (3 vols.), Cambridge: Cambridge University Press

Cutler, Antony *et al.* (1977–8), *Marx's 'Capital' and Capitalism Today* (2 vols.), London: Routledge and Kegan Paul

Daniel, Charles E. (1972), 'Hard work, good work and school work: an analysis of Wenzeslaus Linck's conception of civic responsibility', in Lawrence P. Buck and Johnathan W. Zophy (eds.), *The Social History of the Reformation,* Columbus, Ohio: Ohio State University Press, pp. 41–51

Datta, Amlan (1974), *Perspectives of Economic Development*, London: Macmillan

Datta, Lois-Ellin (1967), 'Family religious background and early scientific creativity', *American Sociological Review*, 32, pp. 626–35

Dauphin-Meunier, A. (1955), *L'Église en Face du Capitalisme*, Paris: Librairie Arthème Fayard

Dawe, Alan (1971), 'The relevance of values', in Arun Sahay (ed.), *Max Weber and Modern Sociology*, London: Routledge and Kegan Paul, pp. 37–66

Deane, Phyllis (1979), *The Evolution of Economic Ideas*, Cambridge: Cambridge University Press

Demereth, N. J. and Hammond, Phillip E. (1969), *Religion in Social Context: Tradition and Transition*, New York: Random House

de Roover, Florence Edler (1966), 'Andrea Banchi, Florentine silk manufacturer and merchant in the fifteenth century', in William M. Bowsky (ed.), *Studies in Medieval and Renaissance History*, vol. 3, Lincoln, Nebr.: University of Nebraska Press, pp. 223–85

de Roover, Raymond (1941), 'A Florentine firm of cloth manufacturers: management and organization of a sixteenth-century business', *Speculum*, 16, pp. 3–33

(1955), 'Scholastic economics: survival and lasting influence from the sixteenth century to Adam Smith', *Quarterly Journal of Economics*, 69, pp. 161–90

(1958), 'The story of the Alberti Company of Florence, 1302–1348, as revealed in its account books', *Business History Review*, 32, pp. 14–59

(1963a), 'The scholastic attitude towards trade and entrepreneurship', *Explorations in Entrepreneurial History*, Second Series, 1, pp. 76–87

(1963b) *The Rise and Decline of the Medici Bank, 1397–1494*, Cambridge, Mass.: Harvard University Press

(1967), *San Bernardino of Siena and Sant' Antonino of Florence: The Two Great Economic Thinkers of the Middle Ages*, Boston: Harvard Graduate School of Business Administration

(1978), The development of accounting prior to Luca Pacioli according to the account-books of medieval merchants', in A. C. Littleton and B. S. Yamey (eds.), *Studies in the History of Accounting*, New York: Arno Press, pp. 114–74

Dickens, A. G. (1971) *Reformation and Society in Sixteenth-Century Europe*, London: Thames and Hudson

Dixon, Keith (1973), *Sociological Theory: Pretence and Possibility*, London: Routledge and Kegan Paul

Dobb, Maurice (1951), *Studies in the Development of Capitalism*, London: Routledge and Kegan Paul

Dux, Günter (1973), 'Religion, Geschichte und sozialer Wandel in Max Webers Religionssoziologie', in Constans Seyfarth und Walter M.

Sprondel (eds.), *Seminar: Religion und gesellschaftliche Entwicklung: Studien zur Protestantismus–Kapitalismus – These Max Webers,* Frankfurt am Main: Suhrkamp, pp. 313–37

Ehrenburg, Richard (1928), *Capital and Finance in the Age of the Renaissance: A study of the Fuggers and Their Connections,* London: Cape

Eisen, Arnold M. (1975), 'Called to order: Max Weber's theory of rationalization and its relation to the Puritan idea of the "calling" ', Unpublished BPhil. thesis, University of Oxford

(1979), 'Called to order: the role of the Puritan Berufsmensch in Weberian sociology', *Sociology,* 13, pp. 203–18

Eisenstadt, S. N., ed. (1968a), *The Protestant Ethic and Modernization,* New York: Basic Books

(1968b), 'The Protestant ethic in an analytical and comparative framework', in Eisenstadt (ed.), *The Protestant Ethic and Modernization,* New York: Basic Books, pp. 3–45

(1971), 'Some reflections on the significance of Max Weber's sociology of religions for the analysis of non-European modernity', *Archives de Sociologie des Religions,* 32, pp. 29–52

(1973), 'The implications of Weber's sociology of religion for understanding processes of change in contemporary non-European societies and civilizations', in C. Y. Glock and P. E. Hammond (eds.), *Beyond the Classics? Essays in the Scientific Study of Religion,* New York: Harper and Row, pp. 131–55

Eldridge, J. E. T. (1971), 'Weber's approach to the sociological study of industrial workers', in Arun Sahay (ed.), *Max Weber and Modern Sociology,* London: Routledge and Kegan Paul, pp. 97–111

Eldridge, J. E. T., ed. (1972), *Max Weber,* London: Nelson

Elton, G. R. (1978), *The Practice of History,* London: Collins/Fontana

Evans, Austin P. (1921), 'The problem of control in medieval industry', *Political Science Quarterly,* 36, pp. 603–61

Evans-Pritchard, E. E. (1937), *Witchcraft, Oracles and Magic Among the Azande,* Oxford: Clarendon Press

Fanfani, Amintore (1935), *Catholicism, Protestantism and Capitalism,* London: Sheed and Ward

Featherman, David L. (1971), 'The socioeconomic achievement of white religio-ethnic subgroups: social and psychological explanations', *American Sociological Review,* 36, pp. 207–22

(1972), 'Achievement orientations and socioeconomic career attainments', *American Sociological Review,* 37, pp. 131–43

Ferguson, Adam (1966), *An Essay on the History of the Civil Society, 1767,* Edinburgh: Edinburgh University Press

Fischer, H. Karl (1968a), 'Kritische Beiträge zu Professor Max Webers

Abhandlung "Die protestantische Ethik und der Geist des Kapitalismus" ',
in Johannes Winckelmann (ed.), *Max Weber, 'Die protestantische Ethik' II: Kritiken und Antikritiken,* München: Siebenstern Taschenbuch, pp. 11–26 (first published 1907)

(1968b), 'Protestantische Ethik und "Geist des Kapitalismus": Replik auf Herrn Professor Max Webers Gegenkritik', in Johannes Winckelmann (ed.), *Max Weber, 'Die protestantische Ethik' II: Kritiken und Antikritiken.* München: Siebenstern Taschenbuch, pp. 38–43 (first published 1908)

Fischoff, Ephraim (1944), 'The Protestant ethic and the spirit of capitalism – the history of a controversy', *Social Research,* II, pp. 53–77

Fisher, F. J. (1957), 'The sixteenth and seventeenth centuries: the dark ages in English economic history?', *Economica,* new series, 24, pp. 2–18

Forcese, Dennis P. (1968), 'Calvinism, capitalism and confusion: the Weberian thesis revisited', *Sociological Analysis,* 29, pp. 193–201

Forsyth, P. T. (1910), 'Calvinism and capitalism', *Contemporary Review,* 97, pp. 728–41; 98, pp. 74–87

Frank, Andre Gunder (1971), *Sociology of Development and Underdevelopment of Sociology,* London: Pluto Press

(1978), *Dependent Accumulation and Underdevelopment,* London: Macmillan

Freund, Julien (1968), 'L'éthique économique et les religions mondiales selon Max Weber', *Archives de Sociologie des Religions,* 26, pp. 3–25

(1979), 'German sociology in the time of Max Weber', in Tom Bottomore and Robert Nisbet (eds.), *A History of Sociological Analysis,* London: Heinemann, pp. 149–86

Fullerton, Kemper (1928), 'Calvinism and capitalism', *Harvard Theological Review,* 21, pp. 163–95

Fusfield, Daniel B. (1957), 'Economic theory misplaced: livelihood in primitive society', in Karl Polanyi *et al.* (eds.), *Trade and Market in the Early Empires,* Glencoe, Ill.: Free Press, pp. 342–56

Gabel, Joseph (1969), 'Une lecture marxiste de la sociologie religieuse de Max Weber', *Cahiers Internationaux de Sociologie,* 44, pp. 51–66

Geertz, Clifford (1955–6), 'Religious belief and economic behavior in a Central Javanese town: some preliminary considerations', *Economic Development and Cultural Change,* 4, pp. 134–58

George, Charles H. (1957), 'English Calvinist opinion on usury, 1600–1640', *Journal of the History of Ideas,* 18, pp. 455–74

George, Charles H. and George, Katherine (1958), 'Protestantism and capitalism in pre-revolutionary England', *Church History,* 27, pp. 351–71

(1961), *The Protestant Mind of the English Reformation, 1570–1640,* Princeton, NJ: Princeton University Press

Gerth, H. H. and Mills, C. W. (1970), 'Introduction: the man and his work', in Gerth and Mills (eds.), *From Max Weber: Essays in Sociology*, London: Routledge and Kegan Paul, pp. 3–74

Giddens, Anthony (1970), 'Marx, Weber, and the development of capitalism', *Sociology*, 4, pp. 289–310

(1971), *Capitalism and Modern Social Theory: An Analysis of the Writings of Marx, Durkheim and Max Weber*, London: Cambridge University Press

(1972), *Politics and Sociology in the Thought of Max Weber*, London: Macmillan

(1976), 'Introduction', in Max Weber, *The Protestant Ethic and the Spirit of Capitalism*, 2nd edn, London: Allen and Unwin, pp. 1–12

Gide, Charles and Rist, Charles (1915), *A History of Economic Doctrines: From the Time of the Physiocrats to the Present Day*, London: Harrap

Gilchrist, J. (1969), *The Church and Economic Activity in the Middle Ages*, London: Macmillan

Gimpel, Jean (1975), *La révolution industrielle du Moyen Age*, Paris: Éditions du Seuil

Goldenweiser, Alexander (1938), 'The concept of causality in the physical and social sciences', *American Sociological Review*, 3, pp. 624–36

Goldthorpe, John H. (1977), 'The relevance of history to sociology', in Martin Bulmer (ed.) *Sociological Research Methods: An Introduction*, London: Macmillan, pp. 178–91

Goldthwaite, Richard A. (1968), *Private Wealth in Renaissance Florence: A Study of Four Families*, Princeton, NJ: Princeton University Press

Gollin, Gillian Lindt (1967), 'The religious factor in social change: Max Weber and the Moravian paradox', *Archives de Sociologie des Religions*, 23, pp. 91–7

Goodman, Mark Joseph (1975), 'Type methodology and type myth: some antecedents of Max Weber's approach', *Sociological Inquiry*, 45, pp. 45–58

Gough, J. W. (1969), *The Rise of the Entrepreneur*, London: Batsford

Gouldner, Alvin W. (1975), 'Anti-minotaur: the myth of a value-free sociology', in his *For Sociology: Renewal and Critique in Sociology Today*, Harmondsworth: Penguin, pp. 3–26

Gras, N. S. B. (1926), 'The economic activity of towns', in C. G. Crump and E. F. Jacob (eds.), *The Legacy of the Middle Ages*, Oxford: Clarendon Press, pp. 435–64

Grassby, Richard (1970), 'English merchant capitalism in the late seventeenth century: the composition of business fortunes', *Past and Present*, 46, pp. 87–107

Greeley, Andrew M. (1964), 'The Protestant ethic: time for a moratorium', *Sociological Analysis*, 25, pp. 20–33

Green, Robert W., ed. (1965), *Protestantism and Capitalism: The Weber Thesis and Its Critics*, Boston: D. C. Heath

Green, V. H. H. (1964), *Renaissance and Reformation: A Survey of European History between 1450 and 1660*, London: Edward Arnold

Groethuysen, Bernard (1968), *The Bourgeois: Catholicism Vs. Capitalism in Eighteenth-Century France*, London: Barrie and Rockliff

Grubb, Isabel (1930), *Quakerism and Industry Before 1800*, London: Williams and Norgate

Halbwachs, Maurice (1925), 'Les origines puritaines du capitalisme', *Revue d'Histoire et de Philosophie religieuses*, cinquième année, pp. 132–54

Hallam, H. E. (1975), 'The medieval social picture', in Eugene Kamenka and R. S. Neale (eds.), *Feudalism, Capitalism and Beyond*. London: Edward Arnold, pp. 28–49

Hamilton, Earl J. (1929), 'American treasure and the rise of capitalism', *Economica*, 9, pp. 338–57

Haney, Lewis H. (1964), *History of Economic Thought*, New York: Macmillan

Hansen, Niles (1963), 'The Protestant ethic as a general precondition for economic development', *Canadian Journal of Economics and Political Science*, 29, pp. 462–74

(1964), 'On the sources of economic rationality' *Zeitschrift für National-ökonomie*, 29, pp. 445–55

Hartwell, R. M. (1971), *The Industrial Revolution and Economic Growth*, London: Methuen

Hauser, Henri (1927), *Les Débuts du Capitalisme*, Paris: Alcan

Heaton, Herbert (1963), *Economic History of Europe*, London: Harper and Row

Helleiner, Karl F. (1951), 'Moral conditions of economic growth', *Journal of Economic History*, 11, pp. 97–116

Herskovitz, Melville J. (1952), *Economic Anthropology*, New York: Knopf

Hertz, Karl H. (1962), 'Max Weber and American Puritanism', *Journal for the Scientific Study of Religion*, 1, pp. 189–97

Higgins, Benjamin (1955), 'The "dualistic theory" of underdeveloped areas', *Economic Development and Cultural Change*, 4, pp. 99–115

Hill, Christopher (1961), 'Protestantism and the rise of capitalism', in F. J. Fisher (ed.), *Essays in the Economic and Social History of Tudor and Stuart England in Honour of R. H. Tawney*, Cambridge: Cambridge University Press, pp. 15–39

(1963), *The Century of Revolution, 1603–1714*, Edinburgh: Nelson

(1964a), 'William Harvey and the idea of monarchy', *Past and Present*, 27, pp. 54–72

(1964b), 'Puritanism, capitalism and the scientific revolution', *Past and Present*, 29, pp. 88–97

(1965a), 'William Harvey (no parliamentarian, no heretic) and the idea of monarchy', *Past and Present*, 31, pp. 97–103

(1965b), 'Science, religion and society in the sixteenth and seventeenth centuries', *Past and Present*, 32, pp. 110–12

(1966), *Society and Puritanism in Pre-Revolutionary England*, London: Secker and Warburg

(1969), *Reformation to Industrial Revolution: A Social and Economic History of Britain, 1530–1780*, London: Weidenfeld and Nicolson

Hill, Michael (1973), *A Sociology of Religion*, London: Heinemann

Hindess, Barry and Hirst, Paul Q. (1975) *Pre-capitalist Modes of Production*, London: Routledge and Kegan Paul

Hirschman, Albert O. (1966), *The Strategy of Economic Development*, New Haven, Conn.: Yale University Press

(1977), *The Passions and the Interests: Political Arguments for Capitalism before its Triumph*, Princeton, NJ: Princeton University Press

Hirst, Paul Q. (1979), 'The necessity of theory', *Economy and Society*, 8, pp. 417–45

Hobson, John (1954), *The Evolution of Modern Capitalism: A Study of Machine Production*, London: Allen and Unwin

Holl, Karl (1959), *The Cultural Significance of the Reformation*, New York: Meridian

Hooykaas, R. (1956), 'Science and reformation', *Cahiers d'Histoire Mondiale*, 3, pp. 109–39

Hoselitz, Bert F. (1962), *Sociological Aspects of Economic Growth*, New York: Free Press

(1965), 'Theories of stages of economic growth', in Hoselitz (ed.), *Theories of Economic Growth*, New York: Free Press, pp. 193–238

Howe, Richard Herbert (1978), 'Max Weber's elective affinities: sociology within the bounds of pure reason, *American Journal of Sociology*, 84, pp. 366–85

Hudson, Winthrop S. (1949), 'Puritanism and the spirit of capitalism', *Church History*, 18, pp. 3–17

Hutchison, T. W. (1953), *A Review of Economic Doctrines 1870–1929*, Oxford: Clarendon Press

Hyma, Albert (1937), *Christianity, Capitalism and Communism*, Ann Arbor, Mich.: Published by the author

(1938), 'Calvinism and capitalism in the Netherlands, 1555–1700', *Journal of Modern History*, 10, pp. 321–43

Israel, Herman (1966), 'Some religious factors in the emergence of industrial society in England', *American Sociological Review*, 31, pp. 589–99

Jaccard, Pierre (1960), *Histoire sociale du Travail: De L'Antiquité à Nos Jours*, Paris: Payot

Jaspers, Karl (1965), *Leonardo, Descartes, Max Weber: Three Essays*,

London: Routledge and Kegan Paul

Jarrett, Bede (1926), *Social Theories of the Middle Ages, 1200–1500*, London: Ernest Benn

Jeannin, Pierre (1972), *Merchants of the Sixteenth Century*, New York: Harper

Johnson, Benton (1962), 'Ascetic Protestantism and political preference', *Public Opinion Quarterly*, 26, pp. 35–46

(1966), 'Theology and party preference among Protestant clergymen', *American Sociological Review*, 31, pp. 200–8

(1971), 'Max Weber and American Protestantism', *Sociological Quarterly*, 12, pp. 473–85

Johnson, E. A. J. (1960), *Predecessors of Adam Smith: The Growth of British Economic Thought*, New York: Augustus M. Kelley

Johnson, Richard (1978), 'Edward Thompson, Eugene Genovese, and socialist-humanist history', *History Workshop*, 6, pp. 79–100

(1979a), 'Culture and the historians', in John Clarke *et al.* (eds.), *Working Class Culture: Studies in History and Theory*, London: Hutchinson, pp. 41–71

(1979b), 'Three problematics: elements of a theory of working-class culture', in John Clarke *et al.* (eds.), *Working Class Culture: Studies in History and Theory*. London: Hutchinson, pp. 201–37

Jonassen, Christen T. (1947), 'The Protestant ethic and the spirit of capitalism in Norway', *American Sociological Review*, 12, pp. 676–86

Jones, Richard Foster (1961), *Ancients and Moderns: A Study of the Rise of the Scientific Movement in Seventeenth-Century England*, St Louis: Washington University Press

Jordan, Heinrich P. (1938), 'Some philosophical implications of Max Weber's methodology', *The International Journal of Ethics*, 48, pp. 221–31

Judt, Tony (1979), 'A clown in regal purple: social history and the historians', *History Workshop*, 7, pp. 66–94

Käsler, Dirk (1975), 'Max-Weber-Bibliographie', *Kölner Zeitschrift für Soziologie und Sozialpsychologie*, 27, pp. 703–30

Kearney, H.F. (1964), 'Puritanism, capitalism and the scientific revolution', *Past and Present*, 28, pp. 81–101

(1965), 'Puritanism and science: problems of definition', *Past and Present*, 31, pp. 104–10

Kedar, Benjamin Z. (1976), *Merchants in Crisis: Genoese and Venetian Men of Affairs and the Fourteenth-Century Depression*, London: Yale University Press

Kennedy, Robert E. (1962), 'The Protestant ethic and the parsis', *American Journal of Sociology*, 68, pp. 11–20

Kim, Hei C. (1977), 'The relationship of Protestant ethic beliefs and values to achievement', *Journal for the Scientific Study of Religion*, 16, pp. 255–62

Kindelberger, Charles P. (1958), *Economic Development*, New York: McGraw-Hill

Kingdon, Robert M. (1972), 'The control of morals in Calvin's Geneva', in Lawrence P. Buck and Jonathan W. Zophy (eds.), *The Social History of the Reformation*, Columbus, Ohio: Ohio State University Press, pp. 3–16

Kitch, M. J. (ed.) (1967), *Capitalism and the Reformation*, London: Longman

Knight, Frank H. (1928), 'Historical and theoretical issues in the problem of modern capitalism', *Journal of Economic and Business History*, 1, pp. 119–36

Kocher, Paul H. (1969), *Science and Religion in Elizabethan England*, New York: Octagon Books

Kolko, Gabriel (1959), 'A critique of Max Weber's philosophy of history', *Ethics*, 70, pp. 21–36

(1960–1), 'Max Weber on America: theory and evidence', *History and Theory*, 1, pp. 243–60

Kosa, John and Rachiele, Leo D. (1963), 'The spirit of capitalism, traditionalism, and religiousness: a re-examination of Weber's concepts', *Sociological Quarterly*, 4, pp. 243–60

Kunkel, John H. (1970), *Society and Economic Growth: A Behavioral Perspective of Social Change*, New York: Oxford University Press

Lachmann, L. M. (1970), *The Legacy of Max Weber*, London: Heinemann

Lane, Frederic C. (1944), *Andrea Barbarigo, Merchant of Venice, 1418–1449*, Baltimore, Md.: Johns Hopkins Press

(1966), 'The rope factory and hemp trade in the fifteenth and sixteenth centuries', in his *Venice and History: The Collected Papers of Frederic C. Lane*, Baltimore, Md.: Johns Hopkins Press, pp. 269–84

Langenfelt, Gösta (1954), *The Historic Origin of the Eight Hours Day: Studies in English Traditionalism*, Stockholm: Almqvist and Wiksell

LaPiere, Richard T. (1934), 'Attitudes vs. actions', *Social Forces*, 13, pp. 230–7

Larrain, Jorge (1979), *The Concept of Ideology*, London: Hutchinson

Laslett, Peter (1975), *The World We Have Lost*, London: Methuen

Lazarsfeld, Paul F. and Oberschall, Anthony R. (1965), 'Max Weber and Empirical Social Research', *American Sociological Review*, 30, pp. 185–99

Le Bras, Gabriel (1963), 'Conceptions of economy and society', in M.M. Postan *et al.* (eds.), *Economic Organization and Policies in the Middle Ages* (*Cambridge Economic History of Europe*, vol. 3), Cambridge:

Cambridge University Press, pp. 554–75
Lecerf, Auguste (1949), 'Calvinism et capitalisme', in his *Études Calvinistes*, Paris: Delachaux et Niestlé, pp. 99–106
LeClair, Edward E., and Schneider, Harold K., eds. (1968), *Economic Anthropology: Readings in Theory and Analysis*, New York: Holt, Rinehart and Winston
Lenski, Gerhard (1963), *The Religious Factor: A Sociological Study of Religion's Impact on Politics, Economics, and Family Life*, Garden City, NY: Doubleday
(1965), 'Comment' [on Babbie], *Review of Religious Research*, 7, pp. 51–3
Letwin, William (1963), *The Origins of Scientific Economics: English Economic Thought, 1660–1776*, London: Methuen
Lewis, W. Arthur (1955), *The Theory of Economic Growth*, London: Allen and Unwin
Lichtheim, George (1971), *Marxism*, London: Routledge and Kegan Paul
Little, David (1966), 'Max Weber revisited: the "Protestant ethic" and the Puritan experience of order', *Harvard Theological Review*, 59, pp. 415–28
(1970), *Religion, Order, and Law*, Oxford: Blackwell
Ludloff, R. (1957), 'Industrial development in sixteenth-seventeenth century Germany', *Past and Present*, 12, pp. 58–75
Luethy, Herbert (1964), 'Once again: Calvinism and capitalism', *Encounter*, 22, pp. 26–38
(1965), 'Max Weber – Luethy's reply', *Encounter*, 24, pp. 92, 94
Lukács, Georg (1972), 'Max Weber and German sociology', *Economy and Society*, 1, pp. 386–98

Macfarlane, Alan (1978), *The Origins of English Individualism: The Family, Property and Social Transition*, Oxford: Blackwell
MacIntyre, Alasdair (1962), 'A mistake about causality in social science', in P. Laslett and W. G. Runciman (eds.) *Philosophy, Politics and Society*, second series, Oxford: Blackwell, pp. 48–70
Madan, G. R. (1979), *Western Sociologists on Indian Society*, London: Routledge and Kegan Paul
Mandrou, Robert (1966), 'Capitalisme et protestantisme: la science et le mythe', *Revue Historique*, 235, pp. 101–6
Marcuse, Herbert (1971), 'Industrialization and capitalism', in Otto Stammer (ed.), *Max Weber and Sociology Today*, Oxford: Blackwell, pp. 133–51
Marshall, Gordon (1975), 'Durkheim and British social anthropology: critique of a methodological tradition – 2', *Sociological Analysis and Theory*, 5, pp. 3–52
(1979), 'The Weber thesis and the development of capitalism in Scotland',

Scottish Journal of Sociology, 3, pp. 173–211

(1980a), 'The dark side of the Weber thesis: the case of Scotland', *British Journal of Sociology*, 21, pp. 419–40

(1980b) *Presbyteries and Profits: Calvinism and the Development of Capitalism in Scotland, 1560–1707*, Oxford: Clarendon Press

(1981), 'Accounting for deviance', *International Journal of Sociology and Social Policy*, 1, pp. 17–45

Marwick, Arthur (1970), *The Nature of History*, London: Macmillan

Marwick, Max (1973), 'How real is the charmed circle in African and Western thought?', *Africa*, 43, pp. 59–71

Marx, Karl (1972), *Capital*, vol. 1, London: Dent (Everyman's Library) (first published 1867)

Marx, Karl and Engels, Frederick (1970a), *Selected Works*, London: Lawrence and Wishart

(1970b), *The German Ideology*, London: Lawrence and Wishart (written 1846)

Mason, S. F. (1953a), 'Science and religion in 17th century England', *Past and Present*, 3, pp. 28–44

(1953b), 'The scientific revolution and the Protestant Reformation', *Annals of Science*, 9, pp. 64–87, 154–75

(1956), *Main Currents of Scientific Thought: A History of the Sciences*, New York: Abelard-Schuman

Masur, Gerhard (1963), *Prophets of Yesterday: Studies in European Culture, 1890–1914*, London: Weidenfeld and Nicolson

Mathias, Peter (1975), *The First Industrial Nation: An Economic History of Britain, 1700–1914*, London: Methuen

Mauro, Frédéric (1970), *Le XVIe Siècle Europeen: Aspects Économiques*, Paris: Presses Universitaires de France

McCormack, Thelma (1969), 'The Protestant ethic and the spirit of socialism', *British Journal of Sociology*, 20, pp. 266–76

McKendrick, Neil (1961), 'Josiah Wedgewood and factory discipline', *Historical Journal*, 4, pp. 30–55

McNamara, Patrick M. (1974), 'A theoretical review (review symposium: the sociology of Andrew M. Greeley)', *Journal for the Scientific Study of Religion*, 13, pp. 79–86

McNeill, John T. (1967), *The History and Character of Calvinism*, New York: Oxford University Press

Means, Richard L. (1965), 'Weber's thesis of the Protestant ethic: the ambiguities of received doctrine', *The Journal of Religion*, 45, pp. 1–11

(1966), 'Protestantism and economic institutions: auxiliary theories of Weber's Protestant ethic', *Social Forces*, 44, pp. 372–81

Meier, Gerald M. and Baldwin, Robert E. (1964), *Economic Development: Theory, History, Policy*, New York: John Wiley

Merton, Robert K. (1968), *Social Theory and Social Structure*, New York: Free Press

Mehl, Roger (1970), *The Sociology of Protestantism*, London: SCM Press

Michaelsen, Robert S. (1953), 'Changes in the Puritan concept of calling or vocation', *New England Quarterly*, 26, pp. 315–36

Miracle, Marvin P. (1976), 'Interpretation of backward-sloping labor supply curves in Africa', *Economic Development and Cultural Change*, 24, pp. 399–406

Miracle, Marvin P. and Fetter, Bruce (1969), 'Backward-sloping labor-supply functions and African economic behavior', *Economic Development and Cultural Change*, 18, pp. 240–51

Mitzman, Arthur (1973), *Sociology and Estrangement: Three Sociologists of Imperial Germany*, New York: Knopf

Moehlman, Conrad Henry (1934), 'The Christianization of interest', *Church History*, 3, pp. 3–15

Molho, Anthony, ed. (1969), *Social and Economic Foundations of the Italian Renaissance*, New York: John Wiley

Mommsen, Wolfgang J. (1959), *Max Weber und die deutsche Politik*, Tübingen: J. C. B. Mohr (Paul Siebeck)

(1965), 'Max Weber's political sociology and his philosophy of world history', *International Social Science Journal*, 17, pp. 23–45

(1977), 'Max Weber as a critic of Marxism', *Canadian Journal of Sociology*, 2, pp. 373–98

Moore, Barrington (1977), *Social Origins of Dictatorship and Democracy: Lord and Peasant in the Making of the Modern World*, Harmondsworth: Penguin

Moore, Robert (1971), 'History, economics and religion: a review of "the Max Weber thesis" thesis', in Arun Sahay (ed.), *Max Weber and Modern Sociology*, London: Routledge and Kegan Paul, pp. 82–96

(1974), *Pit-men, Preachers and Politics: The Effects of Methodism in a Durham Mining Community*, London: Cambridge University Press

Moore, Wilbert E. (1964), 'Labor attitudes toward industrialization in underdeveloped countries', in Bernard Okun and Richard W. Richardson (eds.), *Studies in Economic Development*, New York: Holt, Rinehart and Winston, pp. 381–9

Morris, M. D. (1967), 'Values as an obstacle to economic growth in South Asia: an historical survey', *Journal of Economic History*, 27, pp. 588–607

Mundy, John H. and Riesenberg, Peter (1958), *The Medieval Town*, Princeton, NJ: D. Van Nostrand

Nafziger, Estel Wayne (1965), 'The Mennonite ethic in the Weberian framework', *Explorations in Entrepreneurial History*, second series, 2, pp. 187–204

Nelson, Benjamin (1947), 'The usurer and the merchant prince: Italian businessmen and the ecclesiastical law of restitution, 1100–1550', *Journal of Economic History*, 7 (supplement), pp. 104–22

(1964), 'In defence of Max Weber', *Encounter*, 23, pp. 94–5

(1969), *The Idea of Usury: from Tribal Brotherhood to Universal Otherhood*, Chicago: University of Chicago Press

Nelson, Benjamin (1973), 'Weber's Protestant ethic: its origins, wanderings, and foreseeable futures', in C. Y. Glock and P. E. Hammond (eds.), *Beyond the Classics? Essays in the Scientific Study of Religion*, New York: Harper and Row, pp. 71–130

(1974), 'Max Weber's "Author's introduction" (1920): a master clue to his main aims', *Sociological Inquiry*, 44, pp. 269–77

Nisbet, Robert A. (1970), 'Developmentalism: a critical analysis', in John C. McKinney and Edward A. Tiryakian (eds.), *Theoretical Sociology: Perspectives and Developments*, New York: Appleton-Century-Crofts, pp. 167–204

Oberschall, Anthony (1965), *Empirical Social Research in Germany 1848–1914*, Paris: Mouton

O'Brien, George (1923), *An Essay on the Economic Effects of the Reformation*, London: Burns Oates and Washbourne

Okun, Bernard and Richardson, Richard W., eds. (1964), *Studies in Economic Development*, New York: Holt, Rinehart and Winston

Origo, Iris (1963a), *The Merchant of Prato*, Harmondsworth: Penguin

(1963b), *The World of San Bernardino*, London: Cape

Parenti, Michael (1967), 'Political values and religious cultures: Jews, Catholics, and Protestants', *Journal for the Scientific Study of Religion*, 6, pp. 259–69

Parias, Louis-Henri (n.d.), *Histoire Générale du Travail* (4 vols.), Paris: Nouvelle Librairie de France (F. Sant' Andréa et J-G. Tronche)

Parsons, Talcott (1928), ' "Capitalism" in recent German literature: Sombart and Weber', *The Journal of Political Economy*, 36, pp. 641–61

(1935), 'H. M. Robertson on Max Weber and his school', *The Journal of Political Economy*, 43, pp. 688–96

(1964), 'Evolutionary universals in society', *American Sociological Review*, 29, pp. 339–57

(1966), *Societies: Evolutionary and Comparative Perspectives*, Englewood Cliffs, NJ: Prentice-Hall

(1968), *The Structure of Social Action*, (2 vols.), New York: Free Press (first published 1937)

(1971a), 'Value-freedom and objectivity', in Otto Stammer (ed.), *Max Weber and Sociology Today*, Oxford: Blackwell, pp. 27–50

(1971b), *The System of Modern Societies*, Englewood Cliffs, NJ: Prentice-Hall

Pepelasis, Adamantios, *et al.*, eds. (1964), *Economic Development: Analysis and Case Studies*, New York/Tokyo: Harper and Row/John Weatherhill

Petersen, David L. (1979), 'Max Weber and the sociological study of ancient Israel', *Sociological Inquiry*, 49, pp. 117–49

Pirenne, Henri (1956), *Medieval Cities: Their Origins and the Revival of Trade*, Garden City, NY: Doubleday

Polanyi, Karl (1977), *The Livelihood of Man*, New York: Academic Press

Pollard, Sidney (1963), 'Factory discipline in the industrial revolution', *Economic History Review*, second series, 16, pp. 254–71

(1965), *The Genesis of Modern Management: A Study of the Industrial Revolution in Great Britain*, London: Edward Arnold

Popper, Karl R. (1966), *The Open Society and its Enemies* (2 vols.), London: Routledge and Kegan Paul

Power, Eileen (1941), *The Wool Trade in English Medieval History*, London: Oxford University Press

Prades, J. A. (1969), *La Sociologie de la Religion chez Max Weber*, Louvain: Éditions Nauwelaerts

Prestwich, Menna (1966), *Cranfield: Politics and Profits under the Early Stuarts*, Oxford: Clarendon Press

Rabb, Theodore K. (1962), 'Puritanism and the rise of experimental science in England', *Cahiers d'Histoire Mondiale*, 7, pp. 46–67

(1965), 'Religion and the rise of modern science', *Past and Present*, 31, pp. 111–26

(1966), 'Science, religion and society in the sixteenth and seventeenth centuries', *Past and Present*, 33, p. 148

(1974), 'The expansion of Europe and the spirit of capitalism', *Historical Journal*, 17, pp. 675–89

Rachfahl, Felix (1968a), 'Kalvinismus und Kapitalismus', in Johannes Winckelmann (ed.), *Max Weber, 'Die protestantische Ethik' II: Kritiken und Antikritiken*, München: Siebenstern Taschenbuch, pp. 57–148 (first published 1909)

(1968b), 'Nochmals Kalvinismus und Kapitalismus', in Johannes Winckelmann (ed.), *Max Weber, 'Die protestantische Ethik' II: Kritiken und Antikritiken*, München: Siebenstern Taschenbuch, pp. 216–82 (first published 1910)

Ramsay, G. D. (1943), *The Wiltshire Woollen Industry in the Sixteenth and Seventeenth Centuries*, London: Oxford University Press

Raphaël, Freddy (1970), 'Max Weber et le judaïsme antique', *Archives Européennes de Sociologie*, 11, pp. 297–336

Razzell, Peter (1977), 'The Protestant ethic and the spirit of capitalism: a natural scientific critique', *British Journal of Sociology*, 28, pp. 17–37

Reid, W. Stanford (1962), *Skipper from Leith: The History of Robert Barton of Over Barnton*, Philadelphia: University of Pennsylvania Press

Renouard, Yves (1968), *Les Hommes D'Affaires Italiens Du Moyen Age*, Paris: Librairie Armand Colin

Rex, John (1971), 'Typology and objectivity: a comment on Weber's four sociological methods', in Arun Sahay (ed.), *Max Weber and Modern Sociology*, London: Routledge and Kegan Paul, pp. 17–36

Reynolds, Robert L. (1945), 'In search of a business class in thirteenth-century Genoa', *Journal of Economic History*, 5 (supplement), pp. 1–19

Rickert, Heinrich (1902), *Die Grenzen der naturwissenschaftlichen Begriffsbildung: Eine logische Einleitung in die historischen Wissenschaften*, Tübingen: J. C. B. Mohr (Paul Siebeck).

(1962), *Science and History: A Critique of Positivist Epistemology*, Princeton, NJ: Van Nostrand (first published 1898–1902)

Robertson, H. M. (1933), *Aspects of the Rise of Economic Individualism: A Criticism of Max Weber and his School*, Cambridge: Cambridge University Press

Robertson, Roland (1972), *The Sociological Interpretation of Religion*, Oxford: Blackwell

Rotenberg, Mordechai (1978), *Damnation and Deviance: The Protestant Ethic and the Spirit of Failure*, New York: Free Press

Roth, Guenther (1975), 'Survey review', *Contemporary Sociology*, 14, pp. 366–73

Runciman, W. G. (1969), 'The sociological explanation of "religious" beliefs', *Archives Européennes de Sociologie*, 10, pp. 149–91

(1972), *A Critique of Max Weber's Philosophy of Social Science*, London: Cambridge University Press

Sahay, Arun (1969), 'Hindu reformist ethics and the Weber thesis: an application of Max Weber's methodology', unpublished Ph.D thesis, University of London

(1971), 'The importance of Weber's methodology in sociological explanation', in Sahay (ed.), *Max Weber and Modern Sociology*, London: Routledge and Kegan Paul, pp. 67–81

(1972), *Sociological Analysis*, London: Routledge and Kegan Paul

Salomon, Albert (1945), 'German sociology', in Georges Gurvitch and Wilbert E. Moore (eds.), *Twentieth Century Sociology*, New York: The Philosophical Library, pp. 586–614

Salzman, L. F. (1926), *English Life in the Middle Ages*, London: Oxford University Press

Samuelsson, Kurt (1961), *Religion and Economic Action*, London: Heinemann

Schluchter, Wolfgang (1979), 'The paradox of rationalization: on the relation of ethics and the world', in G. Roth and W. Schluchter (eds.), *Max Weber's Vision of History: Ethics and Methods*, Berkeley, Calif.: University of California Press, pp. 11–64

Schmidt, Gert (1976), 'Max Weber and modern industrial sociology: a comment on some recent Anglo-Saxon interpretations', *Sociological Analysis and Theory*, 6, pp. 47–73

Schoenfeld, Eugene (1964), 'A preliminary note on love and justice: the effects of religious values on liberalism and conservatism', *Review of Religious Research*, 16, pp. 41–6

Schumpeter, J. (1974), *Capitalism, Socialism and Democracy*, London: Unwin

Scoville, Warren C. (1960), *The Persecution of Huguenots and French Economic Development, 1680–1720*, Berkeley, Calif.: University of California Press

Sée, Henri (1927), 'Dans quelle mesure Puritains et Juifs ont-ils contribué aux progrès du capitalisme moderne?', *Revue Historique*, 155, pp. 57–68

—— (1928), *Modern Capitalism: Its Origins and Evolution*, London: Noel Douglas

Selbourne, David (1980), 'On the methods of history workshop', *History Workshop*, 9, pp. 150–61

Seliger, Martin (1979), *The Marxist Conception of Ideology*, Cambridge: Cambridge University Press

Seyfarth, Constans (1973), 'Protestantismus und gesellschaftliche Entwicklung: zur Reformulierung eines Problems', in Constans Seysfarth und Walter M. Sprondel (eds.), *Seminar: Religion und gesellschaftliche Entwicklung: Studien zur Protestantismus–Kapitalismus – These Max Webers*, Frankfurt am Main: Suhrkamp, pp. 338–66

Seyfarth, Constans and Sprondel, Walter M., eds. (1973), *Seminar: Religion und gesellschaftliche Entwicklung: Studien zur Protestantismus–Kapitalismus – These Max Webers*. Frankfurt am Main: Suhrkamp

Sheehan, James J. (1966), *The Career of Lujo Brentano: A Study of Liberalism and Social Reform in Imperial Germany*, Chicago: University of Chicago Press

Simmel, Georg (1978), *The Philosophy of Money*, London: Routledge and Kegan Paul (first published 1900)

Smelser, Neil J. (1976), *Comparative Methods in the Social Sciences*, Englewood Cliffs, NJ: Prentice-Hall

Smith, Anthony D. (1973), *The Concept of Social Change: A Critique of the Functionalist Theory of Social Change*, London: Routledge and Kegan Paul

Sombart, Werner (1902), *Der Moderne Kapitalismus* (2 vols.), Leipzig: Duncker und Humblot

—— (1903), *Die deutsche Volkswirtschaft im neunzehnten Jahrhundert*,

Berlin, Georg Bondi

(1951), *The Jews and Modern Capitalism*, Glencoe, Ill.: Free Press (first published 1911)

(1967), *The Quintessence of Capitalism*, New York: Howard Fertig (first published 1913)

Sorokin, Pitirim (1966), *Sociological Theories of Today*, New York: Harper and Row

Stark, Werner (1966), 'The Protestant ethic and the spirit of sociology', *Social Compass*, 13, pp. 373–7

(1977), *The Sociology of Knowledge: An Essay in Aid of a Deeper Understanding of the History of Ideas,* London: Routledge and Kegan Paul

Stedman Jones, Gareth (1976), 'From historical sociology to theoretical history', *British Journal of Sociology*, 27, pp. 295–305

Stimson, Dorothy (1948), *Scientists and Amateurs: A History of the Royal Society*, New York: Henry Schuman

Stone, Lawrence, ed. (1965), *Social Change and Revolution in England, 1540–1640*, London: Longman

Strauss, Leo (1953), *Natural Right and History*, Chicago: University of Chicago Press

Strieder, Jacob (1929), 'Origin and evolution of early European capitalism', *Journal of Economic and Business History*, 2, pp. 1–19

Summers, Gene *et al.* (1970), 'Ascetic Protestantism and political preference: a re-examination', *Review of Religious Research*, 12, pp. 17–25

Supple, B. E. (1963), 'The great capitalist manhunt', *Business History*, 6, pp. 48–62

Sutton, F. X. (1965), 'The social and economic philosophy of Werner Sombart: the sociology of capitalism', in Harry Elmer Barnes (ed.), *An Introduction to the History of Sociology*, Chicago: University of Chicago Press, pp. 316–31

Swanson, Guy E. (1967), *Religion and Regime: A Sociological Account of the Reformation*, Ann Arbor, Mich.: University of Michigan Press

Sweezy, Paul M. *et al.* (1954), *The Transition from Feudalism to Capitalism*, New York

Tawney, R.H. (1925), 'Introduction', in Thomas Wilson, *A Discourse Upon Usury* (1572), London: Bell and Sons, pp. 1–172

(1972), *Religion and the Rise of Capitalism*, Harmondsworth: Penguin (first published 1926)

Tenbruck, Friedrich H. (1980), 'The problem of thematic unity in the works of Max Weber', *British Journal of Sociology*, 31, pp. 316–51

Therborn, Goran (1976), *Science, Class and Society: On the Formation of Sociology and Historical Materialism*, London: New Left Books

Thomas, Keith (1964), 'Work and leisure in pre-industrial society', *Past and Present*, 29, pp. 50–62

Thompson, E. P. (1967), 'Time, work-discipline, and industrial capitalism',

Past and Present, 38, pp. 56–97

(1978), *The Poverty of Theory, and Other Essays*, London: Merlin Press

Thompson, James Westfall (1960), *Economic and Social History of Europe in the Later Middle Ages (1300–1530)*. New York: Frederick Ungar

Thrupp, Sylvia L. (1941), 'Social control in the medieval town', *Journal of Economic History*, 1 (supplement), pp. 39–52

(1942), 'Medieval gilds reconsidered', *Journal of Economic History*, 2, pp. 164–73

(1948), *The Merchant Class of Medieval London (1300–1500)*, Chicago: University of Chicago Press

(1972), 'Medieval industry, 1000–1500', in Carlo M. Cipolla (ed.), *The Middle Ages* (*Fontana Economic History of Europe*, vol. 1), London: Collins/Fontana, pp. 221–73

Tigar, Michael E. and Levy, Madeleine R. (1977), *Law and the Rise of Capitalism*, New York: Monthly Review Press

Tilgher, Adriano (1931), *Work: What It has meant to Men through the Ages*, London: Harrap

Torrance, John (1974), 'Max Weber: methods and the man', *Archives Européennes de Sociologie*, 15, pp. 127–65

Trevor-Roper, H. R. (1963), 'Religion, the Reformation, and social change', in *Historical Studies 4* (papers read before the Fifth Irish Conference of Historians), London: Bowes and Bowes, pp. 18–44

Troeltsch, Ernst (1912), *Protestantism and Progress: A Historical Study of the Relation of Protestantism to the Modern World*, London: Williams and Norgate

(1931), *The Social Teaching of the Christian Churches* (2 vols.), London: Allen and Unwin (first published 1911)

Turksma, L. (1962), 'Protestant ethic and rational capitalism', *Social Compass*, 9, pp. 445–73

Turner, Bryan S. (1974), *Weber and Islam*, London: Routledge and Kegan Paul

Unwin, George (1927), *Studies in Economic History: The Collected Papers of George Unwin*, London: Macmillan

van der Sprenkel, Otto B. (1963), 'Max Weber on China', *History and Theory*, 3, pp. 348–70

von Schelting, Alexander (1934), *Max Webers Wissenschaftslehre: Das logische Problem der historischen Kulturerkenntnis; Die Grenzen der Soziologie des Wissens*, Tübingen: J. C. B. Mohr (Paul Siebeck)

Villard, Henry H. (1963), *Economic Development*, New York: Holt, Rinehart and Winston

Wagner, Helmut (1964), 'The Protestant ethic: a mid-twentieth century view', *Sociological Analysis*, 25, pp. 34–40

Walker, P. C. Gordon (1937), 'Capitalism and the Reformation', *Economic History Review*, 8, pp. 1–19

Wallerstein, Immanuel (1974), *The Modern World-System: Capitalist Agriculture and the Origins of the European World-Economy in the Sixteenth Century*, New York: Academic Press

Walzer, Michael (1963), 'Puritanism as a revolutionary ideology', *History and Theory*, 3, pp. 59–90

———(1966), *The Revolution of the Saints: A Study in the Origins of Radical Politics*, London: Weidenfeld and Nicolson

Ward, Richard J., ed. (1967), *The Challenge of Development: Theory and Practice*, Chicago: Aldine

Warner, R. Stephen (1970), 'The role of religious ideas and the use of models in Max Weber's comparative studies of non-capitalist societies', *Journal of Economic History*, 30, pp. 74–99

Wax, Rosalie, and Wax, Murray (1955), 'The Vikings and the rise of capitalism', *American Journal of Sociology*, 61, pp. 1–10

Webb, John (1962), *Great Tooley of Ipswich: Portrait of an Early Tudor Merchant*, Suffolk Records Society Publication

Weber, Marianne (1975), *Max Weber: A Biography*, London: John Wiley (first published 1926)

Weber, Max* (1905), 'Die protestantische Ethik und der "Geist" des Kapitalismus', *Archiv für Sozialwissenschaft und Sozialpolitik*, 20, pp. 1–54; 21, pp. 1–11

———(1907), 'Kritische Bemerkungen zu den vorstehenden "Kritischen Beiträgen"', *Archiv für Sozialwissenschaft und Sozialpolitik*, 25, pp. 243–9

———(1908), 'Bemerkungen zu der vorstehenden "Replik"', *Archiv für Sozialwissenschaft und Sozialpolitik*, 26, pp. 275–83

———(1910a), 'Antikritisches zum "Geist" des Kapitalismus', *Archiv für Sozialwissenschaft und Sozialpolitik*, 30, pp. 176–202

———(1910b), 'Antikritisches Schlusswort zum "Geist des Kapitalismus"', *Archiv für Sozialwissenschaft und Sozialpolitik*, 31, pp. 554–99

———(1923), *General Economic History*, London: Allen and Unwin

———(1924), *Gesammelte Aufsätze zur Soziologie und Sozialpolitik*, Tübingen: J. C. B. Mohr (Paul Siebeck)

———(1947), *Gesammelte Aufsätze zur Religionssoziologie*, 1, Tübingen: J. C. B. Mohr (Paul Siebeck) (first published 1920)

———(1950), 'The social causes of the decay of ancient civilization', *Journal of General Education*, 5, pp. 75–88 (first published 1896)

———(1960), *Ancient Judaism*, Glencoe, Ill.: Free Press (first published 1917–19)

———(1962), *The Religion of India: The Sociology of Hinduism and Buddhism*, Glencoe, Ill.: Free Press (first published 1916–17)

*The chronology of Weber's writings is explained in the Appendix on pages 174–9.

(1964), *The Religion of China: Confucianism and Taoism*, New York: Macmillan (first published 1916)

(1968), *Economy and Society* (3 vols.), New York: Bedminster Press (first published 1922)

(1969), *The Methodology of the Social Sciences*, New York: Free Press (previously published 1904, 1906, 1917–18)

(1970a), 'The Protestant sects and the spirit of capitalism', in H. H. Gerth and C. W. Mills (eds.), *From Max Weber: Essays in Sociology*, London: Routledge and Kegan Paul (previously published 1906, 1920)

(1970b), 'The social psychology of the world religions', in Gerth and Mills, op. cit. (first published 1916)

(1970c), 'Religious rejections of the world and their directions', in Gerth and Mills, op. cit. (first published 1916)

(1970d), 'Politics as a vocation', in Gerth and Mills, op. cit. (first published 1919)

(1970e), 'Science as a vocation', in Gerth and Mills. op. cit. (first published 1919)

(1970f), 'Capitalism and rural society in Germany', in Gerth and Mills, op. cit. (first published 1906)

(1971), *The Protestant Ethic and the Spirit of Capitalism*, London: Unwin (previously published 1905, 1920)

(1972a), 'Methodological introduction for the survey of the society for social policy concerning selection and adaptation (choice and course of occupation) for the workers of major industrial enterprises', in J. E. T. Eldridge (ed.), *Max Weber*, London: Nelson, pp. 103–55 (written 1908)

(1972b), 'Georg Simmel as sociologist', *Social Research,* 39, pp. 155–63 (written 1908)

(1975), *Roscher and Knies: The Logical Problems of Historical Economics,* New York: Free Press (first published 1903–6)

(1976), *The Agrarian Sociology of Ancient Civilizations*, London: New Left Books (first published 1909)

(1978), 'Anticritical last word on "the spirit of capitalism", by Max Weber', *American Journal of Sociology,* 83, pp. 1105–31 (first published 1910)

Weinryb, Elazar (1975), 'The justification of a causal thesis: an analysis of the controversies over the theses of Pirenne, Turner, and Weber', *History and Theory,* 14, pp. 32–56

Welch, Michael R. (1978), 'Religious non-affiliates and worldly success', *Journal for the Scientific Study of Religion,* 17, pp. 59–61

Weyembergh, Maurice (1971) *Le voluntarisme rationnel de Max Weber*, Bruxelles: Palais des Académies

White, Lynn (1969), 'The iconography of *Temperantia* and the virtuousness of technology', in Theodore K. Rabb and Jerrold E. Seigel (eds.), *Action* and Conviction in Early Modern Europe: Essays in Memory of E. H. Harbison, Princeton, NJ: Princeton University Press, pp. 197–219

Whitteridge, Gweneth (1965), 'William Harvey: a royalist and no parliamentarian', Past and Present, 30, pp. 104–9

Whyte, William F. and Williams, Lawrence K. (1968), Toward an Integrated Theory of Development: Economic and Non-Economic Variables in Rural Development, Ithaca, NY: New York State School of Industrial and Labor Relations

Williams, Raymond (1973), 'Base and superstructure in Marxist cultural theory', New Left Review, 82, pp. 3–16

Williamson, Harold F. and Buttrick, John A., eds. (1962), Economic Development: Principles and Patterns, Englewood Cliffs, NJ: Prentice-Hall

Wilson, Bryan R., ed. (1977), Rationality, Oxford: Blackwell

Wilson, Charles (1958), Mercantilism, Historical Association Pamphlet 37, general series, London: Routledge and Kegan Paul

   (1967), 'Trade, society and the state', in E. E. Rich and C. H. Wilson (eds.), The Economy of Expanding Europe in the Sixteenth and Seventeenth Centuries (Cambridge Economic History of Europe, vol. 4), Cambridge: Cambridge University Press

Winter, J. Alan (1974a), 'Elective affinities between religious beliefs and ideologies of management in two eras', American Journal of Sociology, 79, pp. 1134–50

   (1974b), 'Quantitative studies of the applicability of the Weber thesis to post-World War II USA: a call for redirected efforts', Review of Religious Research, 16, pp. 47–58

Yamey, B. S. (1949), 'Scientific bookkeeping and the rise of capitalism', Economic History Review, 1, pp. 99–113

   (1975), 'Notes on double-entry bookkeeping and economic progress', Journal of European Economic History, 4, pp. 717–23

Yinger, J. Milton (1967), Religion, Society and the Individual: An Introduction to the Sociology of Religion, New York: Macmillan

   (1970), The Scientific Study of Religion, London: Collier-Macmillan

Zaret, David (1980a), 'Ideology and organization in Puritanism', European Journal of Sociology, 21, pp. 83–115

   (1980b), 'From Weber to Parsons and Schutz: the eclipse of history in modern social theory', American Journal of Sociology, 85, pp. 1180–1201

Index

(There are no entries under frequently recurring words such as capitalism, protestant, spirit of capitalism, etc.)